The Concept of Injustice

The Concept of Injustice challenges traditional Western justice theory. Thinkers from Plato and Aristotle through to Kant, Hegel, Marx and Rawls have subordinated the idea of injustice to the idea of justice. Misled by the word's etymology, political theorists have assumed injustice to be the logical opposite of justice. Heinze summons ancient and early modern texts, philosophical and literary, with special attention to Shakespeare, to argue that injustice is not primarily the negation, failure or absence of justice. Injustice is the constant product of regimes and norms of justice. Justice is not always the cure for injustice, and is often its cause.

Eric Heinze is Professor of Law and Humanities at Queen Mary, University of London. His most recent publications on legal theory have appeared in the *Oxford Journal of Legal Studies*, *Ratio Juris*, the *International Journal of Law in Context*, *Legal Studies*, *Social & Legal Studies*, *The Canadian Journal of Law and Jurisprudence*, *Law and Critique*, *Law and Literature* and *Law and Humanities*.

The Concept of Injustice

Eric Heinze

a GlassHouse book

First published in 2013
by Routledge
2 Park Square, Milton Park, Abingdon, Oxofordshire OX14 4RN

Simultaneously published in the USA and Canada
by Routledge
711 Third Avenue, New York, NY 10017

First issued in paperback 2014
Routledge is an imprint of the Taylor & Francis Group, an informa company

A GlassHouse Book

© 2013 Eric Heinze

The right of Eric Heinze to be identified as author of this work has been asserted by him in accordance with sections 77 and 78 of the Copyright, Designs and Patents Act 1988.

All rights reserved. No part of this book may be reprinted or reproduced or utilised in any form or by any electronic, mechanical, or other means, now known or hereafter invented, including photocopying and recording, or in any information storage or retrieval system, without permission in writing from the publishers.

Trademark notice: Product or corporate names may be trademarks or registered trademarks, and are used only for identification and explanation without intent to infringe.

British Library Cataloguing in Publication Data
A catalogue record for this book is available from the British Library

Library of Congress Cataloging in Publication Data
Heinze, Eric.
  The concept of injustice / Eric Heinze.
    p. cm.

  1. Justice. 2. Justice (Philosophy) 3. Justice in literature. I. Title.
  JC578.H44 2012
  340'.114—dc23
                                                        2012012975

ISBN 13: 978-0-415-52441-4 (hbk)
ISBN 13: 978-0-415-63479-3 (pbk)

Typeset in Garamond
by Keystroke, Station Road, Codsall, Wolverhampton

For István

νόμος ὅδ', οὐδὲν ἕρπει
θνατῶν βιότῳ πάμπολύ γ' ἐκτὸς ἄτας.*

Sophocles, *Antigone* 613–14 (Ant [RJ])

* '[Y]our law prevails:
   no towering form of greatness
   enters into the lives of mortals
   free and clear of ruin.' Ant 686–89.

Contents

Sources ix

1 Nietzsche's echo 1

   1.1 Introduction 1
   1.2 A mutual exclusion? 4
   1.3 Plan of this book 10

PART I
Classical understandings 13

2 Injustice as the negation of justice 15

   2.1 Introduction 15
   2.2 Typical expressions of mutual exclusion 16
   2.3 Injustice within isolated contexts 22
   2.4 Injustice and anti-rationalism 28
   2.5 Injustice within systemic contexts 33
   2.6 A dialectic of injustice 36
   2.7 Historicist dialectics of injustice 42
   2.8 The partial incommensurability of justice and injustice 45

3 Injustice as disunity 50

   3.1 Introduction 50
   3.2 Disunity as the primary cause of injustice in Plato 50
   3.3 Disunity as a major element of injustice in Aristotle 60
   3.4 Disunity as metaphysical injustice in Christianity 63
   3.5 The dialectic of unity and individuality in modernity 67

| 4 | Injustice as mismeasurement | 79 |

    4.1 Introduction 79
    4.2 Suum cuique as an empty formalism 79
    4.3 Suum cuique as a decisive element 86
    4.4 Injustice as failure of reciprocity 90
    4.5 Transition to a post-classical concept of justice 93

PART 2
Post-classical understandings   97

| 5 | Injustice as unity | 99 |

    5.1 Introduction 99
    5.2 Antigone: conventional versus critical contexts 100
    5.3 Macbeth: unity as the source of disunity 103
    5.4 Talbot: merit and myth 109

| 6 | Injustice as measurement | 114 |

    6.1 Introduction 114
    6.2 'Will much impeach the justice of the state' 115
    6.3 'Pageants of the sea' 118
    6.4 'Like a golden fleece' 120
    6.5 'Mine own teaching' 121
    6.6 'The complexion of a devil' 126
    6.7 'Kindness' 130
    6.8 'As swift as yours' 138
    6.9 'As much as he deserves' 140
    6.10 'Le plus beau, le plus fort' 144

| 7 | Measurement and modernity | 153 |

    7.1 Introduction 153
    7.2 'I'll counterpoise' 154
    7.3 'To set a gloss' 160
    7.4 'If things be measured equal to their worth' 171
    7.5 'My spirit's split in two' 182

Bibliography   198
Index   207

Sources

The following is a list of works that require the identification of a standard reference, due to multiple editions.

The Bible (references are to IBS-UK, 2009)
Eccl	*Ecclesiastes*
Ep Rom	*Epistle to the Romans*
Gen	*Genesis*
Lvt	*Leviticus*
Matt	*Matthew*
NIV-UK	*The New International Version, United Kingdom edition*

Sophocles (references are to Sophocles, 1984, unless otherwise indicated)
Ant	*Antigone*
Ant [RJ]	*Antigone* in Sophocles, 1891
Oed	*Oedipus Tyrannus*

Herodotus (references are to Herodotus, 2008)
His	*The Histories*

Plato (references are to Plato, 1997, unless otherwise indicated)
Alc	*Alcibiades*
Ap	*Apology*
Cri	*Crito*
Euthphr	*Euthyphro*
Euthphr [HC]	*Euthyphro* in Plato, 1961
Grg	*Gorgias*
L	*Laws*
L [HC]	*Laws* in Plato, 1961
Lch	*Laches*
Ltr 7	*Seventh Letter*
M	*Meno*
Phd	*Phaedo*

Phdr	*Phaedrus*
Prt	*Protagoras*
R	*Republic*
R [Bur]	*Republic* in Plato, 1903
R [HC]	*Republic* in Plato, 1961
Smp	*Symposium*
Stm	*Statesman*
Tht	*Theaetetus*

Aristotle (references are to Aristotle, 1984, unless otherwise indicated)
An Post [Ba]	*Posterior Analytics* in Aristotle, 1993
De Int	*On Interpretation*
Meta	*Metaphysics*
NE	*Nicomachean Ethics*
NE [By]	*Nicomachean Ethics* in Aristotle, 1894
NE [Ir]	*Nicomachean Ethics* in Aristotle, 1999
Pol	*Politics*
Pol [Re]	*Politics* in Aristotle, 1998
Pol [Si]	*Politics* in Aristotle, 1992

Augustine (references are to Augustine, 1984)
CD	*Civitas Dei (City of God)*

Aquinas (references are to Aquinas, 2000)
ST	*Summa Theologica*

Dante (references are to Alighieri, 2007, unless otherwise indicated)
DM	*De Monarchia (On World Government)* in Alighieri, 1949
Inf	*Inferno*
Inf [Ci]	*Inferno* in Alighieri, 1954
Par	*Paradiso*
Par [Ci]	*Paradiso* in Alighieri, 1970
Pur	*Purgatorio*
Pur [Ci]	*Purgatorio* in Alighieri, 1957

Erasmus (references are to Erasmus, 1997)
ECP	*The Education of a Christian Prince*

Shakespeare (references are to Wells, 1982, unless otherwise indicated; citation forms follow MLA, 2003)
Ado	*Much Ado about Nothing*
ARD2	*Arden Shakespeare* (2nd series) (Ellis-Fermor *et al.*, eds)
ARD3	*Arden Shakespeare* (3rd series) (R. Proudfoot *et al.*, eds)
AWW	*All's Well that Ends Well*

Sources xi

CAM4	New Cambridge Shakespeare (P. Brockbank et al., eds)
Cym	Cymbeline
Err	The Comedy of Errors
1H4	Henry IV, Part One
2H4	Henry IV, Part Two
H5	Henry V
1H6	Henry VI, Part One
H8	Henry VIII
Ham	Hamlet
JC	Julius Caesar
Jn	King John
LLL	Love's Labours Lost
Lr	King Lear
Mac	Macbeth
MM	Measure for Measure
MND	A Midsummernight's Dream
MV	The Merchant of Venice
NOR2	The Norton Shakespeare (2nd edn) (S. Greenblatt et al., ed.)
Oth	Othello
OXF4	Oxford Shakespeare (individual plays, S. Wells, ed.)
PEN2	New Penguin Shakespeare (T. Spencer, ed.)
Per	Pericles
R2	Richard II
R3	Richard III
Rom	Romeo and Juliet
Shr	The Taming of the Shrew
TGV	Two Gentlemen of Verona
Tim	Timon of Athens
Tit	Titus Andronicus
Tmp	Tempest
TN	Twelfth Night
Tro	Troilus and Cressida
Wiv	The Merry Wives of Windsor
WT	The Winter's Tale

Hobbes (references are to Hobbes, 1998)
Lev   *Leviathan*

Milton (references are to Milton, 1991)
PL   *Paradise Lost*

Corneille (references are to Corneille, 1980a–c)
Cid   *Le Cid*
Cid-1660   *Le Cid* (1660 version)

Cin   *Cinna*
Méd   *Médée*
Mél   *Mélite*
PC-OC   *Œuvres complètes de Pierre Corneille*

Racine (references are to Racine, 1999)
Andr   *Andromaque*
Brt   *Britannicus*
JR-OC   *Œuvres complètes de Jean Racine*

Locke
LT   *Letter Concerning Toleration* (references are to Cahn, 2002)
STCG   *Second Treatise of Civil Government* (references are to Locke, 1988)

Voltaire
DP   *Dictionnaire philosophique* (references are to Voltaire, 1961)
L14   *Le Siècle de Louis XIV* (references are to Voltaire, 1958)

Rousseau (references are to Rousseau, 1980a–d)
CS   *Du Contrat Social (The Social Contract)*
EP   *Discours sur l'Économie Politique (Discourse on Political Economy)*
GP   *Considérations sur le gouvernement de Pologne (Considerations on the Government of Poland)*
JJR-OC   *Œuvres complètes de Jean-Jacques Rousseau*
OI   *Discours sur l'origine de l'inégalité (Discourse on the origin of inequality)*
OI-Gour   *Discourse on the origin of inequality*, in Rousseau, 1997
SA   *Discours sur les sciences et les arts (Discourse on the Sciences and Arts)*

Kant (references are to Kant, 1968a–d)
EF   *Zum ewigen Frieden (Perpetual Peace)*
GMS   *Grundlegung zur Metaphysik der Sitten (Groundwork for the Metaphysics of Morals)*
KpV   *Kritik der praktischen Vernunft (Critique of practical reason)*
MS   *Die Metaphysik der Sitten (The Metaphysics of Morals)*

Schiller (references are to Schiller, 2003)
WT   *Wilhelm Tell*

Hegel (references are to Hegel, 1970a–c)
Äs   *Vorlesung über die Ästhetik (Introductory Lectures on Aesthetics)*

GPR	*Grundlinien der Philosophie des Rechts* (*Elements of the Philosophy of Right*)
PhG	*Phänomenologie des Geistes* (*Phenomenology of Mind*)

Bentham (references are to Bentham, 1843)
CE	*A Critical Examination of the Declaration of Rights*

Mill
Lib	*On Liberty* (references are to Mill, 1982)
Ut	*Utilitarianism* (references are to Mill, 1957)

Marx and Engels (references are to Marx and Engels (MEW), 1956c)
JF	*Zur Judenfrage* (*On the Jewish Question*)
Kap	*Das Kapital* (*Capital*)
KGP	*Kritik des Gothaer Programms* (*Critique of the Gotha Programme*)
KHR	*Zur Kritik der Hegelschen Rechtsphilosophie* (*Critique of Hegel's Philosophy of Right*)
MkP	*Manifest der kommunistichen Partei* (*The Communist Manifesto*)
ÖpM-1	*Ökonomisch-philosophische Manuskripte* (1844), *Erstes Manuskript* (*Economic-philosophical manuscripts* (1844), *First Manuscript*)
ÖpM-3	*Ökonomisch-philosophische Manuskripte* (1844), *Drittes Manuskript* (*Economic-philosophical manuscripts* (1844), *Third Manuscript*)

Nietzsche (references are to Nietzsche, 1999)
AsZ	*Also sprach Zarathustra* (*Thus Spoke Zarathustra*)

Freud (references are to Freud, 1999a, 1999b)
MIA	*Massenpsychologie und Ich-Analyse* (*Mass psychology and Ego-Analysis*)
UK	*Das Unbehagen in der Kultur* (*Civilisation and its Discontents*)

Chapter 1
Nietzsche's echo

οὐ γὰρ τὸ ποιεῖν τὰ ἄδικα ἀλλὰ τὸ πάσχειν φοβούμενοι ὀνειδίζουσιν οἱ ὀνειδίζοντες τὴν ἀδικίαν. οὕτως, ὦ Σώκρατες, καὶ ἰσχυρότερον καὶ ἐλευθεριώτερον καὶ δεσποτικώτερον ἀδικία δικαιοσύνης ἐστὶν ἱκανῶς γιγνομένη.[1]

1.1 Introduction

The quote above, from Plato's *Republic*, translates as follows: 'Those who reproach injustice do so because they are afraid not of doing it but of suffering it. So, Socrates, injustice, if it is on a large enough scale, is stronger, freer, and more masterly than justice.'[2] That proclamation sounds as impudent today as it did over two millennia ago when Plato placed it in the mouth of the sophist Thrasymachus. The *Republic* still stands as Plato's peremptory reply to the question, 'What is justice?'[3] Generations of readers have witnessed one of Western philosophy's great showdowns: the pugnacious Thrasymachus sings the praises of injustice, as Socrates strains to shoot down his arguments one by one. Power or wealth, Socrates' proto-Nietzschean[4] nemesis urges, are handily acquired through unjust actions. The select few, the clever and the daring, ought not to toil when they can prosper[5] through force or stealth. Law and justice are risible weapons, forged by a mediocre, cowardly multitude, the weak and the meek, who, at the hands of the powerful, merit not justice but disdain.[6]

Many of us, like Socrates, disagree. We assume justice to be better than injustice. We assume that 'doing what's unjust is actually the worst thing there is'.[7] Countless children grow up with some version of that lesson. For us

---

1 R [Bur] 1.344c.
2 R 1.344c.
3 R 1.331b–c.
4 See, e.g., Zehnpfennig, 2001, p. 50; Annas, 1981, p. 37.
5 Cf. e.g., Grg 491e–92c.
6 Cf. Grg 483b–c, 488b–d. Cf. also Annas, 1981, pp. 48–49; Shklar, 1990, pp. 33–35; Klosko, 2006, pp. 3–4.
7 Grg 469b. Cf. Grg 477e.

adults, it is too obvious for discussion.[8] Our mediatised political and ethical debates never ask what justice and injustice 'are'. They focus on particular issues. Is it just or unjust to go to war? To lower taxes? To prohibit addictive substances? To open marriage and child rearing to same-sex partners? Lurching towards pragmatism, our hunch seems to be that such questions can be decided without our having to examine concepts of justice and injustice more broadly. We often believe that, by attending to the specific, concrete problems, one by one, we can work progressively towards justice throughout society as a whole, towards overall justice *someday*.

If justice is nevertheless so conspicuously superior to injustice, in the eyes of adults and children alike, we would certainly expect one who does take the time to ponder it in abstraction – Plato, the founder of systematic ethical and political theory in the Western canon – to have little difficulty demonstrating the point. After a few volleys, Socrates does seem to prevail: '[A] just person (δίκαιος) has turned out to be good and clever, and an unjust one (ἄδικος) ignorant and bad.'[9] On closer reading, however, what leaps out is how unpersuasive Socrates' replies to Thrasymachus are. One interlocutor, Plato's brother Glaucon, notes that Socrates has left crucial points of Thrasymachus's challenge unanswered. Perhaps all that matters for injustice to prevail is for unjust people to *appear* just.[10] Glaucon tells the legend of a poor shepherd who had found a magic ring. It enabled him to turn invisible while he committed unjust acts. He 'seduced the king's wife, attacked the king with her help, killed him, and took over the kingdom'.[11] At that point of achieving absolute power, the shepherd no longer needs to fear justice. In becoming king, he effectively becomes the law. He becomes law's source, power and authority. He becomes the arbiter of justice. It is he who will now decide what is and is not just.[12]

Glaucon, still playing devil's advocate, suggests to Socrates that we would not hesitate to do injustice if we knew with certainty that no harm, and indeed great personal good, would come to us as a result of doing it.

> Now, no one, it seems, would be so incorruptible that he would stay on the path of justice or stay away from other people's property, when he could take whatever he wanted from the marketplace with impunity, go into people's houses and have sex with anyone he wished, kill or release from prison anyone he wished, and do all the other things that would make him like a god among humans. [. . .] This, some would say, is a great proof that one is never just willingly but only when compelled to

8 Cf. Alc 113d.
9 R 1.350c.
10 R 2.361a–b.
11 R 2.360a–b.
12 Cf. R 1.340e–41a.

be. [. . .] [W]herever [a] person thinks he can do injustice with impunity, he does it. Indeed, every man believes that injustice is far more profitable to himself than justice.[13]

No enterprise becomes more desperate or more suspicious in Plato's writings than his hundreds of pages of mind-numbing acrobatics to establish what we mostly take to be trivially obvious, namely, that justice is better than injustice. Children will readily agree[14] that justice is better because it is fairer, making society happier, more prosperous, more peaceful. The more Plato tries to defend justice on those or any other grounds, however, the less convincing his arguments become. Plato claims, for example, that any perpetrator of injustice, even Glaucon's shepherd, always ends up more miserable than the victim. '[A] just person is happy, and an unjust one wretched',[15] even if the unjust person has gained great power or wealth by inflicting, with impunity, horrendous brutality upon those who are just. Socrates insists that individuals who commit injustice must ultimately end up more miserable than their victims. Any unjust agent, be it an individual or a group, always becomes tormented,[16] 'miserable',[17] 'an enemy to itself'.[18] Neither through argument nor example, however, does Socrates show that unjust people do in fact suffer much despair at all, let alone pangs sharper than those suffered by their victims. Nor can we, looking back on a further 2,500 years of history, do much to bolster Socrates' view. Hitler, Stalin, Pol Pot, Ceaucescu, Kim Il Sung, Saddam, Qadaffi or Kim Jong-Il may have faced bad ends – and some of them suffered not even that – but, for the most part, not terribly protracted ones, compared to what they inflicted,[19] and compared to their decades of relishing power, wealth, and often glory.[20] '[C]urrent events quite suffice', Socrates is reminded in another exchange, to show 'that many people who behave unjustly are happy'.[21]

Plato does sometimes add afterlife myths about divine or ultimate justice.[22] But those tales scarcely reassure us. His other brother, Adeimantus, reminds Socrates that, in ancient Athens as today, any supernatural order that will reward the just or punish the unjust remains shrouded in doubt. Perhaps 'the

---

13 R 2.360b–d. Cf. R 2.359a. The point is made not only allegorically, but also with references accepted by the interlocutors as historically accurate, at Grg 470d–71d.
14 Cf. Alc 110c.
15 R 1.354a.
16 Cf. Grg 492e–508c.
17 Grg 508b.
18 R 1.352e.
19 On brutality and torture practiced with impunity under positive law, see, e.g., Grg 473b–c.
20 Cf. Grg 471a–d. Cf. also 479a, e.
21 Grg 470d (the young immoralist Polus speaking).
22 R 10.614a–21d; Grg 523a–27e; Phd 81c–82c, 107d–14c; L 927a.

gods don't exist or don't concern themselves with human affairs'.[23] Christianity will later hail divine justice to urge us that 'it is not the kind of suffering but the kind of person who suffers that is important'.[24] But why would we believe that Christianity's divine order exists?

Countless Western thinkers, in their various ways, will rush to the defence of justice, from Aristotle, Augustine and Aquinas through to Locke, Rousseau, Kant, Hegel, Mill or Marx, and many more in our own day. It remains questionable whether they can defeat Thrasymachus's views any more convincingly than Plato does. Little in their work tackles Thrasymachus's challenge head-on. To be fair, Socrates does add other arguments. He claims, for example, that persons united by 'a common unjust purpose' – we need only recall a long line of Mafia films – inevitably render themselves unable to attain it. They become wracked not only by the internal psychological divisions of each unjust person, but by inter-personal strife.[25] Once again, however, history often suggests otherwise, scarcely showing that high-minded projects inevitably prosper better than despotic ones. The Weimar Republic hardly flourished better than the Third Reich. Elevating justice above injustice, and even clearly distinguishing them, remains a complicated business.

1.2 A mutual exclusion?

For all their differences, Socrates and Thrasymachus share a crucial assumption. Most of us share it with them. Without it they would have no disagreement at all. They both presuppose that justice and injustice form a mutually exclusive pair, not merely as a matter of empirical observation, but as a tautology. Injustice by definition negates justice; justice by definition negates injustice. In Aristotle's words, 'the just will be both the lawful and what is fair, and the unjust will be both the lawless and the unfair'.[26]

The justice or injustice of some acts is, of course, debatable. Consider the age-old controversies about whether it is ever justified to sacrifice one person to save many; or the debates concerning how much force counts as 'reasonable' to ward off a physical attack. Consider also complex factual scenarios, including armed conflict or natural calamites, in which a web of human actions, variously just or unjust, may become impossible to disentangle. For Plato and most of his successors, Aristotle or Aquinas, Kant or Hegel, Mill or Marx, Rawls or Dworkin, the fact that some scenarios are ethically complex in no way means that justice becomes inscrutable.[27] The binarism therefore remains intact.

---

23 R 2.365d.
24 CD 1:8.
25 R 1.351c.
26 NE [Ir] 5.1.1129^{b}1.
27 See, for example, Aristotle's discussion of legal and ethical complexity in the context of equity at NE 5.10.

Insofar as Socrates deems justice superior to injustice, it is precisely because the one term is assumed to negate the other that Thrasymachus can construct, in symmetrical opposition, his argument that injustice is better than justice. If 'unhappy' is the opposite of 'happy', if 'untrue' is the opposite of 'true', then, in the same way, 'injustice' and 'justice', must be mutually defined opposites. When Aristotle writes, 'if the unjust is unfair (ἄδικον ἄνισον), the just is fair (δίκαιον ἴσον)', he deems that observation to be 'true to everyone without argument'.[28]

What would it mean if there were something incorrect about that seemingly obvious, seemingly necessary, assumption? On the one hand, it is easy enough to note that terms can function as mutually exclusive without sharing an etymological link, such as terms like 'good' and 'bad', or 'right' and 'wrong'. On the other hand, and more importantly, as I shall argue, it is far from obvious that an etymology of logical opposition strictly corresponds to mutually exclusive realities. A long tradition has emerged in the West, embodying what can be called the 'classical model' of justice. That binary model relentlessly mirrors the etymology which renders 'injustice' a sheer negation of justice. A hallmark of programmatic theorists, from Plato and Aristotle through to Aquinas, Locke, Rousseau, Hegel, Mill, Marx, or Rawls, is that they explain injustice by assuming that some model of justice must be identified, such that injustice becomes, by definition, that which opposes or negates all, or some necessary part of the model: '[L]aws that accord with the correct constitutions must be just, and those that accord with the deviant constitutions not just.'[29]

A common approach for those theorists – whom I shall call 'classical' solely to denote their shared assumption of that strict, binary relationship between the concepts of 'justice' and 'injustice' – is to turn one part of their efforts towards condemning historical or existing injustices, and then another, towards elaborating an alternative programme, designed to foster justice. They attempt to spell out the conditions of a just society in step-by-step detail, on the assumption that injustice is, or results from, the absence or negation of those conditions.[30] In this book, I shall refer to 'programmatic' theorists to denote writers, often landmark figures in Western thought, who do not contemplate justice only in essayistic or impressionistic ways – although those can certainly be incisive, as countless authors from Montaigne and Voltaire to Benjamin and Arendt remind us – but who propose frameworks for restructuring much or all of society. The West's first programmatic justice theory is Plato's *Republic*.[31]

---

28 NE [Ir] 5.3.1131^{a}13–14. Cf. Prt 331a–b.
29 Pol [Re] 3.11.1282^{b}12–13. Cf. Aristotle's distinction between 'true' or 'correct' and 'perverted' or 'deviant' constitutional orders. Pol 4.2.1289^{a}26–30, and, generally, Pol 3.7.
30 Cf. Shklar, 1990, pp. 15–17.
31 Although some observers have deemed the *Republic* to be a parody, it is not the case that Aristotle or most scholars since have viewed its core arguments that way. See, e.g., NE 2.2–5. See also, e.g., Rice, 1998, pp. 123–25.

The tradition continues through to John Rawls's *A Theory of Justice* (1999), and is still pursued.

It could be argued that Plato does indeed respond to Thrasymachus's challenge, not through this or that argument, but through the entirety of the *Republic*; and that only in contemplation of the complete work can any response emerge. Leaving aside one obvious problem with that reply, namely that it would almost require a review of the whole of Platonic philosophy before we could decide whether Thrasymachus's challenge has been met, it also overlooks a more basic point. Book I of the *Republic* mirrors the style of Plato's more typically 'Socratic' dialogues. A 'What is X?' question is posed, 'What is justice?', and various replies are considered and debated, with no clear solution yet reached. The remainder of the *Republic* is different, prompting some scholars to surmise that Plato added Books II–X later.[32] By the end of Book II, the open-ended debate is progressively vanishing. Socrates now acts less in his peremptorily 'Socratic' role of challenging others' beliefs, and more as a mouthpiece for Plato's ideas, with little airing of serious challenges or contrary views. Gone is the Socrates who unveils others' ignorance while proclaiming his own. It is in that philosophical moment of uncertainty, as Socrates pursues not justice within his own theories but injustice within others', that systematic western justice theory, if not all of Western ethical and political philosophy, is born. Once Plato then turns ethical and political philosophy towards programmatic justice theory, that Socratic moment goes missing. The following 25 centuries will be dominated by programmatic theories that collapse the concept of injustice into a derivative of this or that particular justice theory, a straightforward negation of this or that particular concept of justice.

In questioning the relationship of mutual exclusion between the concepts of justice and injustice, my aim will not be to swing to the opposite extreme, towards a nihilist view that justice and injustice are meaningless or wholly relative concepts. I shall ask only whether the relationship between the two involves greater complexity. I shall certainly acknowledge everyday senses in which the binarism seems to work well enough. Moreover, as my interest in this book is in grasping injustice, I shall not propose anything more constructive than that workaday binarism, as any greater task would fall under the domain of justice theory, and not of injustice theory. I shall argue, however, that the traditional binarism tells us less about injustice than either our institutional practices or our programmatic theories have generally assumed. We overlook the reach and the complexity of injustice, we impoverish our understanding of it, when we instinctively obey the arbitrary dictates of etymology, theorising injustice as a sheer negation of something else.

---

32 See, e.g., Annas, 1981, pp. 16–18; Zehnpfennig, 2001, p. 29; Pappas, 2003, pp. 27–30. It is later editors, and not Plato, who divided the dialogue into books.

I shall challenge the classical binarism by arguing that injustice must primarily be seen as a product, not a negation, of criteria generally deemed necessary to justice. My aim is not to argue, as do the traditional approaches, expressly or by implication, that injustice arises because criteria generally thought necessary to justice have been misapprehended. In other words, I shall not argue, along the lines of the classical binarism, either that we have identified the wrong criteria for justice, and must instead adopt other criteria, or that we have identified the right criteria, but have applied them wrongly, and must instead apply them in some other way. I shall instead argue that injustice arises primarily from criteria that we generally deem to be necessary to justice *as they are*, and which are applied in ways that we all deem equally necessary *as they are*. Those criteria are mostly of two types. Above all, and particularly in modernity, they are criteria of *measurement*. However, on some alternative theories, such as Platonic or indeed Marxist ones, those criteria may, in either sweeping or at least in partial attempts to transcend the plagues of measurement *über alles*, instead emphasise criteria of socio-political *unity*. I shall argue that it is not merely this or that criterion of unity or of measurement, but rather unity and measurement as such, under any conception, which, simultaneously, are indispensible to justice, yet necessarily − that is, not merely through being 'negations' or 'failures' of such justice[33] − generate injustice.

The task of understanding injustice is not fundamentally about 'replacing' either or both of those criteria, which would entail the destruction of justice altogether. Nor can this book explain everything that injustice is or can be, nor examine its many manifestations in detail. My argument in this book will be limited to the suggestion that one condition, a necessary even if not a sufficient one, for understanding injustice, is to abandon the age-old assumption of its straightforward relationship of mutual exclusion with some conceptually prior notion of justice. Despite 2,500 years of theorists beavering away under the binarist assumption, any such notion remains as hazy today as when Plato first staged a Socrates and a Thrasymachus trying, and failing, to hash out the matter. Thrasymachus is Socrates' shadow, not his nemesis. Plato's Socrates cannot solve the problem of justice, as the classical binarism would in principle do, by erasing Thrasymachus or what he stands for. On the surface, it may well be that Socrates advocates justice and Thrasymachus advocates injustice, each in pristine, polar opposition to the other. More fundamentally, however, Thrasymachus is not only a partisan of injustice, but also a creation of justice, of the very thing that Socrates pursues and Plato so fervently wishes to implement.

Two millennia of philosophy have constantly delivered theories aiming to exhaust the concept of justice, to pin down its essence or core, with some concomitant theory of injustice explained or implied as its negation. The

---

33 Cf. Shklar, 1990, p. 22.

West's long train of justice theories has nevertheless left us not with the one theory upon which we generally agree, but with each theory inadvertently doing little more than to set limits to the others, each time rendering all the more conspicuous the illusion of a distinct theory of injustice as the manifest opposite of justice. My reply to the question 'What is injustice?' will not be: 'Injustice is *not* the opposite of justice', although it will come close. Rather, my reply will be: 'Injustice is not *solely* the opposite of justice, even if it is merely and simply the opposite in certain conventional senses.'

No study of injustice can be exhaustive. Everything ever spoken or written on any ethical or political topic in some sense concerns injustice, whether it be religious or secular, expository or artistic, tragic or comic, sociological or psychological, programmatic or essayistic, speculative or empirical. *Innombrables sont les récits du monde*[34] – innumerable are the narratives of the world, and innumerable are our accounts of injustice. Every cry about power, abuse, deceit, conquest, exclusion, hierarchy, brutality, domination, subordination, or corruption is about injustice, be it only, with Thrasymachus or Nietzsche, as a celebration. Any writer on the topic is, therefore, in a bind. On the one hand, if only small numbers of prior writers are included, one or another reader will wonder at the exclusion of others; on the other, to try to include every writer whom some reader somewhere may deem germane to the problem of justice would be like insisting that the grains of sand on the beach are not to be estimated, but must instead be counted individually.

What applies across that breadth of sources applies to many thinkers in detail. There is scarcely a work by Plato, for example, which does not underscore the primacy of justice as an object of enquiry,[35] even where the immediate topic at hand appears remote from politics in the ordinary sense.[36] Similar observations pertain to figures from Augustine or Aquinas to Rousseau or Marx. Even if the same cannot so obviously be said about figures like Locke, Kant or Mill, whose epistemological works are presented as facially distinct from ethics, nevertheless the intricacy of all such writers' views on political, social or legal matters far surpasses what can be encompassed in this book.

Today's neo-Aristotelians, neo-Thomists, neo-Kantians, neo-Hegelians, neo-Marxists, or latter-day students of other classic writers or traditions, have largely shed various orthodoxies originally associated with those intellectual figureheads. Those disciples have often distilled and updated what they see as their philosophies' crucial contributions, in ways that would require closer study if this book's aim were to sketch an overview, let alone to assess the strengths and weaknesses, of classical justice theories. The writers examined in this book are chosen not for purposes of evaluating the ultimate merits of

---

34 Barthes, 1977, p. 7.
35 See Cairns, 1942, p. 359.
36 See, e.g., Phdr 247d; Smp 209a; Tht 167c, 172a–73d, 175b–76e.

their ideas – and even less for pondering various revisions of those ideas, as if this book were searching for yet another justice theory – but only insofar as they shed light on the classical binary model. For the most part, I shall draw upon two kinds of writers. I shall examine programmatic theories for insight into how their binarist assumptions lead them to theorise injustice; and I shall examine some early modern literary texts for evidence about how their authors problematise the binary view precisely at a stage in Western history when many of today's dominant notions of justice make an unmistakable appearance.

This book puts one central question to each of the various programmatic theorists: 'To what extent do your theory's core principles necessarily generate injustice?' That question seems, at first, rhetorical. Each theorist would presumably provide the same reply, namely, that the theory proposed promises the least possible injustice, less than any rival theory. If I then ask, 'But what, in your model society, is the cause even of that residual injustice?' (which I suspect to be more than merely residual), each would presumably point back to the traditional binarism, assuming injustice to be a mere negation of justice. 'Even the best justice theory', they would reply, 'cannot be perfect. Injustice therefore arises to the extent that justice, in one or another area, fails to operate as entailed by the theory.' A problem with our 2,500 years of programmatic justice theorists is that they see injustice only as an accident or a privation, and not as a substantive product of justice as *they* conceive it.

Solely in passing, as it is not this book's focus, I would add that the consequences of nuancing the traditional binarism may be of some interest for theories of justice within the Mosaic monotheisms – Judaism, Christianity or Islam. That is not an urgently important, but is a particularly evident, consequence of the thesis that justice necessarily produces injustice. If this book's thesis holds, we shall have to say to all three of them: either you can do law, or you can do justice, but you can never do both. Whatever your theodicy may be, you necessarily turn God into a deliberate and systematic doer of injustice by persisting in the idea that your concept of justice can be implemented programmatically as law while remaining justice. You can certainly pursue justice in aspirational terms ('God wills us all to pursue justice', 'God's justice is mysterious', 'God performs justice through love', etc.). But you can never implement your ideas of justice in codified form, because any such form of justice necessarily and actively – and not merely by 'human imperfection' – generates injustice, which a perfectly just God can never will, not even to 'test us' or to 'teach us lessons' or to 'improve us in the long run'.

A perfectly just God can perhaps will a justice that we do not understand (if it makes sense to talk about God's 'will' in such prosaic terms), but cannot, on any non-contradictory notion of 'perfection', specifically will us to undertake systemic injustice, and therefore cannot ordain justice in the kind of programmatic form that must inevitably have that result. You must therefore renounce programmatic law, if you wish only justice; or you must renounce justice, if you either practice or desire programmatic law. You can certainly render justice in individual cases, applying, for example, 'Thou shalt not murder'. Injustice, however, must inhere in your justice theory as it inheres in any other theory *qua* programmatic justice theory.

My thesis in this book might have come as no surprise, then, to those Greeks who were laconic about the suggestion that gods can do unjust things,[37] or to Confucians, Taoists, Buddhists or Shintoists amenable to the idea of injustice as inherent in a world order in ways not crucially linked to divinities who have a supernatural and overarching will or plan for human beings.[38] Nor ought it to come as a surprise to those Jews, Christians or Muslims who have long understood that justice, as a spiritual concept, can never translate into conclusively and comprehensively codified regimes. But, as I say, questions of religious law as such will not be central to this book.

1.3 Plan of this book

This book divides into two parts. The task of Part 1, entitled 'Classical understandings', will be to examine ways in which Western thought has grasped injustice solely as a negation of justice. I begin, in Chapter 2, by considering how the word's fateful etymology sets the stage for our longstanding assumption of mutual exclusion between justice and injustice. I acknowledge that, in many everyday contexts, for purposes of expedient problem solving, the traditional binarism appears to be accurate. I argue that the standard binarism works only insofar as justice and injustice are theorised or applied in institutional or intellectual abstraction from the systemic contexts of ethics and politics. As mentioned, while rejecting the dogma that justice and injustice are, by definition, co-extensive opposites, each always just the flip side of the other, I equally reject the view at the opposite extreme, that justice and injustice are altogether meaningless or relative. I describe the two concepts instead as 'partially commensurable', partially binary, up to the point that straightforward mutual exclusion does accurately account for their relationship; but also, therefore, as 'partially incommensurable', partially non-binary, insofar as their relationship surpasses that point. By understanding the limits of the two concepts' commensurability, we can set the stage for considering, in Part 2, injustice as something not merely derivative of a theory of justice, but as requiring a theoretical approach of its own, to the extent of its incommensurability, its non-binary relationship, with the concept of justice. Key to those two concepts' incommensurability is what I shall identify as the systemic, as opposed to the isolated, contexts within which they must be analysed.

In Chapters 3 and 4, I further argue that, despite the variety of justice theories, Plato and Aristotle already correctly identify two defining features

---

37 See, e.g., Ant 671, 695–98. Cf. R 2.379e–80a.
38 See, e.g., Hsi and Tsu-Ch'ien, 1967, pp. 5–34.

among programmatic theories: *unity* and *measurement*. Measurement in particular, as the key criterion of justice in modernity, and traditionally entailing *mismeasurement* as the criterion of injustice, will be the most important concept in this book. Unity, too, must nevertheless be examined, in view of its role in traditional theory and in view of its inherent link to measurement. In Chapter 3, I examine unity more as an element of traditional justice theories, which has generally implied disunity as its opposite, and therefore as injustice. The West's first programmatic theory also provides its greatest illustration of a unity theory in the *Republic*, echoed strongly among writers otherwise as different as Dante, Rousseau and Marx. In Chapter 4, I turn to measurement as the other central element of traditional justice theories, already recognised by Plato, and prominent in Aristotle. Unity, after all, remains a distant, holistic ideal. No one norm can easily articulate it, and even an entire legal system does so only with difficulty. Measurement, on the other hand, structures virtually every concrete, ordinary norm of any existing legal regime, from the most vital of substantive norms to the most ancillary of procedural norms; and it similarly pervades any programmatic justice theory. Injustice then becomes, on the binary model, mismeasurement – application of the wrong measure, or misapplication of the right one.

The goal of Part 2, entitled 'Post-classical understandings', is to look beneath the surface of the classical model, at a more complex relationship between injustice and justice. In a post-medieval age, Europe will brim with justice theories, from Erasmus through to Locke. I shall argue that literary works, as the law and literature movement has long suggested, already offer critical insights into the inherently complex relationship between injustice and justice. In Chapter 5, after a preliminary examination of the ancient *Antigone*, I turn to unity theories of justice in some early modern texts to examine how injustice arises not primarily, as the traditional binarism would have it, from the sheer breach of positive norms of justice, but from the opposite, namely, the rigorous pursuit of principles of justice, regardless of the socio-political contexts in question.

Even those examples, however, provide only a taste of the origins of injustice, since, again, unity remains an older and abstract ideal. In Chapters 6 and 7, I therefore focus on measurement. In Chapter 6, I examine Shakespeare's *The Merchant of Venice*. That play merits particular attention, as its socio-legal world, in several respects, anticipates the emerging conditions of modernity. In its proto-capitalist setting, any pursuit of justice constantly collapses into criteria of measurement, entailing systematic injustice as the constant product of principles of justice. In Chapter 7, those patterns are traced further through early modernity, with special attention devoted to Shakespeare's later collaborative effort with Thomas Middleton, *Timon of Athens*, and to two works of Pierre Corneille – his first, early comedy *Mélite* and his more familiar drama *Le Cid*.

Citations to canonic sources, subject to multiple editions, refer either to established lineation systems, or to original textual divisions, wherever they are specific enough. Where page numbers are required, standard editions are used. Translations from modern languages are mine, unless otherwise indicated. For Corneille, as my purposes are more analytic than poetic, I have retained conventional iambic pentameter, with rhymed endings. Despite recent translators' preferences for free verse,[39] the rhyming pattern, as I explain in Chapter 7, is often germane to the substantive point it is used to express, often concerning comparison and rivalry, which the strict metre and rhyme more faithfully convey. Italics within cited sources are noted as such regardless of their function, but for those German texts which employ intermittent spacing for emphasis, in lieu of italics, my notes refer to 'emphasis'.

Ideas in this book were first presented at a staff seminar held in the UK at the University of Warwick in November 2010. Many thanks to those who attended, and to Alan Norrie, Paul Raffield and Gary Watt for their incisive replies. Many thanks also to those who attended a second seminar, held in March 2011 at the University of Leicester, and in particular to Claire Grant, who organised and chaired the discussion, and provided valuable feedback. Thanks also to Roger Cotterrell, Andrew Heinze and Jo Murkens for their comments on an early draft, and to Colin Perrin, Melanie Fortmann-Brown and the Routledge staff for their support, along with Hayley Chelsom and Heather Jones.

---

39 See, e.g., Corneille, 1975.

Part I

Classical understandings

Chapter 2

Injustice as the negation of justice

ὁρῶμεν δὴ πάντας τὴν τοιαύτην ἕξιν βουλομένους λέγειν δικαιοσύνην, ἀφ' ἧς πρακτικοὶ τῶν δικαίων εἰσὶ καὶ ἀφ' ἧς δικαιοπραγοῦσι καὶ βούλονται τὰ δίκαια· τὸν αὐτὸν δὲ τρόπον καὶ περὶ ἀδικίας, ἀφ' ἧς ἀδικοῦσι καὶ βούλονται τὰ ἄδικα.[1]

2.1 Introduction

From its etymology, injustice appears solely as not-justice, not-X. By definition, not-X becomes meaningful only insofar as X is meaningful. In this chapter, I shall examine how that etymology reflects a concept of injustice arising out of disputes construed, for practical, institutional or speculative purposes, in isolation from their social contexts. A core function of traditional, bipolar litigation is to distil disputes from those contexts, in the sense, for example, of rendering opposing parties amenable to all-or-nothing ascriptions of 'winner' and 'loser'. Within the bounds of traditional positive law, those tags correspond, respectively, to determinations of 'just' and 'unjust'. In that way, dominant legal norms and processes preserve conventionally dualist assumptions about injustice as the negation of justice, and justice as the negation of injustice.

It would miss the point to seek some outright overthrow of that traditional dualism. Purely conventional understandings of many legal or ethical terms, like 'reasonable' or 'intentional', are woven into the fabric of socio-legal life, as are their conventional opposites, such as 'unreasonable' or 'unintentional'. Rarely do we witness clean breaks from everyday understandings of such familiar normative concepts. It is in that respect, and this will be the chapter's first main point, that there is indeed an undeniable level of 'commensurability' or 'coextension', through the familiar relationship of mutual exclusion, between

---

1 NE [By] 5.1.1129^{a}7–12. 'We see that all men mean by justice that kind of state which makes people disposed to do what is just and makes them act justly and wish for what is just; and similarly by injustice that state which makes them act unjustly and wish for what is unjust.'

the concepts of 'justice' and 'injustice'. That conventional dualism, reflected in everyday legal norms and processes, does therefore bring us part of the way towards understanding injustice. We cannot deny that, in many customary contexts, speaking about justice and injustice as opposites 'does the trick'. It 'serves all intents and purposes' for routine ethical or legal discussions – many of a so-called pragmatic bent would see justice and injustice as nothing else – which may not appear to require a deeper approach.

Injustice certainly does arise within the context of disputes isolated or distilled for practical, institutional, or speculative purposes. We have grown accustomed to contriving artificial situations, both institutionally, in our political and legal practices, and intellectually, in our habits of casual as well as academic ethical reasoning. The second main point of this chapter will nevertheless be to recall that, in a more fundamental sense, injustice emerges out of broader social, economic, cultural, ethical and political contexts – a perfectly familiar idea, although its consequences for the concept of injustice have been neglected. I shall attempt to show that, as injustice must above all be understood within those broader contexts, its relationship to justice ceases to be one of sheer mutual exclusion.

Those two main points will yield the following result, which is this chapter's overriding aim. At the level of specific disputes, discretely isolated for everyday institutional or hypothetical purposes, the concepts of justice and injustice do indeed commonly form a mutually exclusive pair. To that degree, the two concepts readily appear to be 'commensurable' or 'coextensive'. Beyond that limit, they become incommensurable, and injustice can no longer be grasped as a sheer negation of justice. Accordingly, the concepts of justice and injustice can be seen as partially commensurable, and therefore, by definition, partially incommensurable. In the book's subsequent chapters, it is that locus of partial incommensurability which will be analysed for purposes of pursuing a concept of injustice, as something other than the sheer opposite of some, often questionable, concept of justice.

2.2 Typical expressions of mutual exclusion

The etymology of 'injustice' turns one reality into the negation of a prior reality. 'Prior' in that sense does not mean temporally prior. To the contrary, the desire for justice is often felt only after an injustice has already occurred.[2] The etymology nevertheless suggests that justice is conceptually prior to injustice, such that injustice as 'not-justice' depends for its meaning upon some presupposed concept of justice. That etymology has persisted from ancient through to modern languages (ἀδικία, *iniustitia*, *ingiustizia*, *injusticia*, *Ungerechtigkeit*, *onrechtvaardigheid*).

---

2 See this chapter, Section 2.4.

Standard dictionary definitions recapitulate that etymology. *The Oxford English Dictionary* indicates as its first definition of 'injustice' precisely '[t]he opposite of justice'.[3] In *The New Oxford Dictionary of English*, we find 'lack of ... justice'.[4] *Webster's New Universal Dictionary of the English Language* defines 'injustice' as 'the quality of being unjust or unfair',[5] with 'unfair' displaying a parallel etymology. *Webster's Third New International Dictionary* includes the cognate notions 'unfairness' and 'iniquity',[6] which, of course, are no more determinate than 'injustice' itself. Dictionaries from other languages also reveal circular or question-begging definitions.[7]

Some definitions offer an affirmative content, but that, too, is inadequate. A definition like 'violation ... of the rights of another',[8] for example, applies only within the context of sufficiently rights-based regimes.[9] In the *Republic*, Plato imagines a just society conspicuous for its absence of rights in any familiar sense. Law in the *Republic* aims at harmonising interests,[10] not at the primacy of rights.[11] It certainly lacks anything like Locke's early modern schema of rights as foundational of the legal order,[12] or Ronald Dworkin's view of rights as 'trumps'.[13] Nor is Plato's the only model that eschews any clear foundation in the language of rights. Bentham notoriously challenges early modern notions in their various natural-law meanings, famously rejecting them not merely as 'nonsense', but, in view of their elevated, higher-law claims, as 'nonsense upon stilts'.[14] Marx equally rejects classical concepts of rights-based legal regimes as falsely universalist, functioning in reality to secure only the privilege of the property-owning classes,[15] at the price of oppression of the proletariat. It is problematical, then, to assume that talk of injustice presupposes talk about rights. The only accurate dictionary definitions turn out to be the tautological ones, which preserve the binarism of injustice as the opposite of justice.

At first glance, the concepts of justice and injustice in everyday practice seem indeed to pair off logically, reflecting both their shared etymology and the dictionary definitions. Specific instances of injustice indeed appear to be plain

---

3 *OED*, 1989, v. 7, p. 982.
4 *New Oxford*, 1989, p. 940.
5 *Webster's New Universal*, 1976, p. 944.
6 *Webster's Third New Int'l*, 1976, v. 1, p. 1164.
7 See, e.g., *Le Petit Robert*, 1977, p. 1005; *Duden*, 1989, p. 1603; *Wolters'*, 1992, p. 788.
8 *Webster's Third New Int'l*, 1976, v. 1, p. 1164.
9 The brief entry in *Black's Law Dictionary* adds nothing to the standard *Oxford* or *Webster* definitions. See *Black's*, 2004, p. 857. *The Oxford Dictionary of Law* omits entries altogether for 'injustice' or 'unjust'. However, it includes 'justice', defined as a 'moral ideal ... not synonymous with law' since 'it is possible for a law to be unjust'. *Oxford Law*, 2009, p. 310.
10 See this book, Chapter 3, Section 3.2.
11 See generally Heinze, 2007a.
12 STCG chs 5, 7–9.
13 See Dworkin, 1977, pp. 22–31.
14 CE art 2.
15 JF, MEW 1: 364–66.

and simple not-justice. Assume, for example, that a suspect is falsely accused of a crime, that a husband is violent, or that a child is starving. Assume also that all three scenarios arise as a result of human agency – the child is starving, for example, due to malice or neglect, and not because of a natural catastrophe or some other circumstance beyond human control.[16] In each of those cases, and we could find many more, the suggestion of injustice seems already 'built in' from the outset. Injustice, in each case, becomes precisely the negation of the justice that we accept as inherent within the notions of truthful accusations, peaceful husbands, or care for children. By extension, we grasp the rendering of justice in such cases as, in turn, negations of the injustice: the falsely accused suspect is released, the violent husband is restrained, the starving child is fed. There is even more than one possible result for each negation in that latter sequence. Some alternatives would be, for example: the false accusation is punished, the violent husband is prosecuted, the child's parents are investigated.

From the assumption that justice manifests through truthful accusations, peaceful husbands, or nourished children, injustice does indeed appear to be straightforward not-justice: the accusation is false, the husband is violent, the child is starving. Just as obviously, just as tautologically, justice re-surfaces when those negations are, in turn, plainly and simply negated, becoming, so to speak, not-not-justice, for example: the falsely accused suspect is released, the violent husband restrained or the starving child fed. Such simple sequences of injustice negating justice, and justice negating injustice, seem to confirm the etymological suggestion, and the customary assumption, that justice and injustice define each other in binary pairings: 'It's financial management, then, that gets rid of poverty, medicine that gets rid of disease, and justice that gets rid of injustice.'[17]

Those who accept the traditional, binary view will freely admit that not all examples are straightforward. Propositions such as 'Strict regulation of markets promotes a more just society', or 'The death penalty achieves natural justice', spark more controversy than 'Children should be nourished'. Nevertheless, however controversial a proposed norm may be, the basic logical structure remains constant. To the extent that some state of affairs satisfying that norm is accepted or assumed to be just, then, to that same extent, some opposite state of affairs, constituting a violation of the norm, is unjust. On that familiar view, certain controversial applications may raise difficulties, but the mutually defining relationship between justice and injustice remains intact. I am not arguing that formal logic cannot accommodate a more complex relationship between justice and injustice,[18] but only that such complexity has not formed part of the dominant popular or programmatic understandings of those terms.

16 Cf. Shklar, 1990, pp. 1–5, 51–82.
17 Grg 478a–b.
18 See, e.g., Malinowski, 2001. Cf., e.g., Heinze, 2003a, 2005.

Our traditional models of bipolar litigation follow the familiar pattern, defining each dispute so that it may culminate in a decision about which party wins and which loses, about which party's cause, within the bounds of legal convention, is just, and which – be it only through the trivial notion that the loser's case is less just than the winner's – is unjust. If, like Montagues and Capulets, two households have feuded, with members of each having caused harm to members of the other, litigation may proceed from a long list of charges and counter-charges, with the aim of determining the 'winner' or 'loser', the justice and injustice, point by point. Admittedly, some methods of alternative dispute resolution are not bipolar in that sense. Even those, however, often take place in the shadow of potential bipolar resolution. In any event, techniques of alternative dispute resolution cannot yet be said to represent the traditional or prevailing methods or understandings of Western law in modernity.

We observe, then, four typical ways in which the meaning of 'injustice' draws upon a conceptually prior assumption of justice: the word's etymology; its standard dictionary definitions; its application within hypothetical ethical reasoning to instances of justice and injustice examined in isolation; and its institutional application within litigation structured along bipolar lines. All four of those settings would accommodate countless discrete disputes, generating predictable sequences of justice and injustice negating each other in turn. They represent the relationship of mutual exclusion assumed more generally within programmatic justice theories. As the classical Western model of theorising injustice as the opposite of justice emerges with Plato, he writes several works, such as *Apology*, *Protagoras* or *Gorgias*, to challenge the injustice of familiar socio-political attitudes or practices. Those become complementary to other works, such as the *Republic* or *Laws*, which present justice as requiring something different from that existing order of things, some alternative socio-political order, and which, in its ideal form, represents justice, such that greater or lesser degrees of injustice emerge from greater or lesser departures from it. Many writers will follow that path. Figures as different as Aristotle, Rousseau or Marx divide their attention between, on the one hand, reviewing the problems or imperfections, hence the injustices, of earlier or existing societies, and, on the other, explaining how justice would result from the better societies that they propose. Others, such as Kant, Fuller or Rawls, albeit not undertaking such systematic surveys of past or existing conditions, nevertheless make obvious their view that injustice equates with the departures from their own models.

In 'Das Problem der Gerechtigkeit' ('The Problem of Justice'), Hans Kelsen attacks the classical natural law tradition, as he embarks upon his project of strictly separating matters of justice from matters of legal validity.[19] This

---

19 Kelsen, 1960, pp. 357–62.

exponent of modern positivism challenges natural law doctrines as mistaken insofar as those doctrines qualify norms contrary to the dictates of justice to be 'not law'. Of course, contrary to Kelsen's thesis, not all natural law theories take that step, or indeed are even as similar to one another in their content or aims as Kelsen argues.[20] But that difficulty in Kelsen is unimportant for my present interest, which is the traditional assumption of mutual exclusivity between justice and injustice. The noteworthy point is that, even for Kelsen, as long as that supposed error in natural law reasoning is avoided, the binarism of justice and injustice as mutually exclusive opposites remains strictly intact. The qualification of 'just' or 'unjust' in no way becomes irrelevant or meaningless to his positivist project. It instead flows from a *Gerechtigkeitsnorm*, a norm of justice, albeit strictly independent of the legal system. An attribution of 'just' or 'unjust' is one that

> states either that the act *is*, as it – according to a given norm of justice (*Gerechtigkeitsnorm*) – *ought* to be, in other words, that the act is worthy (*wertvoll*), because it has a positive justice-value (*Gerechtigkeitswert*); or that the act, being the opposite, is not – according to that norm of Justice – as it ought to be, in other words, that the act is unworthy (*wertwidrig*), because it has a negative justice-value.[21]

Kelsen's analysis of the concept of justice in his essay consists of critiquing a variety of formulations, mostly classical, but also theories, as different as Kantian and Marxist, that carry us into post-Enlightenment modernity. However radical may be Kelsen's rethinking of law, and however persuasive or unpersuasive we may consider his separation of law from justice to be, Kelsen's residual concept of justice still emphatically recapitulates the classical model. Such absolute adherence to the traditional binarism means that each of Kelsen's analyses of one or another theory of justice *ipso facto* becomes an analysis of a precisely corresponding and coextensive theory of injustice. The attributions 'just' or 'unjust' become, respectively, a conformity with, or a departure from, any given norm of justice.

Although not expressly citing Kelsen, Chaïm Perelman's essay 'De la Justice' ('On Justice') undertakes a review, similar to Kelsen's, of familiar justice theories. Their difference is that Kelsen's aim is critical, while Perelman, in a constructive vein, aims to distil some essence or core of justice. Recalling, like Kelsen, a series of maxims, such as 'to each according to his merits' or 'to each according to his needs', Perelman argues that no one recipe of that type can ever suffice. Not only are we likely to disagree about them, but different ones may be appropriate to different circumstances. Each of them nevertheless,

---

20 Cf. Heinze, 2007b, pp. 329–36.
21 Kelsen, 1960, p. 358 (Kelsen's emphasis).

on Perelman's view, instantiates one common, 'purely formal'[22] definition of justice: 'We can therefore define formal or abstract justice as *a principle of action according to which beings belonging to the same essential category must be treated in the same way.*'[23] Leaving aside questions about the meanings of Perelman's operative terms, or the merits of his definition, what remains common to all of the theories of justice which he subsumes under that formal definition is the corollary that injustice again becomes, for that master theory and therefore for each of its instantiations, the straightforward opposite or negation of justice.[24]

Despite that persistence of the binarist assumption as logically self-evident, and therefore conceptually prior to any particular ethical viewpoints or debates, a challenge to the binarist assumption might nevertheless seem unsurprising. Again, complex issues often display no obvious justice or injustice, but rather a mixture of both. Such issues often involve ambiguous or conflicting fact patterns, strongly reliant upon interpretation or viewpoint. As Plato or Aristotle, Rousseau or Kant, Mill or Marx, Fuller or Rawls nevertheless illustrate, even that complexity does not change the traditional binarist assumption that, insofar as some given state of affairs can be called just, there is some opposite state of affairs that is by definition unjust. For Perelman, complexity and disagreement shroud justice not because the binarism at any point breaks down, but only because different people apply, or different situations warrant, different criteria of justice.[25] All of those criteria nevertheless remain binarist, as reflected in Perelman's meta-formula and in each of its instantiations.

We might try to assail the traditional binarism through a well-worn strategy, along the following lines.

> *Socrates' and Thrasymachus's respective assumptions need not be mutually exclusive. Each can be correct at, so to speak, a different level. Socrates' insistence on the superiority of justice may be right as a matter of ethical principle, but Thrasymachus's opposite view often prevails in the bitter world of everyday practice.*

That *distinguo*, however, presents no real challenge to the binarism. It merely leads to the practical conclusion that we all need to *try harder* to avoid injustice in practice. And that is only another trivially obvious inference, which leaves the binarism wholly intact: justice is good, injustice is bad, good and bad are mutually exclusive, and therefore so are justice and injustice. Accordingly, on

---

22 Perelman, 1990, p. 31.
23 Perelman, 1990, p. 30 ('On peut donc définir la justice formelle ou abstraite comme *un principe d'action selon lequel les êtres d'une même catégorie essentielle doivent être traités de la même façon.*') (Perelman's italics)).
24 Perelman, 1990, p. 34.
25 Perelman, 1990, p. 31.

that view, we must pursue the ideal that justice is good even if, in practice, injustice often defeats it.

Plato makes clear that Socrates' and Thrasymachus's dispute runs deeper than that hackneyed theory-*versus*-practice distinction. Thrasymachus does not argue that injustice merely happens to triumph in practice, despite justice being better in theory. He recites his praise for injustice not merely as a descriptive account of actual practice, but as correct in principle. Thrasymachus announces that 'complete injustice is more profitable than complete justice'.[26] Injustice is better in practice precisely because it is better in theory. Thrasymachus proclaims a principle as absolute as the symmetrically opposite principle embraced by Socrates, who, for his own part, equates justice with the virtue or excellence of human beings (ἀνθρωπεία ἀρετή).[27] Justice, for Plato's Socrates, regardless of whether or how often it prevails in fact, is better in practice precisely because it is better in theory. (Similar challenges yield similar results. For example, the commonplace that 'there are always winners and losers', or the utilitarian view that sacrifices must be made to achieve greater goods, far from undermining the binarism, seek only to justify it.)

2.3 Injustice within isolated contexts

The binary scheme succeeds largely through the successive examination of examples – such as the falsely accused suspect, the violent husband, or the starving child – extracted from their broader social, ethical or political contexts. It is easy to overlook that transformation from broader to isolated contexts, because the transformation does not manifest as complex or arcane, but as altogether familiar and routine. Much everyday reasoning about justice and injustice, like much institutionalised legal practice, uncritically assumes that transformation.

In Shakespeare's *Henry V*, the humble foot soldier Michael Williams protests, unaware he is doing so to the disguised King, his doubts regarding the battle about to take place against the French. '[I]f the cause be not good, the King himself hath a heavy reckoning to make, when all those legs and arms and heads chopped off in battle shall join together at the latter [Judgment] day and cry all, "We died at such a place".'[28] If Williams fails to reason more comprehensively about the overall ethical or political justifications either for pacifism or for armed conflict, and if his imagery is at best allegorical, at worst superstitious, it is not because he is less educated than the nobles. Nor is there any obvious reason to find that he has reached, by ordinary standards, an unsatisfactory conclusion. His style of raising a plausible objection without

---

26 R 1.348b.
27 R 1.335c.
28 H5, 4.1.129–32.

exhausting all relevant principles and permutations is the method by which we generally undertake day-to-day ethical reasoning. The high-born Prince Hamlet's delays and deliberations about revenging the murder of his father by killing his uncle, the present King Claudius,[29] are no different in that respect. They encompass anything but a systematic examination of the ethics or politics of regicide. What Shakespeare's foot soldier reminds us is not only that ethical deliberation often inclines towards particular, concrete problems, but also that the lines between the particular and the general are often mutable. Does Williams oppose all war on all grounds? Or some wars but not others? Or only the present war against France?

Our everyday ethical reasoning often compels us to focus on immediate problems, with limited reference to their broader socio-political contexts or theories. That insight may seem obvious and pragmatically necessary, but has plagued Western ethical thought with formidable difficulties, as we often end up at one or another of two opposite, yet equally unsatisfying, extremes. In Plato's *Meno*, Socrates famously challenges the suggestion that we can reason about the virtue of this or that norm or event, in abstraction from a broader notion of justice as such. He questions whether we can grasp human ἀρετή, human virtue or excellence, which Plato strongly links to justice, solely by lining up isolated examples of it. When Socrates asks Meno, 'What do you yourself say that virtue is?',[30] Meno replies in the style of everyday reasoning.

> First, if you want the virtue of a man, it is easy to say that a man's virtue consists of being able to manage public affairs . . .; if you want the virtue of a woman, it is not difficult to describe: she must manage the home well, preserve its possessions, and be submissive to her husband;[31] the virtue of a child, whether male or female, is different again, and so is that of an elderly man, if you want that, or if you want that of a free man or a slave. And there are many other virtues, so that one is not at a loss to say what virtue is. There is virtue for every action and every age, for every task of ours and every one of us.[32]

Meno concludes by suggesting that the same kind of step-by-step description could be made of κακία, 'vice' or 'wickedness'[33] (which is the opposite of virtue, precisely as ἄδικος – unjust – is the opposite of δίκαιος – just).

Socrates rejects Meno's reply. He rejects the suggestion that we can reason about such individual instances in practical or hypothetical isolation.

---

29 See, e.g., Ham 3.3.73–95.
30 M 71d.
31 The *Republic* will admit all qualified persons to the rank of guardians and philosopher kings, be they men or women. R 7.540c.
32 M 71d–72.
33 M 72a.

Something more is needed, he suggests, namely, an understanding of some essential or universal element, which he calls the εἶδος, the 'Idea' or 'Form', by which we can know that each of the items on Meno's list does or does not qualify as virtuous.[34] To the query, which can be paraphrased for present purposes, 'How can we know that this or that norm or event is just without first knowing what justice is?', Plato proposes an absolute reply (although that absoluteness might be seen to be modified in a later work such as the *Laws*). He suggests that we cannot judge any particular norm or event to be just without first knowing, in some conclusive way, what Justice is in itself.[35] Although the *Republic* or *Laws* offer detailed accounts of justice, nothing in Plato, or from any subsequent philosopher, ever provides an exhaustive definition of the terse kind that *Meno*'s Socrates, at least on an ordinary or surface reading, seems to seek. We are left, then, with two opposed styles of reasoning about justice and injustice: on the one hand, our everyday, more-or-less particularist style of ethical reasoning, which, overly bound to its immediate context, risks losing sight of fundamental or systemic elements, and, on the other, Plato's universalist ideal of reason, which seems impossible to achieve, and is perhaps therefore inherently misconceived.

Many philosophers since Plato have sought to bridge that divide. A comprehensive review would take us far afield, and is unnecessary for now. My aim in challenging the exclusive binarism between justice and injustice is to argue only that such a dualism misleadingly relies upon ethical situations treated in institutional or intellectual isolation. In order to wage that challenge, it becomes necessary to develop some notion of what it means to reason broadly or narrowly, that is, in greater or lesser institutional or intellectual isolation, about injustice. Aristotle identifies the so-called 'golden mean' as a methodological principle for ethical reasoning, while declining to seek any definitive or universal essence or 'Form' of virtue in Plato's sense.[36] Aristotle reviews a series of individual virtues, drawing largely upon prevailing values of his day.[37] He focuses on his discrete examples, provisionally allowing broader political contexts, such as those examined in his *Politics*, to be methodologically suspended. Indeed, Meno's approach, describing human virtue as determined in each case by humans' various social roles, would not be altogether mistaken for Aristotle, and might indeed be said to anticipate it.[38] '[A] human being',

---

34 M 72c. The concept of an εἶδος of virtue is introduced in *Meno* in a quest for a unified definition, without the express metaphysical assumption of Forms' independent existence, as espoused in the *Republic, Phaedo* and elsewhere. *Meno*'s discussion is not, however, incompatible with that metaphysics.
35 See, e.g., R 6.508b–e; Phd 75c–d; M 72c–d.
36 NE 1.6.
37 See this chapter, Section 2.6.
38 See, e.g., Pol 1.13.1260^{a}9–36.

Aristotle claims, 'will deliberate better about particulars'.[39] He applies the principle of the mean to bravery, for example, describing it as something achieved by avoiding either the defect of cowardice, or the excess of foolhardiness.[40] He analyses temperance as a quality achieved by avoiding bodily excesses, but also by avoiding the defect of inhumanly shunning pleasures.[41]

To some extent, then, Aristotle endorses the kind of particularist ethical reasoning which Plato problematises in *Meno* (even if he later moves towards it in the *Laws*). When we sit with friends discussing a current ethical or political problem – liberalising access to drugs, the rights and wrongs of euthanasia, or freedom of speech – doing so via reference to some detailed and overarching theory of justice raises difficulties at any number of levels, not least whether we could ever agree upon which theory to apply: Mainstream liberal? Extreme libertarian? Anarchist? Neo-Kantian? Neo-Marxist? And would we even agree on what any of those theories entails? It certainly cannot be a requirement, in order for us to reason about the justice of this or that particular issue, that we first be able to present and to defend some comprehensive and indeed definitive theory of justice. That requirement would exclude most people, and arguably everyone. Traditional courtroom adjudication formalises that pragmatic, everyday necessity, by limiting disputes to specified norms and fact scenarios. It suspends judgment on the totality of background social, political, economic or cultural circumstances, in order to reach a decision about which party wins or loses, about which is just or unjust, under existing norms and procedures. The impression of a strictly binary relationship between justice and injustice thrives on those pragmatics of everyday ethical reasoning.

That method of 'concrete', problem-by-problem, examination is not, then, only an everyday, institutional or indeed commonsensical approach. Aristotle formally elevates it to the level of critical philosophy. He embraces the more abstract principle of seeking an appropriate 'mean' between extremes of conduct or attitudes, as a strategy for simultaneously drawing upon conventional Greek values, yet leaving them open to critical scrutiny and re-evaluation.[42] In applying the mean to a sequence of moral qualities, such as bravery, temperance, magnanimity or friendliness,[43] he nevertheless leaves his analytic approach strongly anchored in the method of isolated, case-by-case ethics. He does so not because he deems the justice or injustice of broader socio-political arrangements to be irrelevant – his overall philosophical project will consist in demonstrating the opposite[44] – but because it can be difficult

---

39 Pol [Re] 3.15.1186^{a}20.
40 NE 3.6–4.9.
41 NE 3.11.
42 NE 2.2.1104^{a}11–26, 2.8–2.9.
43 NE 3.6–4.9.
44 See, e.g., NE 2.1.1103^{b}3–6, 5.2.1130^{b}22–29.

to attain any understanding of socio-political justice in the broadest sense without, at some point, examining discrete ethical problems in close, and to some degree methodologically isolated detail. The more Aristotle isolates ethical problems, the more our 'yes' or 'no' becomes effectively built into the question posed. Who could disagree that the excess represented by rashness or the defect of cowardice are both inferior to the mean of courage? In the same way, who could disagree that falsely accused suspects, violent husbands, or a starving child represent injustices?

The observation that judgments about justice and injustice must, to some extent, isolate controversies from their broader socio-political contexts is hardly new. Nor is the observation that traditional means of adjudication do largely the same. It is not those points in themselves that I wish to stress, but only the point that those processes of institutional or intellectual isolation of ethical problems sustain our assumption of injustice as the tautological opposite of justice, as becomes particularly clear from the study of programmatic justice theorists. Kant, too, begins his approach to the problem of justice by seeking some general principles, and then demonstrating them largely through sequences of specific applications, which he sometimes calls *Kasuistik* – casuistry. He translates the problem of justice into the problem of the capacity of human reason to ascertain principles for the exercise of freedom.[45] He elaborates a system of justice, along more rule-bound, legalist lines than are pursued by Aristotle, through the application of practical ethical reason, beginning by explaining his fundamental rule of human freedom, the 'categorical imperative'.[46] His next step is, first, to apply it to a few discrete examples of ethical problems,[47] and then more comprehensively to a system of norms.[48] Even Mill's ethical method is not altogether different from Kant's in that sole respect. Mill's focus, like Kant's, is on freedom as a decisive principle of justice. In *On Liberty*, Mill proposes his own rule, the well-known 'harm principle', early on,[49] and then elaborates his system of just results by treating a series of relatively general or particular social problems one by one.[50] Aristotle, Kant and Mill, then, as different as they are on many points, each proceed by announcing a founding principle – Aristotle's mean, Kant's categorical imperative, Mill's harm principle – and then applying it to a series of practical problems in some greater or lesser degree of pragmatic, methodological isolation, strongly sustaining a concept of justice and injustice as mutually exclusive. While rejecting strictly axiomatic approaches, particularly as associated

---

45 See, e.g., KpV, Vorrede, Werkausgabe 7: 107; §5, Werkausgabe 7: 138; §8, Anmerkung II(1), Werkausgabe 7: 160.
46 GMS, Werkausgabe 7: 28, 51 *et passim*.
47 See, e.g., GMS, Werkausgabe 7: 29–30.
48 MS §§ 1–62, Werkausgabe 8: 353–477.
49 Lib ch. 1.
50 Lib chs 2–5.

with Kant,[51] Hegel, too, does not shun a serial, problem-by-problem approach,[52] even while he seeks to apply broader, more contextual and synthetic notions of historical and social process.[53] My suggestion is not that analyses of justice via the sequential examination of discrete examples is the unique approach in Western ethical thought nor even within the whole of the writings of those particular theorists, who do develop broader views of justice, beyond isolated instances. Nor am I arguing that such a method of ethical enquiry is deeply misguided, given how it recalls our everyday style of problem-by-problem reasoning, even if, in the manner of Aristotle, Kant or Mill, it goes a step further by supplying, in each instance, an overarching principle.

We nevertheless witness a conspicuous feature of the problem-by-problem method. The more problems are treated in hypothetical isolation, the more they reinforce the classical, binary model, by creating an impression that they are amenable to answers in straightforward, 'built in' terms of right-or-wrong, just-or-unjust. Shakespeare's foot soldier transforms the problem into one of easy resolution through his assumption 'If the cause be not good', which builds in a reply of 'just' or 'unjust' from the outset. Obviously, if the cause is not good, if it is not just, then it is unjust. To be sure, the King's manipulations of both secular and divine law in Act One, to justify his militarism,[54] add force to his soldier's assumption. But it is an assumption nonetheless, lacking any exhaustive exposition of the rights and wrongs of the expedition. My point at this stage is not to rehearse those rights and wrongs with a view towards finding the ethically or politically satisfying solution, but only to signal how the transformation of the problem into a context of isolated, abstracted ethical reason reinforces the binarist assumption that a straightforward response of 'just' or 'unjust' can be elicited.

In Shakespeare's *Henry VI, Part One*, the famed soldier John Talbot must decide whether to allow his son, the young John, to join what is, by that time, a hopeless battle against the French, already turning into a massacre of English troops. The father faces a Corneillian tragic choice: a dutiful parent cannot send the child to a certain and strategically pointless slaughter, and nor can he condemn his son to the badge of dishonour that would haunt a young man who had failed to join in solidarity with his desperate compatriots.[55] And we can compound Lord Talbot's ethical dilemma much further. For example, we can add questions, which that play, and much of the Shakespearean corpus, perpetually invites us to contemplate, about the dubious ethics and legality of that particular war, or about the equally dubious ethics of the aristocracies who are directing it, or about the ethics of war altogether, or about the ethics

---

51 See, e.g., PhG, Werke 3: 310–22.
52 See GPR §§ 41–340, Werke 7: 102–502.
53 See this chapter, Section 2.7.
54 H5 1.2. Cf. 2H4 4.3.342–45.
55 1H6 4.5–6.

of parents' and children's duties to each other, to their families, or to their nations.

No clear line can be drawn around Talbot's conundrum, which would dictate that it 'all boils down' to a choice between some principle X and its opposite. Insofar as Aristotle discusses bravery, for example, he does not claim that it can wholly resolve a dilemma such as Talbot's. He instead offers insight only insofar as the dilemma involves the problem of bravery, such that any conclusions we can draw end up being built into the problem posed. The young Talbot would plausibly err on the side of excess to plunge rashly into a battle to which he can provide no real succour, yet would just as plausibly, certainly from the young man's own perspective, err on the side of cowardice if he were to decline assistance to his countrymen. On its own terms, insofar as the problem of bravery ends up being distilled from the broader ethical complexity of the situation, it yields a clear, binary resolution to the question, 'Is young Talbot brave?', already decided in the sheer posing of it through that technique of de-contextualising, normative isolation, and to which we scarcely have room to answer anything but 'Yes'. Young Talbot could indeed be said to display bravery *qua* bravery, if there were such a thing as bravery *qua* bravery, that is, bravery, or any other ethical quality, existing in isolation from an opaque texture of social and political circumstances. If the distillation of the question from its ethical matrix builds in the response from the outset, that is the effect of isolating complex ethical dilemmas for immediate resolution, namely, to make the problem seem amenable to a yes-or-no, right-or-wrong resolution, leaving justice and injustice appear as straightforward alternatives. The style of isolated reasoning is always pragmatically necessary yet always ethically inadequate, always a pursuit, yet simultaneously a betrayal of justice.

2.4 Injustice and anti-rationalism

The cry 'It's unfair!' is uttered by the youngest children. That gut response often recurs throughout our lives. Injustice as not-justice may suggest a conceptually prior notion of justice, but feelings of injustice originate often in visceral responses. They largely lack any sense of antecedent or distinctly formulated concepts of justice. Notwithstanding etymology, it is often injustice, not justice, that represents the primordial, gut experience.[56] In that sense, if the two terms must be linked by an etymological bipolarity, it would seem more realistic to reverse the etymology, making 'injustice' the experientially primordial term, and 'justice' its more abstract, more theorised derivative. Consider, for example, using a term like 'bad' as that primordial, conceptually foundational term, and the more speculative 'unbadness' to denote whatever ideal ethical circumstances we might envisage as its remedy.

---

56 Cf. Shklar, 1990, pp. 16, 21.

Leaving aside the sense of strangeness of such an unfamiliar word, it is also unsatisfactory in principle. Not everything that is bad is necessarily unjust, since injustice implies ethical capacity or agency. Earthquakes can be bad, but are not in themselves unjust. The difficulty of finding a more closely synonymous term only underscores the entrenchment in our language of an existential awkwardness, whereby 'injustice', the experientially primordial notion, is cast as etymologically and conceptually derivative, while 'justice', the more abstract and speculative notion, is cast as etymologically and conceptually prior and foundational. Feelings that one has been treated badly or – to resume for the time being our conventional language, because 'badly' remains inadequate – unjustly, particularly for those who have faced a history or an intensity of unjust treatment, or who belong to groups with such a background, can prompt cries or emotions of injustice, regardless of whether or how a particular situation's rights and wrongs might have been reasoned.

From various perspectives, figures such as Wittgenstein,[57] Heidegger[58] or Merleau-Ponty[59] all set limits to any rationalist reduction of words and language either to dictionary definitions, or to definitively circumscribed extra-linguistic entities. They explain language as anchored in, and inevitably expressing or reflecting, broader personal or social contexts, as manifested by our everyday exclamations about injustice or unfairness. Presumably, in a situation of outrage, phrases like 'It's wrong', 'It's terrible' and 'It's horrible', lacking any etymological symmetry with some opposite term, can nevertheless substitute for 'It's unjust' or 'It's unfair', with little difference in the perception or emotion expressed.

Within the law and literature movement, storytelling has figured as a crucial innovation, as witnessed, for example, within Critical Race Theory. Storytelling seeks to elicit social and personal complexities that cannot be grasped either by the language of terse and general norms, or by the language of traditional, abstract-universalist, or 'disembodied' ethical or legal theory. 'For many minority persons', writes the American scholar Richard Delgado, 'the principle instrument of their subordination . . . is the prevailing *mindset* by means of which members of the dominant group justify the world as it is'.[60] That mindset may, for example, be overtly racist, 'with whites on top and browns and blacks at the bottom'.[61] But it can also be diffuse. It can persist within a society whose formally adopted legal regime embraces values cast in the universalist language of 'liberty', 'democracy', 'due process' or 'equal protection'.[62] Those norms may have been legislated with the best will in the

---

57 Wittgenstein, 1984, pp. 225–485.
58 Heidegger, 1979, pp. 160–69.
59 See, e.g., Merleau-Ponty, 1945, pp. 203–32.
60 Delgado, 1989, p. 2413 (Delgado's italics).
61 Delgado, 1989, p. 2413. Cf., on 'ascriptive injustice', Shklar, 1990, pp. 38–39.
62 Cf., e.g., Karst, 1996, p. 1783.

world by a liberally minded elite, yet may be applied with little regard to relationships of power and subordination that systematically pervert the very fairness that those norms are designed to promote. In a US Supreme Court case like *McCleskey v. Kemp*,[63] racism looms even as the most well-intentioned judges insist that the formally universalist norms of equal protection and due process are adequate. Racism disempowers, despite those formal, abstract, universalist promises of empowerment. According to Delgado, '[t]he attraction of stories should come as no surprise. For stories create their own bonds, represent cohesion, shared understandings, and meanings.'[64] Our gut sense of injustice might even lead us to believe that a scholarly examination is altogether futile, intellectually arid, counterproductive and a waste of time that might be better spent battling actual injustices in the world. That feeling can prompt the belief that it is not concepts or definitions, models or theories of injustice that we need, but above all compassion and common sense. To import a familiar notion, I may not be able to define injustice, but 'I know it when I see it'.

That idea of a visceral sense of injustice nevertheless presents difficulties. People become outraged by all sorts of things – certainly by war, poverty, oppression, exploitation, or discrimination. Many people, however, have inveighed against what they felt to be not only the human injustice, but even the divine injustice, of individuals practicing homosexuality, or of women pursuing individual autonomy, or of laws imposing rules for racial equality. Nuremberg rallies and Ku Klux Klan lynch mobs exhibit no lack of visceral outrage motivated by their own sense of injustice. Members of such groups also display an intense compassion for other members of their kind. In defining the constituent concepts of politics as *Freund* and *Feind* – friend and foe – Carl Schmitt depicts justice and injustice in terms evocative of such emotional responses.[65] Yet any decision by 'neutral', 'outside' observers – and who is to choose them? – not to admit all outrage, but to decide first which outrages do and do not count as ethically principled, only generates a vicious circle. It merely presupposes the very concept of injustice, as an already critically reflected concept, that we had invoked those emotional responses for the purpose of seeking in the first place.

Hobbes sketches a portrait of human beings as, by nature, selfish and brutal, requiring 'civilisation' in order to secure peace and survival. Rousseau protests, postulating supposedly universal, pre-cultural feelings of empathy and compassion. Rousseau becomes only one of a long line of thinkers who believe in the universality of innate and benign human feelings, as a foundation for a

---

63 *McCleskey v. Kemp*, 481 U.S. 279 (1987) (rejecting claims that death penalty sentencing contained racist bias).
64 Delgado, *supra* n. 60.
65 Schmitt, 1996 *passim*. Cf. Freud's notion of the 'narcissism of small differences'. MIA sec 6; UK sec 5. Cf. also Lévi-Strauss, 1987, pp. 19–26.

universal sense of justice or injustice. Rousseau accuses Hobbes of confusing cause with effect, insisting that civilisation, and its concomitant forces of rivalry, competition and acquisitiveness, lead only to ever greater alienation of individuals from others and from their communities. Civilisation is not the cure but the cause of our ever greater callousness or indifference towards human suffering, hence our blindness to injustice. Beyond those nefarious effects of civilisation, the natural human instinct towards the suffering of another is pity and tenderness.[66] Those instincts become quasi-psychic bonds, among, for example, the indigenous Swiss partisans of Schiller's arch-Rousseauvian *Wilhelm Tell*, who nevertheless draw sharp distinctions between indigenous insider and imperial outsider, self and other, friend and foe.[67]

After centuries of deliberation, however, it remains questionable whether that or countless similar attempts succeed in identifying essential or universal human emotions, and therewith reliable sentiments of outrage. If countless episodes of brutality throughout history somehow confirm Rousseau's views about corrupting civilisation as the culprit, the status of any 'natural man', instinctively just, lurking below, nevertheless remains as elusive today as when Rousseau proposed it.[68] One might argue that even the youngest children display a spontaneous sense of justice and injustice when, for example, they sit in a group, and expect that a distribution of treats should be fair, for example, one for each child.[69] Yet even that simple scenario already involves habituation within socio-cultural contexts.[70] A lower-born child trotted in to play with a 17th-century prince might well witness the prince receiving the lion's share of gifts, praise and attention not as an injustice, but as divinely ordained justice, performed, if for no other reason, to remind all underlings of their natural, God-given inequality. No horror, nor even surprise, is suggested when a servant's offspring is killed to feign the murder of a king's grandson in Jean Racine's *Andromaque*, which elevates the mother as one of the Baroque's paragons of virtue, one of literature's great foes of injustice. Quite the contrary, it is presented as an obvious act, any querying of which would amount to insolence. The summary dispatch of that patently inferior life stands as a pittance for the salvation of King Priam's royal line.[71]

Leaving aside Rousseau's questionable belief in universal human compassion, or equally persistent arguments about the relative influences of 'nature' and 'nurture', the manifest indifference or even callousness that we constantly see displayed by those aware of injustice or even those who commit it – dismissal of the gravity of rape, of torture, of slavery, even of genocide – leaves it difficult

---

66 See, e.g., OI 1 153 ff.
67 WT *passim*.
68 See generally Derrida, 1967a.
69 See, e.g., Perelman, 1990, pp. 54–55.
70 Cf. this chapter, text accompanying nn. 100–1.
71 Andr 1.1.70–76. Cf. commentary at Racine, 1999, p. 201, n. 2.

to believe that anything like pre-cultural universal feelings can be assumed to shed much light on injustice. Even the subtler approaches of a figure like Lévinas[72] nevertheless face the problem of *Eigentlichkeit* – 'authenticity'[73] – when confronted by people who denounce as unjust movements for racial equality, women's rights, gay rights, and the like, again consigning us to the precarious role of deciding which emotions count as distorted, and which count as 'genuinely' human.

Any suggestion that a primordial, phenomenological or ethical-ontological foundation would inevitably deliver only conclusions about justice and injustice that we all can find acceptable therefore remains doubtful. Much is to be said for the phenomenological resistance to the collapse of specific, textured situations into generalised abstractions, for phenomenology's insistence on the irreducible, which can itself be said to define the human.[74] Yet, as we equally resist the idea of dispensing entirely with any concept of justice – can we seriously identify and agree on some better notion to stand as a corrective to our own political and legal regimes? – the fear that 'uniqueness' or 'irreducibility' might overthrow any notion of consistency across cases, across situations and populations, creates anxiety for the phenomenological stance. To be sure, it would be mistaken to construct a simplistic dichotomy between reason and emotion, either with the result of accepting emotion as our sole guide, or dismissing emotion entirely on grounds of an equally simplistic attribution to it of irrationality. What nevertheless remains clear is that the normative proposition 'Jane is unjust' follows with no self-evidence from the fact that Jane has outraged someone.

Anti-rationalist (which does not perforce equate with 'irrational') challenges to traditional, binarist justice theory do not proceed solely at the level of thought and feeling within subjective experience. Foucault, for example, points a way out of that phenomenological dilemma. He suggests a good deal about how law constructs injustice in opposition to a 'justice', which merely institutionalises prevailing power structures, disguising those interests as neutral rationalism. The official designation of social deviants,[75] insanity,[76] or sexual deviance,[77] provide striking examples. Similarly, in-justice, on a Derridean reading,[78] can become ironised as something that becomes its opposite. To be 'in' that which conventionally passes as 'justice' leaves in-justice indeed. Such approaches will pave the way, in the present book, for

---

72 See generally, e.g., Lévinas, 1990a, 1990b. On the 'irreducibly subjective component' of 'victimhood', see Shklar, 1990, p. 37.
73 Cf. Heidegger, 1979, pp. 42–43.
74 See, e.g., Merleau-Ponty, 1945, pp. 496–520.
75 See Foucault, 1975.
76 See Foucault, 1972.
77 See Foucault, 1976.
78 See, e.g., Derrida, 1992.

the post-classical approach of Part 2, which will examine injustice not, unthinkingly following the dictates of etymology, as the sheer, logical opposite of justice, but as deeply intertwined with and indeed products of two elements, unity and particularly measurement, without which we cannot imagine justice.

2.5 Injustice within systemic contexts

Figures like Rousseau or Marx, while retaining detailed theories about how to achieve social justice, do not proceed by anything like a Kantian method of casuistic, problem-by-problem ethical reasoning. They focus from the outset on overall social, economic and political contexts. They are, in that sense, programmatic radicals. From their perspectives, only after prevailing conditions have been thoroughly surpassed would it be meaningful to examine particular ethical problems, let alone in any systematic way.

Justice and injustice matter most where false accusations, violent husbands, starving children, or whatever injustices a given regime generates, arise not merely as random or isolated occurrences, but are endemic. Unjust things can admittedly happen in random, atypical ways. Injustices nevertheless count most when they occur not as spontaneous, offhand incidents, but as a result of cumulative, socio-political processes. The child negligently left to starve in Stockholm embodies a specific injustice, for which we might confidently generate the aforementioned, conventionally binary, sequences: 'It is just for a child to be nourished', 'It is therefore unjust for a child to be starved', 'It is therefore just for a starved child to be fed (or for the child's caretaker to be prosecuted)', etc. By contrast, thousands of children starving in Ethiopia, under circumstances of gross and systemic deprivation, represent injustice manifesting as a pervasive and systemic crisis.

The problem with reducing justice and injustice to mutually exclusive pairings within the context of such a crisis is not that it is logically incorrect (obviously those same binary sequences would apply in Ethiopia: 'It is just for the children to be nourished', 'It is therefore unjust for them to starve', 'It is therefore just for them to be fed', etc.), but that it becomes more conspicuously trivial, giving us a solution that is blatantly obvious, as tautologies do, while leaving the important question, the means to arrive at that solution, undisclosed in any express terms, and indeed often highly disputed. Systemic injustices demand that we examine whole systems and regimes, from multiple, intricately layered, often opaque points of view – historical, social, cultural, economic, ethical, political, legal. For Kantian casuistry, systemic injustice retains a derivative quality, in many instances arguably nothing more than the sum-total of individual instances of injustice. Rousseau or Marx, or indeed Hegel or Foucault, imply a fundamental shift in modern thought about ethics and politics, law and justice, by locating not merely individual or methodologically isolated transactions, but rather overall and systemic social, historical, economic and cultural conditions as the fundamental ground of injustice.

Theories about the kinds of norms, institutions or processes that would produce justice in a context of mass starvation are often complex. They produce age-old disagreements, for example, between ethical universalists and cultural relativists, or between free-marketeers and socialists, or between liberals and communitarians. My point is not to argue that such crises collapse into indeterminacy, but, to the contrary, to observe how disconcerting it would be to claim that we must first stake out some prior agreement about what constitutes justice before we can decide, for example, that mass starvation is unjust.

For the child left starving in a stable and prosperous society, it may indeed appear obvious to conclude that justice is the opposite – feeding the child, which is easy to do without theoretical speculation. For thousands of victims, in a society racked with poverty, oppression, violence or corruption, simply to say that children need to be fed seems almost callously unhelpful. Fundamental injustice in that case is not only about engineering an immediate remedy, but concerns the complex foundations of social, economic, political and legal life. Questions about how existing norms or institutions should be improved in order to create greater justice become divisive, even while we can scarcely be divided, barring the outright ethical nihilism of Thrasymachus or Nietzsche, in observing some fundamental conditions of injustice. In broad, sociopolitically systemic contexts, the sheer negation of injustice, for example, feeding the starving children, emerges more visibly, not as a substantive falsehood, but as an empty tautology. It remains unclear which specific social, economic, political and legal circumstances of justice are negated so as to generate what is nevertheless manifest injustice, except the obvious circumstance of, for example, inadequate food. Injustice as the sheer opposite of justice is not logically wrong, but ethically uninformative and existentially vacuous.[79]

The contrast between a materially prosperous and a poor society, although it exemplifies the point, is not essential to it. Two parallel levels of injustice pertain across societies. On the one hand, isolated scenarios, even within contexts of crisis, can still generate superficially plausible pairings of justice and injustice, as mutually exclusive outcomes, such that there may superficially appear to be little need for anything more. Even under circumstances of grave crises, a petty contract dispute might well be resolved in a generally, or at least provisionally, satisfactory way. On the other hand, injustice at the massive level of systemic socio-political processes cannot in any such obvious or non-trivial way emerge as a sheer negation of some equally manifest scheme of justice. After all, prosperous societies, too, wrestle with core questions of systemic injustice, not least insofar as they become

---

79 Cf. Heidegger, 1995.

beneficiaries, even active accomplices, of injustices that occur beyond their borders.[80] My contrast is not between two fundamentally different types of societies, but between two levels, in any society, at which injustice must be considered. I am certainly not arguing, then, that Sweden has only isolated injustices, and Ethiopia only systemic ones. For any society, it is, above all, systemic injustice, and not isolated injustice, that epitomises injustice, yet does not, as much of the classical Western tradition has assumed, collapse into a justice theory of the programmatic type, whereby injustice would be understood as the straightforward negation of whatever justice is institutionally theorised to be.

Little light is thrown on the problem of injustice through recourse to the traditional concept of *equity*, that is, the longstanding acknowledgment that broadly framed norms may yield unsatisfactory results in certain individual cases, warranting judges or decision-makers to apply appropriate adjustments.[81] Far from overcoming the narrowness of justice conceived in isolated contexts, that notion of equity, without more, can scarcely admit of any other context if it is to make any sense at all as an *ad hoc* corrective precisely to imbalances that arise because of and within isolated normative contexts. Equity has never represented the wholesale replacement of isolated contexts by systemic ones, but rather supports isolated contexts through its method of improvised tinkering. That is not to say that there is anything particularly wrong with equity, no more than with the whole of the regimes within which it is applied. Equity nevertheless serves only as one of the tools, and therefore as a confirmation of, and in no sense as a challenge to, the classical, bipolar model.

The example of mass starvation shows that the problem of systemic injustice lies not with finding it, but with explaining it as something more than the obvious opposite of some notion of justice. To say that some incident of systemic injustice arises as the negation of, for example, a Lockean ideal of justice, but not a Rousseauvian one, or the negation of a utilitarian ideal, but not a socialist one, remains an altogether speculative enterprise in any number of scenarios we could name throughout history. We see, then, a typical difference between ethical reasoning in isolated and in systemic contexts. In isolated contexts, such as conventional legal disputes, a normative framework is largely fixed in advance. Each party cites more-or-less existing law in support of its position. By contrast, once injustice is examined in broader historical or cultural contexts, existing norms themselves, and the entirety of the socio-political regime, come up for question, often in overt and glaring ways.

---

80 In 2012, to name only a routine example, Radio Sweden reported that certain Swedish banks were selling mutual funds including shares 'in an oil company working in a war torn region of Ethiopia despite the banks' own ethical guidelines regarding human rights'. See Radio-Sweden, 2012.
81 See, e.g., NE 5.10; Perelman, 1990, pp. 46–55, 90–91.

Questions as to whether those norms or that regime are themselves just or unjust play the decisive role in any enquiry into injustice.

Consider another example. At the socio-political, 'macro' level, it is easy enough to argue, as a formal matter, that the propositions 'Swedish state laws and practices are fundamentally just' and 'Swedish state laws and practices are fundamentally unjust' stand in a binary, mutually exclusive relationship, to each other. But such purely formal binarisms take us no further. It may be easy enough to designate as mutually exclusive the propositions 'Swedish state laws and practices are fundamentally just' and 'Swedish state laws and practices are fundamentally unjust'. However, without considerable normative and empirical scrutiny, over a range of factors (and we might not even agree about those factors, or about how to scrutinise them), there is no common-sense way of knowing which, if any, of those two propositions to adopt. Once an entire system or process, as opposed to an isolated act, is at issue, any scrutiny requires detailed theories of, or assumptions about, what justice is in general. Even with those, we may fail to settle upon a clear-cut pronouncement that Swedish state laws and practices are 'just' or 'unjust' *simpliciter.*

In addition to providing the context within which much everyday or hypothetical reasoning about justice and injustice, as well as ordinary litigation, takes place, isolated fact patterns are also typical of our media conditioning. It is a commonplace that the mass media noisily cover, for example, high-profile common criminals, but have no comparable practice of assessing the established order as such – not as a matter of unthinking neglect, but because detailed, broad-based assessments remain inimical to the general methods of journalism. Our daily headlines read 'Paedophile Working in Local School' and not 'The Existing Socio-Political Order Slated for Serious Contemplation'. The isolated injustice, the 'concrete' event which can be presented or mediatised as injustice, generates the gripping surface drama.[81a] Once again the point is not that methods of ethical or legal reasoning have remained wholly oblivious to the simplifying effect of isolated contexts, or to the relevance of broader ones (as, for example, a long tradition of legal realism has shown), but only to recall that limited attention has been paid to the tendency of isolated contexts to reinforce the binarist model of justice and injustice.

2.6 A dialectic of injustice

In introducing crises such as mass starvation, my aim is, again, to underscore the systemic, as opposed to random or isolated, character of injustice, as something rooted in political, economic, historical and cultural contexts. That step is more problematical than it may appear, as it seems to entail another vicious circle. As already mentioned, to claim that injustice is more than the

---

81a See Heinze 2012c.

tautological and question-begging opposite of justice, that it is not merely a sum-total of isolated events, seems already to presuppose some substantive notion of injustice. If we can recognise mass atrocities as the kinds of examples that visibly make that point about injustice, then we should presumably be able to identify the ethical principles or values that those examples presuppose, the principles that make *them* examples; and if those examples already presuppose some notion of injustice, then it is misleading to suggest that they are being introduced only as a first step towards a theory of injustice. It would seem that a theory of injustice is already present, which allows them to stand as illustrations.

We have seen Meno take up his discussion with Socrates, boasting that he knows what virtue is. Socrates first argues that Meno does not know,[82] and then adds that he, too, does not know.[83] He declares: 'Nevertheless, I want to examine and seek together with you what it may be.'[84] Meno retorts with what has long been known as 'Meno's paradox', resembling the one that the concept of injustice is putting to us now: 'How will you look for it, Socrates, when you do not know at all what it is? How will you aim to search for something you do not know at all? If you should meet with it, how will you know that this is the thing that you did not know?'[85] The paradox, Aristotle later points out, is that 'you will learn either nothing or what you already know'.[86]

Plato has Socrates reply that the soul carries innate knowledge, and therefore innate knowledge of virtue, which would include innate knowledge of justice and injustice.[87] That knowledge-based theory differs from Rousseau's notion of a universal sense of tenderness or compassion. Socrates in *Meno* instead anticipates Kant's view that a fundamental principle of all ethics or justice inheres within reason *per se*, and therefore within any being possessed of reason. But that rationalist universalism, too, remains problematical, not only because Plato links it to the patently problematical doctrine of the immortality of the soul,[88] but because he remains unclear about how we can reliably pinpoint that innate knowledge within ourselves, particularly since, as a practical matter, our views on justice and injustice constantly differ.[89]

The circularity arising for Meno, substituting his search for virtue with our search for injustice, is that it would appear that we can understand injustice only by articulating some adequate definition of it, yet we can only assess the truth or falsehood of that definition if we already know what injustice is. The task of identifying the principles or values that make some injustices appear

---

82 M 80a–b.
83 M 80c–d. Cf. Prt 327e.
84 M 80d.
85 M 80d.
86 An Post [Ba] 1.1.71^{a}30. Cf. NE 6.3.1139^{b}26–8.
87 M 81c–d.
88 M 81b.
89 Cf. this chapter, text accompanying n. 101.

as manifest atrocities raises difficulties indeed. Recall Thrasymachus urging that injustice is greater than justice, if we can get away with it; that wealth or power are difficult to obtain through honest and applied effort, but easy through theft or murder. Nothing in Thrasymachus's position suggests any limit, not even at the point of waging genocide, slavery, or mass starvation, if doing so with impunity will advance the personal interests of the perpetrator. None of the *Republic's* interlocutors relies either on visceral outrage, common sense, or received wisdom to suggest that Thrasymachus's views are wrong. They want to hear unrelenting reason. They want Socrates to refute his adversary point by point. They want Socrates to spell out why even the most heinous injustices should not be committed by someone who can do so profitably and with impunity. Plato gives us no reason to think that Thrasymachus's view will not ultimately win them over if Socrates fails to provide that refutation (indeed on Socrates' own professed dialectical principle of always obeying only the 'best' argument, in the sense of the argument that best defeats its rivals, while remaining itself undefeated[90]).

There is nevertheless a problem with Meno's paradox. It conceives of the adequate definition or theory as, so to speak, written on a blank slate. It presupposes that we can never stake any claim to knowledge about injustice, or about anything, except insofar as such a claim remains free of prior assumptions, since they would then require the very justification that the definition of theory is charged to provide. In an effort to resolve Meno's paradox, Aristotle rejects any such blank-slate assumption about knowledge altogether, be it in ethics and politics or in other domains: 'All teaching and all learning of an intellectual kind proceed from pre-existent knowledge.'[91] Aristotle never adopts Meno's suggestions that knowledge of virtue, or indeed of justice or injustice, must either be innate, or must rest upon a precise definition, before injustice can be understood. He approaches the paradox differently: '[N]othing prevents us from in one sense understanding and in another being ignorant of what we are learning. What is absurd is not that you should know in *some* sense what you are learning, but that you should know it in *this* way, i.e. in the way and in the sense in which you are leaning it.'[92]

Aristotle argues that the knowledge we can acquire about a thing depends on the kind of thing it is. Some things are not amenable to a definitive statement in the way that others are. We can only look for 'exactness in each area to the extent that the nature of the subject allows'.[93] In that sense, Plato's introduction, in the *Meno*, of a problem in exact geometry, as a model of reasoning generally, is, from Aristotle's perspective, misleading. The goods

---

90 Cri 46b.
91 An Post [Br] 1.1.71^{b}6–9.
92 An Post [Br] 1.1.71^{b}6–9 (Barnes's italics).
93 NE [Ir] 1.3.1094^{b}24–25.

sought by ethics, politics, and law 'exhibit much variety and fluctuation',[94] such that we can only 'indicate the truth roughly and in outline':[95] 'it is just as mistaken to demand demonstrations from a rhetoritician as to accept [merely] persuasive arguments from a mathematician.'[96] Aristotle further claims that 'we need to have been brought up in fine habits if we are to be adequate students of fine and just things, and of political questions generally'.[97] That requirement might itself appear only to replace one paradox with another. If we already know which 'habits' are just, then what is the point of undertaking a long and detailed exploration of ethics or justice? More importantly, if we are undertaking that exploration to discover ethics or justice because they are uncertain, then how can we know which habits are right to have been brought up in, or that those deciding on ethics were indeed brought up in the right habits?

The Platonic *Alcibiades*[98] experiments with the notion that knowledge about justice can be drawn from upbringing and experience,[99] but rejects it as too immersed in the existing culture's unexamined views.

> SOCRATES: When you were a boy . . . sometimes when you were playing knucklebones or some other game, you'd say to one or another of your playmates, very loudly and confidently – not at all like someone who was at a loss about justice and injustice – that he was a lousy cheater and wasn't playing fairly. [. . .] So it seems that even as a child you thought you understood justice and injustice. [. . .]
> ALCIBIADES: I suppose I learned it in the same way as other people.
> SOCRATES: [. . .] from whom? Do tell me.
> ALCIBIADES: From people in general.[100]
> SOCRATES: When you give the credit to 'people in general', you're falling back on teachers who are no good. [. . .] [D]oes it seem to you that people in general actually agree among themselves or with each other about just and unjust people and actions?
> ALCIBIADES: Not in the slightest, Socrates.
> SOCRATES: Really? Do they disagree a huge amount about these things?
> ALCIBIADES: Very much so.

---

94 NE 1.3.1094^{b}15.
95 NE 1.3.1094^{b}24–25. Cf., e.g., NE 2.2.1104^{a}1–9.
96 NE [Ir] 1.3.1094^{b}25–7. Cf. NE 1.7.1098^{a}25–29.
97 NE [Ir] 1.4.1095^{b}5–6.
98 Although a long tradition viewed *Alcibiades* as the best introduction to Plato's thought, it lost favour after the 19th-century philosopher Friedrich Schleiermacher cast doubt on its authorship. See Schleiermacher, 1996, pp. 319–26. Some classicists have nevertheless recently welcomed it back. See, e.g., Pradeau, 2000, pp. 22–29.
99 Alc 110c–d.
100 Cf. Prt 325c–326e, 327e; M 92d–94e.

> SOCRATES: [. . .] Athenians and Spartans and Boetians . . . died at Tanagra, and later at Coronea, including your own father. The disagreement that caused those battles and those deaths was none other than a disagreement over justice and injustice. [. . .] Are we to say that people understand something if they disagree so much about it that in their disputes with each other they resort to such extreme measures?[101]

Aristotle's aim is not to enquire into virtue or justice starting with a *tabula rasa*, from a position of radical ignorance. He does not seek to theorise in the manner of *Meno*'s Socrates, who claims that not only does he not know what virtue is, but that he has 'never yet met anyone else who did know'.[102] To the contrary, as we have seen, Aristotle's ethical writings retain a core of traditional Greek values, those that the Greek male of the citizen class ought presumably to be brought up with, including bravery, temperance, generosity, magnanimity and friendliness. He does not seek radically new ethical values, nor radically new understandings of those familiar values. Plato may not seek fundamentally new values as such, as he equally affirms such traditional virtues as temperance, courage, wisdom and justice,[103] but, at least in the *Republic*, offers radical views about their foundation and of the best circumstances for their achievement. Aristotle more confidently presupposes his reader's overall grasp of them, indeed as achievable under reasonable political circumstances.[104] Aristotle, contrary to *Meno*'s Socrates, exhibits confidence in his knowledge that they are correct and just values, in the sense that knowledge about ethics is simply of a different type than knowledge in the exact sciences.[105] Aristotle certainly innovates in his method of ethical enquiry, but his contributions lie not in introducing substantively new ethical values, either upon a blank slate which had contained none before, or through a revolutionary overturning of old ones. His innovation consists more in integrating longstanding values into a comprehensive understanding of 'the good' and indeed of 'the chief good' (τἀγαθὸν καὶ τὸ ἄριστον), which 'would seem to belong to the most authoritative art and that which is most truly the master art. And politics appears to be of this nature. . . . For even if the end is the same for a single man and for a state, that of the state seems at all events something greater and more complete both to attain and to preserve.'[106]

---

101 Alc 110b–12d. Cf. M 92e–94e; Prt 319b–320b.
102 M 71c. Hutchinson suggests that *Alcibiades's* Socrates, who urges philosophical friendship as a path to knowledge about justice (Alc 132c–33c), reflects later Platonist doctrine. Plato, 1997, p. 558.
103 See, e.g., R 427e.
104 Cf., e.g., Pol 4.1.1289^{a}1–6, 4.11.1295^{a}25–31.
105 NE 1.3.1094^{b}25–7; Cf. NE 6.7.
106 NE 1.2.1094^{a}22–1094^{b}9.

In *Meno*, dialectical reason, in the sense of adherence to the most persuasive argument,[107] must begin upon a blank slate, because any prior assumption would entail a vicious circle. For Aristotle, dialectical reason can begin with prior, familiar ethical views or practices, which remain meaningful and merit attention, but also remain subject to critical scrutiny and revision.[108] That is why he embraces familiar Greek values, while explaining them within a critical, systematic framework. His principle of the mean offers a guide not so much for inventing new ethical principles, but rather for critically, or dialectically, assessing and re-assessing those pre-existing views and practices. Ethical reason can proceed within a context that includes conventional views and practices, without our having either to reject them *ab initio* for lack of that very foundation we are seeking, or to accept them solely on grounds of tradition or authority. Modern Aristotelians have turned precisely that dialectical method against some of Aristotle's own substantive positions, arguing that his fundamental ethical insights can remain intact, while his views on, for example, the inferiority of slaves, women or non-Greeks can be revised.[109]

We can begin a study about injustice drawing upon familiar, widely agreed examples, such as those arising from mass atrocities, with the caveat that our prior notions of injustice remain subject to critical revision, such that, for example, the subordination of women, gays, or ethnic or religious minorities, in various historical contexts, a subordination often ignored and often even praised in many settings, remains subject to re-evaluation. Dialectical reason, in that sense, strikes a balance between one extreme of naïve realism, which would assume truth to be ascertainable spontaneously and uncritically, and the other extreme of relativism, which, denying any such truth, would assume ethics to be altogether illusory. That approach does arguably claim an advantage over a Kantian *tabula rasa* attempt, which – although Kant in practice codifies many of the prevailing values of his own time – does not methodically integrate pre-existing notions into their theories in the way that Aristotle embraces them as being already part of ethical reasoning, even while subject to revision.

Whether that dialectic suffices for a programmatic justice theory still remains uncertain, insofar as criteria for revision, which are still fundamental questions about what is just, are likely to remain controversial. It can nevertheless play a role for a concept of injustice. After all, if something like the trans-Atlantic slave trade, genocides or politically induced mass starvation cannot at some level be recognised as manifestly unjust, on fairly ordinary understandings, then questions arise about whether a discussion is really

---

107 See this chapter, text accompanying n. 90.
108 Cf., e.g., Meta 2.1.993^{a}30–^{b}7.
109 See, e.g., Homiak, 1993.

taking place about justice or injustice at all. When theorists like Hannah Arendt[110] or Emmanuel Lévinas[111] build conceptual perspectives around historical atrocities, in Lévinas's case particularly inspired by phenomenological method, they do so already assuming some sense of injustice that is sufficiently shared to render it meaningful. They do not undertake a *de novo* assertion of those events' injustice for a public that might otherwise have no sense about whether genocide or systemic oppression are or are not unjust. In that respect, something like Aristotle's dialectical approach seems to be at work. Its element of critical revision admittedly remains a precarious enterprise, not readily mustering agreement in controversial instances. But if writers like Arendt or Lévinas can assume certain widely shared feelings of injustice as their point of departure, it is because horrors as extreme as genocide display obvious instances. As with Arendt or Lévinas, most writing about mass injustice – be it in expository prose, or in narrative accounts, such as those of Primo Levi or Elie Wiesel – can assume the injustice to be sufficiently evident.

It seems incorrect to retain any assumption that some articulated justice theory would first have to be provided, allowing us to perform a prior mental negation, before we could grasp even heinous injustices. It is rather our sense of injustice that stakes out the ontologically and conceptually prior moment, and from which we arguably proceed to theorise about justice. Etymologically derivative or negatively defined terms such as 'un-just' and 'in-justice' are not altogether well suited for describing the immediate, systemic realities to which they most glaringly apply. Justice theory and injustice theory indeed emerge as qualitatively different kinds of theories. They approach human experience from certainly related, but not identical, perspectives. Theories of justice can certainly shed light on injustice, but cannot merely substitute for it. Both concepts must be theorised in their own right, without one merely subsuming the other. The classical, programmatic justice theories inevitably rely upon a strongly constructive element. A similarly programmatic theory would be absurd for a distinct theory of injustice, which is obviously not something we are seeking to implement through a constructive project; a theory of injustice is inherently critical, not constructive.

2.7 Historicist dialectics of injustice

The idea of a dialectical understanding of justice or injustice acquires a transformed meaning in the 19th century (leaving aside for now the work of medieval scholasticism), with Hegel and then Marx, who eliminate the

---

110 See, e.g., Arendt, 2006.
111 See generally, e.g., Lévinas, 1990a, 1990b.

functionally open-ended quality of Socratic or Aristotelian dialectic (even if some of Hegel's and Marx's later disciples re-open it), arguing instead that dialectics within reason and history follow a necessary sequence. Through that revised dialectics, Hegel seeks to overcome any lingering indeterminacy, any residual sceptre of relativism, which otherwise appears to surround the ongoing assessment and re-assessment of ethical values within an open-ended dialectic. Yet that degree of certainty eludes us, as Hegelian or Marxist teleologies remain untenable.[112]

On Hegel's view, the justice or injustice of any regime, and therefore *a fortiori* of any isolated act within any such regime, remains partially relative, in the sense that it remains limited to that regime's stage in the entire course of history, with justice as such, justice 'in and for itself' (*an und für sich*), that is, absolute justice, possible only with the realisation of the regime which marks the end, or fulfilment (*Sichselbstwerden*), of history, as presented in his *Grundlinien der Philosophie des Rechts* (*Elements of the Philosophy of Right*). For Hegel, unlike Kant, the justice or injustice of any given regime or situation cannot be assessed in abstraction from the historical moment in which it occurs, a moment that serves only as one step within a teleological development, towards a fulfilment of Being and of history. Justice, an ethical dimension of Being itself, can neither be fully attained nor understood until humanity has realised the aim or end of history – which is simultaneously the realisation of Being itself (Being 'in and for itself', *das an und für sich Sein*), and of the mind (*Geist*) that both is and comprehends Being, in its simultaneously ontological and ethical dimensions, all emerging progressively through history. Justice, like Being or mind, and along with Being and mind, manifests through history.

For Hegel, a historical period, just insofar as it surpasses (*aufhebt*) the injustices of its predecessor, is itself surpassed (*aufgehoben*) through a successor, which, in turn, represents a justice that will both surpass the injustice of its predecessor, and be surpassed by its successor. The Athenian, citizen-governed polis, on that view, surpasses the injustice of an archaic legal regime steeped in the arbitrariness of despotic, monarchical or oligarchic custom that would be dictated to a disenfranchised, disempowered people.[113] It is itself, however, surpassed by a concept of justice, such as the Roman, abstract-universalist concept, which will supersede the Greek concept of justice as something distinct for the Greek citizen.[114] Every such period represents but one step in the historically unfolding process of justice, each stage surpassing injustices of the last, and then surpassed by the justice of the next. Insofar as those historical transitions embody justice at all, it is to the extent that they

---

112 For a standard critique of historicism as teleology, see Popper, 2002b. See also, generally, Popper, 2002a, vols 1 and 2.
113 GPR §356, Werke 7: 509.
114 GPR §357, Werke 7: 510.

necessarily overcome preceding socio-political arrangements. In the same way, they represent injustice when they themselves resist progress into subsequent, necessary arrangements.

Hegel's notion that world history in his time comes to an end, at which point Being and Mind can become fully realised, as identical, in and for themselves, nevertheless entails the conclusion that justice and injustice can fully come into their own as meaningful concepts, as exhibited through the detailed programme of the *Grundlinien*. In the *Grundlinien* Hegel does therefore ultimately retain the binarist model, presenting itself as the complete and highest justice, with departures from it representing lesser justice, and in that sense injustice. For Hegel, the bipolar model of justice and injustice as mutually exclusive concepts or realities applies only with qualification to prior historical moments. A Caesar Augustus, an Oliver Cromwell, or a Robespierre achieve in one historical sense justice, in another sense injustice. Far from being surpassed, that model becomes fully affirmed, fully realised, in Hegel's proposal for the modern state. That approach opposes Kant's, whose categorical imperative inheres in reason as such, and must therefore, by extension, like the Newtonian laws which inspire it, apply absolutely and timelessly, ahistorically, to all ethical problems *per se* at all times and places.

Marx recapitulates Hegel's notion of a historical dialectic, which comes to be known as historical or dialectical materialism, and which similarly catalogues prior historical moments of injustice. He, too, grants earlier historical forms of oppression as inevitable events within a still-unfolding history, progressing towards fully realised justice in communism. Unlike Hegel, Marx sees history realised not in his own time, but in a future world in which socialism will have achieved the progressive 'withering away of the state', to be surpassed by communist society. Capitalism, for Marx, first emerges as an historically progressive force. It serves the historical emergence of justice, insofar as it is necessary for the surpassing of the injustices of feudalism. That capitalism as justice itself becomes injustice, however, as it only replaces one form of class-based exploitation with another. Capitalism as injustice must, in turn, be surpassed by the justice of state-directed socialism, which, in its own turn, must be surpassed through the final dissolution of the state, and the elimination of arbitrarily entrenched hierarchies of power in communism.[115] For Marx as for Hegel, the simple, binary model, as ahistorical or eternal, is too static, and therefore only of relative applicability to pre-communist historical moments. The justice of post-statist communism nevertheless remains unambiguous for Marx, still confirming the model of justice and injustice as mutually exclusive.

On the one hand, Hegelian and Marxist teleological models of history, in their orthodox versions, claim few adherents today. On the other hand, Kant's

115 See, e.g., MkP sec. I.

'clean slate' approach, which means that the categorical imperative applies indifferently to all ethical problems, is similarly embattled. The Aristotelian dialectic inherently implies a historical, without needing a historicist, framework. It is a framework that must necessarily move through history, given Aristotle's theory of ethical knowledge as cumulative, without assuming a fixed historical process or necessary historical outcome.

2.8 The partial incommensurability of justice and injustice

Within traditional, formal logic, the antinomy between 'justice' and 'injustice' remains less than straightforward. If j represents a postulated set of circumstances in which justice prevails, it is not the case that circumstances falling outside that set j necessarily represent injustice.[116] Many circumstances bear no relationship to justice or to injustice. Consider first a trivial example – and a ludicrous example is appropriate, since even seemingly unimportant circumstances or events can nevertheless, in some sense, often be linked to justice or injustice. Assume that I live under that set of just circumstances j. Assume further that my cactus grows most lavishly only when I play Mozart. That does not mean that I violate the circumstances of justice if I play the Bay City Rollers for it, causing it to grow less lavishly. That choice may make me a worse gardener, but not, on ordinary understandings, an unjust person, if my gardening has no broader social consequences. The only point of that example, a commonplace for formal logic, is that the contrary of 'just' is not necessarily 'unjust'. It can also be 'neither just nor unjust'. Similarly, for Aquinas, *malum importat remotionem boni* – all evil is absence of good,[117] but that does not mean that all absence of good is evil, since good can also be said to be absent where neither good nor evil pertain.

Applying that trivial example, in no serious sense can either justice or injustice be attributed to the choice of music played for a cactus. On traditional logic, the set of all things lacking justice encompasses the entirety of the subset of all unjust things, but is also larger than that subset, containing things that fall outside of it, namely those to which neither good nor evil pertain:

> [N]ot every absence (*remotio*) of good is evil. For absence of good can be taken in a privative and in a negative sense. Absence of good, taken negatively, is not evil; otherwise, it would follow that what does not exist is evil, and also that every thing would be evil, because of not having the good belonging to something else. For instance, a man would be evil because he did not have the swiftness of the roe, or the strength of a lion.

---

116 De Int 7–10.
117 ST I q. 48, art 3.

But the absence of good, taken in a privative sense, is an evil; as, for instance, the privation of sight is called blindness.[118]

Not all circumstances, then, that coincide with justice are either necessary or help to promote justice. Beyond trivial examples, however, deciding which circumstances are and are not necessary or helpful for justice, and in what combinations or degrees, is rarely obvious, nor, as I have argued, easy to examine with reference to isolated examples. As a second, less trivial example, assume that jury trials produce just outcomes for cases of commercial fraud. That does not, in strict logic, mean that trials without juries in those cases would produce less just outcomes. It is possible that the outcomes would be similar. It may also be that the justice in those cases further depends on additional elements of the legal system or of the society.

Accordingly, the set i of circumstances constituting injustice is not merely everything falling outside the set j of circumstances constituting justice. Each set contains different kinds of elements. We cannot straightforwardly isolate one element within j, and then assume it to have an obvious opposite, falling within set i. Take a third example. Even if it is true that, under a given set of circumstances c_1, a minimally regulated market fosters just social conditions, that does not mean that, under some other set of circumstances c_2, a more regulated market fosters injustice. The relationships between markets and social conditions are more intricate, indeed as a matter of logic, but also as a matter of socio-economics.

Without pursuing that enquiry further, the important point for now is that injustice does not merely include everything not falling under the, already theoretically problematical, category of 'justice'. Nor, however, does that observation mean that no relationships of simple opposition, or mutual exclusion, between the concepts of justice and injustice can ever be found. The simpler sequences of binarisms, within intellectually or institutionally isolated contexts, as noted at the outset, are plausible enough, as far as they go. We have seen, however, that those relationships nevertheless become more complex – often preserving their strict binarism only in a trivial, purely formal way – as their broader socio-political contexts, the contexts that most matter, are introduced. While it would be inaccurate, then, to attribute a relationship of 'total incommensurability' to the concepts of justice and injustice, as there is certainly some partial overlap between them, the two concepts remain only partially commensurable; they are, therefore, are also partially incommensurable.

The partial incommensurability of justice and injustice places one limit on rationalism, and another on irrationalism. It limits rationalism, as we have seen, by challenging any notion that we grasp injustice through a logical negation of some prior, articulated understanding of justice. When, for

---

118 ST I q. 48, art 3.

example, Kant purports, through the application of the categorical imperative, to generate essential norms of a legal system,[119] he leaves ample doubt about whether he has hit upon a regime of justice to which people would generally wish to subscribe. A long line of readers, certainly from Hegel or Marx onwards, have rejected not only various individual positive norms proposed by Kant, but more generally the assumptions about rigorously individual, autonomous, de-historicised and de-contextualised agents, which, at least on some readings, inevitably underpin the categorical imperative.[120] If Kant's theory of justice is therefore open to question, any Kantian notions of injustice that flow from assuming and applying his norms or principles can equally be contested. Similar results follow from other rationalist or formulaic approaches, such as Locke's scheme of natural rights or Mill's harm theory. If we nevertheless maintain some grasp at least of gross cases of injustice, even when such rationalist approaches seem inadequate, then the concept of injustice does appear to place some limit upon rationalist justice theory: the absence of consensus on rational principles of justice need not eclipse our widely shared sense of injustice, at least in heinous cases.

At the same time, the partial incommensurability that is also by definition a partial commensurability between the concepts of 'justice' and 'injustice', sets a limit to naïve irrationalism. It bars the suggestion that, because we can grasp some significant measure of injustice intuitively, or through wide consensus, we can generally and indifferently grasp justice and injustice that way – put briefly, that we 'just don't need theory'. Some great minds, looking askance at the whole enterprise of abstract or programmatic theory, have certainly doubted that a sense of justice requires abstract reasoning. 'We've needed centuries', quips Voltaire, 'to discover only some of the laws of nature. The wise man needs but a day to know the duties of man.'[121] Setting aside the questionable truth of that claim even on its own terms, our conspicuous dearth of 'wise men', or criteria for identifying them, renders such a maxim useless. Hegel grasps the inadequacy of both extremes. On the one hand, he rejects the simplistic rationalism that would fundamentally derive ethics, politics or law from abstract, definitively formulated rules. On the other hand, he does not view that rejection as swinging to the opposite extreme of sheer irrationalism. Even if his particular versions of history and culture are wanting, his recognition of the contexts within which they embed ethics, politics and law represents an intellectual advance, situated between those two extremes.

The partial incommensurability of 'justice' and 'injustice' limits, then, both the rationalist and irrationalist extremes that would render theories of justice or injustice untenable. Those limits also entail limits both on ethical

119 Cf. this chapter, text accompanying nn. 46–48.
120 Cf. this chapter, text accompanying n. 51.
121 Voltaire, 1964, p. 313. ('Il a fallu des siècles pour connaître une partie des lois de la nature. Un jour suffit au sage pour connaître les devoirs de l'homme.'). Cf. Tolstoy, 1993.

absolutism and on ethical relativism. In view of the ongoing disagreements not only about the substance of justice theory, but even about the criteria relevant to it – legal, ethical, political, economic, sociological, or cultural – ethical relativism becomes tempting. If we then proceed to combine ethical relativism with simplistic binarism, we run the risk of falsely extrapolating from the indeterminacy of justice to a view that injustice must, by definition, be equally indeterminate. Insofar as the simplistic binarism is mistaken, then, that extrapolation is equally mistaken. Even if the controversies surrounding justice theory mean that it rarely delivers uncontested results, the urgent realities, and the ethical primacy, of much injustice persist in highlighting the implausibility of relativism.

Yet we have seen that the immediacy of much injustice does not dictate any obvious justice theory, hence the equal impossibility of ethical absolutism. Certain inflictions of harm unquestionably, and in that sense absolutely, result in injustice, such as political corruption leading to mass starvation. A sheer negation would suggest that prevention or redress of the injustice entails an equally absolute instance of justice, for example, the political corruption should be eliminated. Once again, however, that latter claim is too question-begging as to specific ends and means to amount to a theory, let alone an absolutist one. The sheer diversity of theories that might support the claim preclude us from recognising any one of them as absolute. In post-Holocaust ethical theory, Auschwitz certainly stands for the unacceptability of relativism, for the proposition that some acts can only be seen as categorically unjust, that is, as unjust under *any* defensible ethics. Yet no single programmatic justice theory emerges as a result. The bitter irony is that Auschwitz yields overwhelming certainty about injustice, about what should not happen, yet still leaves us little certainty about justice, and about what form justice affirmatively and indeed programmatically takes.[122]

We are confronted with a predicament, in which etymology designates the immediate, concrete, experientially prior thing, injustice, via a more abstract, experientially remote thing, justice. Ordinarily, the opposite configuration would make more sense, namely, for the more obscure or abstract concept to be grasped by starting with a concrete one. A concept like 'incomplete', for example, draws its meaning from 'complete': a poker deck is complete with 52 cards, incomplete with fewer. The concept of injustice rests upon no such foundation. When we discuss law in ethical terms, although few of us today would call ourselves Platonists, we still fall into binarism's Platonist trap. *Injustice*, the thing that we actually know, everyday, here and now, a peremptory social reality, bears no name at all, except for the derivative, negatively defined, question-begging notion, displayed by its negatively defined etymology. Any attempt to find a substitute, a word not derived from a conceptual abstraction,

---

[122] See Derrida, 1992, p. 63.

instead containing its own immediately descriptive content, shows us how far astray our Platonist mental universe has led us. What other word might we use to denote injustice as an immediate, palpable reality, and not merely a derivative one, not merely a kind of intellectual afterthought?

Since I am accusing our traditional, familiar concept of being abstract and derivative, and since I am accusing it of failing to capture immediate and palpable realities, one might think I am simply looking for a concept that does not take the linguistic form of a negative. One might propose using terms that are not so obviously derivative, such as, for example, 'vice' or 'evil', or perhaps the 'overreaching' or 'outrageousness' (ὕβρις, *hubris*), or the craving of more than one's share (πλεονεξία, *pleonexia*) of ancient Greek thought.[123] Within the European Christian tradition, however, the Manichaean vintage of 'vice' or 'evil' leaves such terms as indeterminate (as indeed are the pre-Christian *hubris* or *pleonexia*) as is the negatively defined 'injustice'. A more neutral, judicially familiar, term like 'unconscionable' might seem preferable, since, as it happens, the modern English language no longer contains the distinct word 'conscionable'[124] that it negates. The problem nevertheless remains that a word like 'unconscionable' carries no more obvious content than words like 'vice' or 'evil'. No sooner are such substitutions proposed that it becomes clear that the problem is not fundamentally linguistic. We must understand injustice in some other way.

---

123 See, e.g., Grg 483c, 483e–84a, 488e–89a.
124 *The Oxford English Dictionary* designates 'conscionable' as 'apparently obsolete'. See *OED*, 1989, v. 3, pp. 755–56.

Chapter 3

Injustice as disunity

> ... così, a l'orazion pronta e divota,
> li santi cerchi mostrar nova gioia
> nel torneare e ne la mira nota.[1]
>
> Dante Alighieri

3.1 Introduction

In this and the next chapter, I shall examine, respectively, *unity* and *measurement* as two core elements of programmatic justice theories. Some theories place greater emphasis on unity, some on measurement, while others underscore the importance of both. According to the traditional binarism, injustice would result from straightforward negations of either or both of those elements. Injustice would result either from disunity or from mismeasurement. The aim of this chapter is to understand the role of unity in traditional justice theories.

3.2 Disunity as the primary cause of injustice in Plato

'[A] harmony is something invisible, without body, beautiful and divine in the attuned lyre, whereas the lyre itself and its strings are physical, bodily, composite, earthy and akin to what is mortal.'[2] Drawing upon that kind of Pythagorean comparison between order in the soul (ψυχή) or in the universe (κόσμος), and order in the tuned lyre,[3] Plato will suggest that there is only one state of being perfectly tuned, but many states of being un-tuned; one

---

1 Par 14.22–24:

> ... so at my lady's prompt and humble plea
> the sacred circles showed yet greater joy
> in their dance and in their heavenly harmony. (Par [Ci])

2 Phd 85e–86a.
3 Cf. Lch 188d, R 1.349e, L 1.654e–655b. Cf. Goyard-Fabre, 1992, p. 63.

state of a body in perfect health, but infinite kinds and combinations of illness;[4] one way for an individual, or a society, to be wholly just, but many ways for them to be unjust. Plato's medical analogies are particularly frequent. Today too, as in antiquity, we find an ever-expanding lexicon for ill-health: heart diseases, lung diseases, kidney diseases, liver diseases, skin diseases,[5] but good health is always just good health. The absence of heart disease is called good health. The absence of lung disease is called good health, and so forth. Similarly, for Plato, there are endless ways for a single individual to be unjust, for example, through murder, theft and fraud, but the opposite of those things – *not* committing murder, *not* committing theft, and the rest – is always the same one thing: justice. '[T]here is one form (εἶδος) of virtue (ἀρετῆς), and an unlimited number of forms of vice (κακίας)'.[6]

Plato's *Republic* will examine many ways for a society to be unjust, while seeking the single best way for it to achieve justice.[7] What is important about that ambition is not the particular arrangements it adopts – guardians do *x* and workers do *y*; mathematics is taught later than gymnastics, and so forth – but the assumption itself. Whether a given society adopts the *Republic's* or some other arrangements, injustice can always take a thousand forms, while justice can only ever take one. '[O]utrageousness (ὕβρις, *hubris*) has as many names as the forms it can take, and these are quite diverse'.[8]

It is in the *Republic* that Plato most systematically pursues the question, 'What is justice?' He declares early on his intention to provide a dual response. An understanding of the just society, justice in the polis, will be sought as a model for understanding the just individual, or justice in the psyche or soul:[9] 'We say, don't we, that there is the justice of a single man', that is, that a given individual does just or unjust things, or has a just or unjust character, 'and also the justice of a whole city?', that is, that a polis as such has more or less just or unjust laws, institutions or practices.[10] As the investigation unfolds, it nevertheless becomes clear that not merely two, but three, distinct levels are inter-linked. The cosmos, too, like the tuned lyre, represents a balanced ordering, hence the inter-relationships of order and justice at the levels of cosmos, polis and psyche. Plato focuses on two, however, as humans exert no control over the cosmos as a whole, which is an ordering that stands as an object not of action but of contemplation, allowing us to draw analogies to those realms in which we can indeed act to achieve greater or lesser levels of

---

4 M 72d; R 4.405d–06b.
5 Cf. R 3.405d; L 1.646b.
6 R 4.445c.
7 Cf. Perelman, 1990, p. 93.
8 Phdr 238a.
9 R 2.368c–369b.
10 R 2.368e.

harmony or justice.[11] For Plato, we can actively choose, or decline, to tune the lyre, but can never choose what constitutes such attunement.

Plato sets as his aim the ideal of a best possible attunement of those two levels of polis and psyche with the inherent ordering of the cosmos. Again, he does introduce afterlife myths that would integrate the cosmos even more directly into the active, deliberative choices and actions of individuals, as our afterlives would reflect the justice with which we act during our mortal lives.[12] Although partly drawn from pre-existing legends,[13] Plato's tales of the hereafter are nevertheless introduced in a speculative vein. They stand apart from the dialectic of the principle discussion, with no obvious indication that the interlocutors will be persuaded by them. That tentativeness about the manner in which, or the degree to which, individual acts and choices entail cosmic consequences contrasts with the interaction between human and divine forces that will emerge in Christian justice theory, in which the universal order will play a central and constant role. Plato's idea of an eternal Form of justice will also add a cosmic or metaphysical level to the analysis of the polis and the psyche, but, even more so than the afterlife myths, Plato can introduce the theory of Forms only as a novelty, and not as the kind of acknowledged metaphysical bedrock that later Christian thinkers would confidently attribute to God. In *Parmenides*, Plato problematises the theory of Forms, and in works deemed to have been written after the *Republic*, such as *Statesman* or *Laws*, he no longer relies upon it.

Regardless of whether we focus on justice in the polis and psyche, or additionally introduce their relationship to a cosmic order, the salient condition for the possibility of justice in the *Republic* remains the element of unity – the absence of conflicting forces, the absence of components striving for irreconcilable ends, both within the body politic and within the human being. It is that harmony of all participating forces which can be said to represent the defining feature of justice, be they the various necessary functions fulfilled by citizens across the polis, or the various drives, thoughts and feelings within the individual. '[D]oing the one work that is his own, [the citizen] will become not many but one, and the whole city will itself be naturally one not many.'[14] Under that model, injustice arises through opposed conditions, when disharmony, or disunity, afflicts those same elements, either internally, or between or among one another: 'Is there any greater evil (κακὸν) we can mention for a city than that which tears it apart and makes it many instead of one? Or any greater good (ἀγαθὸν) than that which binds it together and makes it one?'[15] The good statesman would 'pay regard to the internal warfare

---

11 Cf. R 9.592b.
12 See this book, Chapter 1, text accompanying n. 22.
13 Cf., e.g., Wilcox, 1976, p. 43 (noting the limited status of divine retribution in Homer).
14 R 4.423d. Cf. Goyard-Fabre, 1992, pp. 46–51.
15 R 5.462a. Cf. Pol 2.2.1261ª14–15.

which arises, from time to time, within the city, and is called ... *faction*.[16] Political or individual injustice depart from cosmic order not, as in Christianity, as sin, not as a direct offense against the will of a God pervasively active in human affairs, but nevertheless in such a way as to confirm that justice and injustice are not relative or subjective notions. Political and individual action harmonise with an objective natural order to generate justice, or depart from it to generate injustice.

Plato's emphasis on unity is not self-evident or platitudinous, as emerges from the difficulty he has refuting Thrasymachus's anti-justice views. The *Republic* portrays those views substantively, but also narratively. Thrasymachus is offensive, violent, disruptive and contemptuous of the co-operation,[17] the inter-personal unity, required in order for a critical discussion to take place. His aggressive push forward mirrors Socrates' diffident pulling back.[18] Thrasymachus expresses injustice as disunity in word and deed. Plato's rejection of ethical relativism emerges from his disagreement with the views of those sophists who renounce any ethically meaningful unity of cosmic and human order.[19] Socrates condemns the inverted natural law of the orator Callicles, the disciple of Gorgias who maintains that the cosmic order, the order of nature is indeed relevant, but only insofar as nature, far from a theatre of justice, is the stage of overtly aggressive domination and conquest, such that the cosmic order, if relevant at all, would dictate not a higher law of justice, but an ethos of 'might makes right', with supreme injustice as the greatest prize.[20]

The view that justice requires unity does, then, have its problems. First, it may seem obvious or trivial. It comes as no surprise to suggest that justice ought to promote unity over discord or faction. Plato's insistence on unity, however, suffices to show how un-obvious unity is. The *Republic* certainly departs from today's dominant institutional understandings. Again, our legislatures, courts and regulatory bodies apply norms and procedures to more-or-less isolated problems. They do so with little regard to the degree or character of overall unity within society as a whole. In large, administratively complex societies, that task would be unthinkable. Our political rhetoric may routinely invoke slogans about unity; however, legislatures or administrative bodies, even if specifically tasked with improving or harmonising conditions over broad populations, do so issue-by-issue, with little attention to, let alone agreement on, overarching socio-political unity. It does therefore matter whether or to what extent a theory emphasises unity as a crucial element of justice.

Second, it might be argued that unity is not an element of justice at all, and that Plato and others confuse means with ends. On that view, if unity is indeed

---

16 L [HC] 1.628a (translator's italics); cf. L 3.679e, 4.708b–d.
17 R 1.336a–b.
18 R 1.327c.
19 Cf., e.g., Tht 167c, 172a–d.
20 Grg 483c–d.

a human goal, then it is more as a by-product than as a specific component of justice. A best possible justice theory will entail the most satisfied population. That population will, in turn, be least likely to fragment, and will therefore *end up* unified. Unity is therefore a, or the, desirable aim of justice, but is not any specific part of it. By extension, one might argue that unity is therefore an overall 'political' goal, but not any particular component of 'law' as such. Kelsen's and Perelman's overviews of justice theories, for example, review a host of traditional models or maxims, but wholly ignore the principle of unity. In 'Das Problem der Gerechtigkeit', part of Kelsen's analysis consists of reviewing and critiquing a variety of conceptions, from ancient to Kantian and Marxist, and from the familiar maxims 'To each his own' or 'Do unto others', to Kant's more intricately formulated categorical imperative and Aristotle's rule of the 'mean', to principles of revenge (*Vergeltung, lex talionis*) or proportionality. Perelman examines 'to each according to his merits', 'to each according to his needs', and similar maxims of remedy and distribution.

Part of Kelsen's error in 'Das Problem der Gerechtigkeit' consists in pondering the concept of justice by reviewing and critiquing only measurement theories. He assumes the classical model, such that injustice arises only from mismeasurement, as determined only through discrete legislative, administrative and judicial acts. Examining only measurement theories, Kelsen inadvertently reveals the reductionist, mechanist assumption of justice as the sheer sum-total of de-contextualised, case-by-case instances of legislation, administration or adjudication. His essay collapses the concept of justice into sheer formulas or algorithms for justice, as if the only aim justice theory has ever had has been to perform calculations for the resolution of isolated disputes, the entirety of the legal system being nothing more than the total set of norms and institutions aimed at providing those resolutions. Small wonder that Kelsen, like many legal theorists – including many who believe themselves to have moved on from the starting point of orthodox, mechanistic positivism; and unlike most political philosophers, who rarely have had much use for *that* particular starting point in the first place – can only ever understand a figure like Plato in risibly brief and dismissive terms. Kelsen has little more to offer about, if not ignoring entirely, other theories placing greater or lesser value on unity as a distinct aim of justice, such as those of Rousseau or Hegel.[21] Kelsen treats even Marx, whose theories shout unity,[22] only as a measurement theorist. In fairness, of course, even Kelsen's reductionism surpasses much of today's dominant Anglo-American tradition of post-positivist legal theory, which scarcely seems able to identify anything of interest within two millennia of justice theories at all.[23]

---

21 See this chapter, Section 3.5.
22 See this chapter, Section 3.5.
23 See Heinze, 2007b.

For Kelsen and Perelman, both modernists, justice amounts, then, to sheer measurement. That omission is unsurprising for the positivist Kelsen, who seeks indeed to distinguish the aims and operation of law from those of politics, and who would arguably view unity as a 'purely political' aspiration. Yet even Perelman seems to assume some such view, as the justice theories he reviews all suggest that it is solely the perception of fair measurement that a population will see as just. Leaving aside the thorny questions about differences between 'law' and 'politics', or between 'ends' and 'means' in law, it is important to recall, as even Kelsen does, that the very idea of theorising about *justice* – regardless of whether we view that task, as Kelsen does, to be distinct from theorising about *law* – is inherently normative, and is normative at both large and small scales of human activity. To distinguish that task, therefore, from ethical, political or indeed legal (in its normative dimension) theory would involve artificial boundaries to be drawn among those spheres, luring us into the age-old trap of assuming that conventionally different words must correspond to fundamentally different realities. The *Republic* alone suffices to show, regardless of our agreements or disagreements with it, that unity can be deemed to be not only a crucial aim of law, but can also pervade the minutiae of its norms, institutions and practices, as the details of Plato's model society constantly remind us.

Third, the ideal of political unity in Plato's theory may seem Draconian, conformist, or simply implausible. Certainly, some of the requirements introduced, from music composed only in Dorian and Phrygian, but never in Lydian modes,[24] to naked, adult, mixed-sex gymnastic exercises[25] either strike the modern reader as parody, or, if construed literally, seem to reduce to a regime of totalitarian control, a reading of Plato that came to prominence amidst 20th-century experiences of fascism and dictatorship.[26] It is worth recalling of course that, given Plato's famous sense of irony, and some of his more humorous or puzzling passages, some commentators have suspected that the *Republic* is intended only as a satire on utopianism. Few leading scholars today take that view,[27] however, and nor do Aristotle's discussions[28] take the *Republic* in any such vein. Be that as it may, neither a defective model of unity, nor the abuse of a good model, suffice in themselves as grounds for dismissing the ideal of unity altogether. Plato's unity theory is examined here not with an aim of scrutinising Plato, but with the aim of scrutinising unity as such, as an aim or element of justice. My interest for present purposes is in the *Republic* as a theory about the cardinal place for unity as an aim and justification of law and politics.

24 R 3.398e–99d.
25 R 5.452a–b.
26 See, e.g., Popper, 2002a. Cf. Heinze, 2007b.
27 See, e.g., Rice, 1998, pp. 123–25.
28 Pol 2.2–5.

Heinous abuses of unity ideals in Nazi, Stalinist, Maoist and other totalitarian regimes spurred an equal and opposite reaction in liberal theories, which, in turn, have rendered unity epiphenomenal, a by-product of a regime otherwise working well. Plato, Rousseau and Marx, the three most absolute of programmatic Western unity theorists,[29] embrace an essential ingredient of unity, namely the necessity to reconstruct the entirety of society by reconstructing human beings in their entirety. All three witness how complex, market-driven legal regimes fragment society, alienating individuals from it, from one another, and from themselves, leaving the pursuit of self-interest as the only available, and therefore seemingly natural, life plan. Individuals must therefore be wholly re-made into beings fundamentally concerned with social welfare, and social justice, not as a threat to, but as part and parcel of, their own welfare and of the justice of their individual circumstances.[30] Marx cites from Rousseau's *Contrat Social* with approval.

> One who dares attempt to govern a people must feel able to change, so to speak, human nature, to transform each individual, who, in himself, is a perfect, solitary whole, a part of a greater whole of which each individual receives, in some sense, his life and his being; to substitute independent, physical existence for partial, moral existence. One must rid man of his own capacities and give him instead some that are foreign to him, and which he cannot use except with the aid of others.[31]

In other words: which he cannot use except in a state of pervasive unity with others.

Plato's emphasis on unity as the essence of justice remains important if only because so many subsequent theories maintain some version of that ideal. Few dismiss it expressly, with the exception of the most extreme libertarianism or anarchism, and even their exponents often insist that unity is in fact greater where it is unconstrained and voluntary, as opposed to being government-directed.[32] Plato's emphasis on unity sheds light on what it means to think of injustice fundamentally as disunity. The role of unity requires attention all the more, as, despite its centrality for Plato and several other theorists, analyses such as those of Kelsen or Perelman show how easily it is overlooked by legal theorists.

---

29 See this chapter, Section 3.5.
30 Cf., e.g., Heinze, 2007a, pp. 116–20.
31 CS 2: 7, JJR-OC 381–82, cited in JF sec. 1, MEW 1: 370. ('Celui qui ose entreprendre d'instituer un peuple doit se sentir en état de changer pour ainsi dire la nature humaine, de transformer chaque individu, qui par lui-même est un tout parfait et solitaire, en partie d'un plus grand tout dont cet individu reçoive en quelque sorte sa vie et son être, de substituer une existence partielle et morale à l'existence physique et indépendante. Il faut qu'il ôte à l'homme ses forces propres pour lui en donner qui lui soient étrangères et dont il ne puisse faire usage sans le secours d'autrui.') Cf. EP 251–52.
32 See generally Préposiet, 2002.

It is worth at least noting briefly that Plato's particular and pointed suspicion about writing, which extends to the recording of laws and legal records,[33] entails, for Derrida, a view of writing itself as a betrayal or corruption of an author's 'authentic' meaning. Although *The Laws* will certainly embrace written codes and records, the *Republic*'s seeming absence of them would suggest, on Derrida's view, a faith in, and privileging of, some pre-orthographic truth as authenticity. That authenticity, that pure and ultimate reality behind the 'dangerous supplement' of writing,[34] would be reflected in Plato's theory of Forms, and in the almost otherworldly unity ideal which defines his notion of justice. Derrida's challenge to any such privileged moment of authenticity independent of the actually or effectively inscribed utterance becomes a challenge to myths of unity themselves as myths of authenticity. Derrida's approach will be helpful in Chapter 5, where unity as an aim of justice is revisited with the aim of developing a post-classical perspective.

Plato's analysis of both political and individual injustice constantly focuses upon causes of disunity, being political for society, psychological for the individual. He has Socrates in the *Republic* explain that the guardians, the ideal society's stewards of justice, must, by law, amass neither wealth nor luxuries, nor their own private property. They must live with the fewest possible personal comforts beyond the barest material necessities, so as never to place ambitions for private comfort or gain above their constant care for the common weal.[35] Socrates' interlocutor Adeimantus, Plato's other brother present at the discussion, along with Glaucon, raises an objection: '[Y]ou aren't making [the guardians] very happy. . . . The city really belongs to them, yet they derive no good from it.'[36] Adeimantus notes the oddity, certainly if we consider rulers' lifestyles throughout history, that it is the workers, the class without the power, who 'own land, build fine big houses, acquire furnishings to go along with them . . . entertain guests, and [possess] gold and silver and all the things that are thought to belong to people who are blessedly happy'.[37] Socrates, far from flinching, ups the ante: 'and what's more, [the guardians] work simply for their keep and get no extra wages as the others do. [. . .] they'll have nothing to give to their mistresses, nothing to spend in whatever other ways they wish, as people do who are considered happy',[38] that is, 'considered happy' on conventional views.

The *Republic's* ideal society certainly differs from most of history's simultaneously centralised yet non-democratic regimes. Its unusual system of checks

---

33 See, e.g., Stm 295c–e. See also, e.g., Heinze, 2007a, pp. 116–20.
34 See generally Derrida, 1972; Cf. Derrida, 1967a, 1967b.
35 R 3.416c–d. Cf. L 5.742e–43a.
36 R 4.419a.
37 R 4.419a.
38 R 4.420a. Cf. 4.464b–d.

and balances assures that those with power, the guardians, lack personal wealth,[39] and those with wealth, the workers, lack political power.[40] The aim of that constitutional and demographic symmetry is that the potential for class enmity will balance out on both sides, favouring unity over rivalry. Socrates' reply to Adeimantus, as an aspiration, has not aged a day. Few of us could disagree with it: '[I]n establishing our city, we aren't aiming to make any one group outstandingly happy but to make the whole city so, as far as possible.'[41] The binarism of justice and injustice immediately follows. 'We thought that we'd find justice most easily in such a city and injustice, by contrast, in the one that is governed worst.'[42]

In *Statesman*, Plato depicts justice not in terms of the metaphysics of justice as an 'idea' or 'form', but through the more artisanal analogy to weaving, in which separate strands – professions, interests, etc. – are harmonised into a seamlessly unified whole,[43] again recalling the harmony of the tuned lyre. That image is apt for Plato, as weaving requires measuring out, to each strand, its appropriate length and position, *suum cuique*;[44] yet that measuring always serves, and remains subordinated to, the unity of the whole. '[T]his bonding together is more divine, uniting parts of virtue that are by nature unlike each other, and tend in opposite directions.'[45] Without that balancing of interests for the purposes of overcoming factions and forging unity, the opposite state of affairs, injustice, inevitably follows.

> [Socrates]: You're happily innocent if you think that anything other than the kind of city we are founding deserves to be called *a city* (πόλιν).
> [Adeimantus]: What do you mean?
> [Socrates]: We'll have to find a greater title for the [other cities] because each of them is a great many cities, not *a* city. . . . [E]ach of them consists of two cities at war with one another, that of the poor and that of the rich.[46]

Plato pursues that thought, underscoring the interweaving of unity as justice within society as a whole, and unity as justice within the individual.

> [Socrates]: [E]ach of the [non-guardian] citizens is to be directed to what he is naturally suited for, so that, doing the one work that is his own, he

---

39 R 3.416c–e, 4.423e–24a.
40 R 4.419a–20e.
41 R 4.420b; 5.466a.
42 R 4.420b.
43 Stm 279b ff., 304e, 311b–c. Cf. Goyard-Fabre, 1992, p. 64.
44 See this book, Chapter 4, Section 4.2.
45 Stm 310a.
46 R 4.422e (translator's italics).

will become not many but one, and the whole city will itself be naturally one not many.[47]

Shortly thereafter, in an exchange with Glaucon, Socrates explains:

> [Socrates]: [I]n our city more than in any other . . . [w]hen any one of them is doing well or badly, they'll [all-EH] say that 'mine' is doing well or that 'mine' is doing badly.
> [Glaucon]: That's absolutely true.
> [Socrates]: Now, didn't we say that the having and expressing of this conviction is closely followed by the having of pleasures and pains in common?
> [Glaucon]: Yes, and we were right.
> [Socrates]: Then won't our citizens, more than any others, have the same thing in common, the one they call 'mine'? And, having that in common, won't they, more than any others, have common pleasures and pains?
> [Glaucon]: Of course.[48]

It is the West's first programmatic political theory, then, which elaborates the first and the most unequivocal version of the classical model of justice through unity, as a template for injustice through disunity. The many possible manifestations of injustice, like the many kinds of illness, or the many ways for a lyre to be out of tune, all become negations of the one way for the polity to be unified, mirroring the one state of being in good health, or the one way for the lyre to be in tune. Greater or lesser degrees of injustice precisely correspond to greater or lesser degrees of negation of, through departure from or through corruption of, the justice that comes through unity. Plato argues in *The Laws*:

> The first-best society, then, that with the best constitution and code of law, is one where the old saying is most universally true of the whole society. I mean the saying that 'friends' property is indeed common property.' If there is now on earth, or ever should be, such a society . . . if all means have been taken to eliminate everything we mean by the word *ownership* from life . . . in a word, when the institutions if a society make it most utterly one, that is a criterion of their excellence . . . no truer or better will ever be found.[49]

Plato's defiance of democracy, a challenge still heard in our day, draws from his argument that, by placing individual freedom and choice as a supreme

---

47 R 4.423d. Cf. 8.551d, 5.744b–e.
48 R 4.463e–64a.
49 L [HC] 5.739c–d (translator's italics).

value, tacitly placing it above any sense of shared or common welfare, democracy in a sense has no real πολιτεία, no real constitution at all, beyond being the latter being an intellectual abstraction, what we today call 'just a piece of paper'. One instead finds a παντοπώλιον, a 'bazaar' or 'supermarket' of constitutions,[50] each citizen a constitution unto himself, following law unwillingly if it means compromising personal advantage, and arguably not at all, if he can get away with it. For Plato, the risk is that the people will themselves ultimately turn to populism, and its logical conclusion, tyranny, once their internal divisions create excessive instability, at which point 'the most severe and cruel slavery [emerges] from the utmost freedom'.[51]

Plato does not seek any old unity at any price. Order imposed through the coercive and arbitrary rule of the tyrant brings neither justice nor real unity at all, but only overt or latent division.[52] Plato nevertheless describes the decay from comparatively better towards comparatively worse political and legal regimes as the consequence of individuals and groups falling into discord.[53] The pursuit of individual advantage, and social or economic forces that spur us on to that pursuit, are inevitably the cause of division,[54] leading over time to progressively more coercive social relations, required to maintain, yet ultimately never successfully maintaining, unity.[55] The injustice of an oligarchy, for example, is precisely that 'it isn't one city but two – one of the poor and one of the rich – living in the same place and always plotting against one another'.[56]

3.3 Disunity as a major element of injustice in Aristotle

Much of Aristotle's ethical and political theory also places unity at the core of justice, as is evident in his influence on communitarian theorists today.[57] Aristotle develops his own vision of unity echoing through the three levels of cosmos, polis and psyche. He develops a view of justice as the greatest possible perfecting of the nature or ordering (φύσις) of both the individual character and the socio-political collectivity. He nevertheless argues that Plato's *Republic* undermines unity precisely by taking it to an extreme, at the expense of human diversity, which might superficially appear to undermine unity, but remains indispensable to the greatest possible prosperity and cohesion of the polis *qua* collectivity. 'Is it not obvious that a state (πόλις) may at length attain

---

50 R 8.557d.
51 R 8.564a.
52 See, e.g., L 3.697c–98a, 6.776c.
53 See, e.g., R 4.444a–b; 8.545c–d.
54 R 8.547b, 8.550e. Cf. Heinze, 2007a, pp. 100–14.
55 R 8.548e.
56 R 8.551d; cf. R 1.351c.
57 See, e.g., Taylor, 1992; MacIntyre, 2007, pp. 146–64.

such a degree of unity as to be no longer a state? . . . [T]he nature of the state is to be a plurality (πλῆθος γάρ τι τὴν φύσιν ἐστὶν ἡ πόλις).'[58]

The citizens' diverse roles are, for Aristotle, a positive benefit, and not inherently a danger that requires strong constraint: 'The state consists not merely of a plurality of men, but of different *kinds* of men; you cannot make a state out of men who are all alike.'[59] The greatest possible unity would make the polis nothing more than, in a sense, one person, that is, many acting as or fused into one. (Recall the 1651 frontispiece of Hobbes's *Leviathan*, in which all individuals of the realm reduce to faceless points, welded into the one visible figure of the omnipotent sovereign. Our distaste for that image resonates with Aristotle's for Plato's *Republic*.) Aristotle agrees with Plato in identifying discord or factionalism as a source of injustice, and justice-as-unity as its opposite, but disagrees that justice equates with the tightest possible unity.[60]

The *Republic's* metaphysics presents universals as existing independently of particulars. Justice exists as an essentially unified Form, signally instantiated whenever any particular just act is performed. Justice maintains one eternal nature, while injustice is of countless varieties. Aristotle deems that concept of justice excessively, misleadingly unified, as it fails to account for the qualitatively different ways in which states of affairs can be just or unjust (we can recall here his similarity to Meno on that point). On Aristotle's view, 'the just is spoken of in more ways than one' and 'so is the unjust'.[61] Fortuitously murdering an innocent is, then, unjust 'by nature', while driving on the right is, in Britain, unjust by convention, that is, not inherently unjust, but unjust only because some convention is required, and it is therefore neither more nor less unjust than driving on the left would be in France.[62] What nevertheless remains is the mutual exclusion between justice and injustice. Aristotle's attack on excessive unity, either conceptual or political, in Plato, is neither a denial of any unity whatsoever, nor a renunciation of Plato's essential and strict binarism between the concepts of justice and injustice.

Aristotle, then, rejects the *Republic* for imposing too much unity, to the point of extinguishing rather than enforcing the polis's necessary and constructive diversity. On the one hand, motivated by appalling abuses of Athenian democracy,[63] Plato fears that power distributed across many citizens leads to disunity and injustice, through overwhelming incentives to pursue self-interest at the expense of the common good, which leads to factionalism

---

58 Pol 2.2.1261^{a}16–18. As in Plato's *Republic*, it is still the Greek polis being discussed, albeit rendered by some translators as 'city', by others as 'state', and by others as 'city-state'.
59 Pol [Si] 2.2.1261^{a}22–24 (translator's italics).
60 See, e.g., Pol 3.15.1286^{b}1.
61 NE [Ir] 5.1.1129^{a}26–27.
62 See NE 5.7. Aristotle further identifies other senses of justice, such as 'general' and 'special' and 'distributive' and 'rectificatory'. Cf. this book, Chapter 4, Section 4.3.
63 See, e.g., Ap *passim*; Ltr 7.325b–c.

and demagogy. On the other hand, Plato observes the equal abuses of which other constitutions, notably monarchical-tyrannical or oligarchic, are capable.[64] It is unsurprising that, as part of the project of theorising ideal communities in such programmatic writings as the *Republic* and *Laws*, Plato devotes exhaustive attention to regulations governing the minutiae of social and personal life, to a degree, as was mentioned, that often appears more like irony than theory. For Plato, 'too much' unity is a contradiction in terms, like a body being too healthy, a lyre too well tuned, or a circle too round. Aristotle's faith in the citizens' ability to assess their collective needs and interests[65] correlates to an ideal of society for which his favoured norms are presented more in general outline, more in terms of foundational guidelines for engendering civic mindedness among citizens able to rule themselves.

In no way, then, does unity vanish from Aristotle's view of justice, and it is his wish to blend the two age-old ingredients of unity and diversity that appeals to communitarians today. Aristotle's ethical and political theories do aim strongly at social cohesion, generally more so than modern liberal theories. The marginally greater autonomy of citizens in *The Laws* – how great it is can be debated – in comparison to the *Republic*, suggests that Plato is by no means unaware of some constructive role for diversity in the polis, even if that work still makes unity the core ingredient of justice. What is important for present purposes is not to pin Plato or Aristotle down to all-or-nothing views on unity and diversity, but only to show how unity remains a leading value, even for theories, such as Aristotle's, which criticise Plato's view, instead blending unity with values that, seeming contrary to it, might rather strengthen it. If Plato's and Aristotle's views of ethics and politics differ in many ways, they nevertheless agree, then, in adopting some version of the classical model, by correlating justice, in some significant measure, to unity, and injustice to disunity.

> We must consider also in which of two ways the nature of the universe contains the good, and the highest good, whether as something separate and by itself, or as the order of the parts. Probably in both ways, as an army does. For the good is found both in its order and in the leader, and more in the latter; for he does not depend on the order but it depends on him. And all things are ordered together somehow, but not all alike, – both fishes and fowls and plants; and the world is not such that one thing has nothing to do with another, but they are connected. For all are ordered together to one end.[66]

Aristotle strikes a blow on the side of diversity, against stronger Platonic unity, by according privately owned land to all citizens.[67] He preserves Plato's

---

64 R 8.546a–69c.
65 But cf. L 1.643e, 6.762d–e.
66 Meta 12.10.1075^{a}11–18.
67 See, e.g., Pol 7.10.1329^{b}40–30^{a}2, 1330^{a}11. Cf. NE 4.1.1120^{a}5–9.

concern for balancing wealth against power, but does so in a different way, namely, by striking also a counter-blow on the side of unity, so that no one citizen or faction can accumulate either too much power or too much property or wealth.[68] All share in, not necessarily equal, but nonetheless comparable distributions of those goods, a matter to be explored further in the next chapter. Aristotle moreover remains strongly on the side of unity in theorising about the optimal land and population sizes to be held by the whole of the polis. He certainly follows Plato[69] in arguing that 'it is difficult, if not impossible, for a populous state to be run by good laws'.[70]

> [L]aw is order, and good law is good order; but a very great multitude cannot be orderly.... Beauty is realized in number and magnitude, and the state which combines magnitude with good order must necessarily be the most beautiful. To the size of states there is a limit.... [I]f the citizens of a state are to judge and to distribute offices according to merit, then they must know each other's characters; where they do not possess this knowledge, both the election to offices and the decision of lawsuits will go wrong. When the population is very large they are manifestly settled at haphazard, which clearly ought not to be. [...] Clearly then the best limit of the population of a state is the largest number which suffices for the purposes of life, and can be taken in at a single view.[71]

3.4 Disunity as metaphysical injustice in Christianity

Subsequent Western thought, in the Christian tradition, will often mirror one or another version of the classical model, either Plato's overwhelming emphasis on unity, or Aristotle's inclusion of it as an important but not sole factor. For St Augustine, strongly influenced by Platonism,[72] the earthly society (*civitas terrena*) takes countless forms, always more or less imperfect and therefore always more or less unjust. The realm of divine law (*civitas dei*), hence of perfect justice, is one, is eternal, and is unified.[73] Those parallel realms are linked. They are 'two kinds of societies, to which all men of all times belong'.[74]

From a loosely Hegelian perspective, that is, not assuming any strictly teleological path of history, we could say that the role of the binarism, justice as unity and injustice as disunity, becomes simultaneously diminished and enlarged. It is diminished insofar as the ideal of the immediate, inter-personal

---

68 See, e.g., Pol 1.9, 3.13.1284^{b}27, 4.12.1295^{b}34–96^{a}3. Cf. NE 4.1.1120^{b}16–18.
69 R 4.423b, L 5.737d.
70 Pol [Si] 7.4.1326^{a}25.
71 Pol 7.4.1326^{a}30–26^{b}25. Alternatively, 'not so large that it cannot easily be surveyed', Pol [Si]. Cf. L 6.768b.
72 See, e.g., CD 8:5.
73 CD 11:1, 14:28.
74 Fortin, 1987, p. 195. Cf. CD 11:1.

unity of the Greek polis or the Roman republic has vanished, replaced by what Hegel identifies as the detached, anonymous, alienated individual who emerges in the Roman imperial world, which, even as Rome declines, becomes supplanted by the Christian universalist ideal, unifying not the small but immediate and active citizenry of democratic Athens or republican Rome, but only a vast, undifferentiated and subordinated mass.[75] At the same time, justice as unity is enlarged through Christianity's augmentation of cosmic, metaphysical unity under a divine law consciously ordered by the omnipotent and omniscient God. As concrete citizenship and individuality weaken, abstract citizenship and individuality strengthen. While Plato's and Aristotle's visions of individual and social justice and injustice are metaphysically informed, the minutiae of their discussions about justice nevertheless maintain their focus on the polis and the psyche; Christianity will, through the metaphysics of a God deliberating about and intervening in human affairs, embrace the more elevated and abstracted trinity of cosmos, state and individual.

For Augustine, God's 'purpose . . . was that the human race should . . . be bound together by a kind of tie of kinship to form a harmonious unity, linked together by the "bond of peace" (*in unitatem concordem pacis uinculo conligandum*)'.[76] By contrast, 'human society is generally divided against itself'.[77] Cosmic unity in Plato provides a criterion of truth, but does not emerge through an agent consciously acting through or vigilant about human affairs.[78] Christian political theory will more strongly balance those three levels, rendering injustice more overtly a violation of the divinely willed, natural order, in which unity remains central to justice, and injustice represents division and separation of individuals not only from themselves, one another, and their communities, but also from God and God's cosmic plan.

For Aquinas, the eternal law (*lex aeterna*), God's justice, is perfectly unified: '[T]he whole community of the universe is governed by the divine reason [which is] not subject to time, but eternal.'[79] Injustices under human law (*lex humana*) arise from its respectively imperfect, discordant sources: 'Human law has the nature of law in so far as it partakes of reason. . . . But in so far as it deviates from reason, it is called an unjust law, and has the nature, not of law, but of violence.'[80] The mutual exclusion of justice and injustice, injustice as an absence of justice, reflects the mutual exclusion of good and evil, evil as the absence of good.[81] Parallel circumstances emerge at the level of individual justice, that is, of the soul: '[I]n the state of corrupted nature man cannot

---

75 See Kojève, 1975, pp. 71–89.
76 CD 14:1.
77 CD 18:2.
78 Cf., e.g., R 2.365d.
79 ST I-II q. 91 a. 1.
80 ST I-II q. 93, a. 3 ad 2.
81 See this book, Chapter 2, text accompanying n. 117.

fulfil all the divine commandments without healing grace.'[82] Accordingly, 'justice may be brought about in man by a movement *from one contrary the other*, and thus justification implies a transmutation from the state of injustice to the . . . state of justice'.[83]

In Dante's *Paradiso*, which will synthesise Christianity with classicism, and Augustine with Aquinas, the poet wanders through a progressively articulated vision, strongly integrating cosmic, political and individual notions of justice as unity. The blessed are united in themselves, with others, and with God and the universe.

> Le cose tutte quante
> hanno ordine tra loro, e questo è forma
> che l'universo a Dio fa simigliante.
>
> Qui veggion l'alte creature l'orma
> de l'etterno valore, il qual è fine
> al quale è fatta la toccata norma.
>
> Ne l'ordine ch'io dico sono accline
> tutte nature, per diverse sorti,
> più al principio loro e men vicine
>
> onde si muovono a diversi porti
> per lo gran mar de l'essere, e ciascuna
> con istinto a lei dato che la porti.[84]

---

82 ST I-II q. 109, a. 4.
83 ST I-II q. 113, a. 1 (italics added).
84
> '[A]ll things', she began, 'whatever their mode
>   observe an inner order. It is this form
>   that makes the universe resemble God.
>
> In this the highest creatures see the hand
>   of the Eternal Worth, which is the goal
>   to which these norms conduce, being so planned.
>
> All Being within this order, by the laws
>   of its own nature is impelled to find
>   its proper station round its Primal Cause.
>
> Thus every nature moves across the tide
>   of the great sea of being to its own port,
>   each with its given instinct as its guide.' (Par [Ci] 1.103–14)

The *Inferno* meanwhile remains a cauldron of division and cacophony, cut off from the moment of Satan's rebellion as a factious fragment banished from harmonious communion with the totality of God's universe, as the souls of the unjust, not only suffer, but actively perpetuate their own and therefore one another's eternal disintegration and alienation. Hell, perfect and eternal injustice, is perfect and eternal disunity.

> Quivi sospiri, pianti e alti guai
> risonavan per l'aere sanza stelle,
> per ch'io al cominciar ne lagrimai.
>
> Diverse lingue, orribili favelle,
> parole di dolore, accenti d'ira,
> voci alte e fioche, e suon di man con elle
>
> facevano un tumulto, il qual s'aggira
> sempre in quell'aura sanza tempo tinta,
> come la rena quando turbo spira.[85]

Souls in *Purgatorio* have not yet achieved *Paradiso's* experience of perfected, manifest justice. Their harsh regimen nevertheless remains shielded from Satanic division, under the unified government and plan of God.[86] None of those three realms is earthly, but Dante's allegory in *La Divina Commedia* finds its programmatic counterpart in *De Monarchia*, a paradigm of human justice conceived within a universal Christian ideal of justice as divinely ordered unity. '[H]uman society is a totality in relation to its parts, but is itself part of . . . the whole universe. But its parts are well-ordered only on the basis of a single principle (*per unum principium tantum*).'[87] Injustice is the negation of, the discordant departure from, that just ideal. 'Between any two governments, neither of which is in any way subordinate to the other, contention can arise either through their own fault or that of their subjects.'[88]

85
> Here sighs and cries and wails coiled and recoiled
>   on the starless air, spilling my soul to tears.
>   A confusion of tongues and monstrous accents toiled
>   in pain and anger. Voices hoarse and shrill
>   and sounds of blows, all intermingled, raised
>   tumult and pandemonium that still
> whirls on the air forever dirty with it
>   as if a whirlwind sucked at sand. (Par [Ci] 3.22–29)

86 See, e.g., Pur 9.46–49; 10.37–39, 103–08; 11.1–45.
87 DM 1.7.
88 DM 1.10.

Dante further explains that '"being", "unity," and "good" have an order of precedence [in the sense of] priority. For by its nature being is prior to unity and unity prior to the good, because whatever is in the fullest sense a being is most unified, and when most unified it is most good.'[89] Accordingly, injustice, or evil, follows as the negation or the opposite, as the lack of unity.

> [T]he less a thing has complete being, the less unity it has, and consequently it is less good. For this reason it is true in all matters whatsoever that the most unified is the best. . . . Thus we see that at the root of what it means to be good is being one; and the root of what it means to be evil is being many. [. . .] Thus we can see what sin is: it is to scorn unity and hence to proceed toward plurality. [. . .] [W]hatever is good is good because it is unified. And since concord is essentially a good, it is clear that at its root there must be some kind of unity. . . . Now concord is a uniform movement of many wills; in this definition we see that the uniform movement is due to the union of wills, and that this union is the root and very being of concord. [. . .] So we speak of a number of men as being in concord when in moving together toward a single goal their wills are formally united, that is, the form of unity is in their wills.[90]

3.5 The dialectic of unity and individuality in modernity

At the threshold of modernity, Erasmus, in *The Education of a Christian Prince*, still maintains the ideal of justice through unity, negated by injustice through discord. The tyrant 'knows that noble and confident spirits do not tolerate despotism with good grace'. Despotism rather 'stir[s] up dissension and mutual hatred among his subjects, so that one accuses the other and he himself meanwhile becomes more powerful as a result of his people's troubles'.[91] Still drawing upon Scripture and Christian tradition, Erasmus nevertheless builds his arguments upon fundamentally secular ground, rarely invoking any broader metaphysical vision.

The conception of justice as unity, and injustice as disunity, is not only characteristic of the more metaphysically inclined thinkers. Writers of a secular or metaphysically sceptical bent also pursue it. From the emergence of Renaissance humanism or secularism through to our own day, Western theories will swing between stronger and weaker emphases on unity, although it will rarely disappear as an element of justice. Again, even anarchists and libertarians will advocate their views not as hostility towards the concept of

---

89 DM 1.15.
90 DM 1.15.
91 ECP 29.

unity, but, to the contrary, as hostility towards a state apparatus which they view as corrosive of social and human ties, ties that can become genuine and cohesive only insofar as they are freely chosen within contexts liberated from repressive political constraints, to be regulated instead only where urgently necessary, for example, to prevent physical harm.[92]

Hobbes steeps his writing in Biblical references, while his vision of exclusive and undivided, hence unified sovereignty, finds its justifications on secular grounds.[93] His fear, too, is of faction and discord. Unity, even if coercive, stands as the peremptory political imperative. Hobbes betrays little of the meditation upon concepts of justice and injustice *per se* that preoccupy Plato or Aristotle, and less of the concomitant vocabulary, not least in view of his subjectivist ethics.[94] Peacekeeping, stability and order become for Hobbes the very content of justice, or displace justice *per se* through concepts relating to public welfare, the public good, or the common weal. Even if Hobbes's terminology changes, the fundamental binarism of justice – or that which stands in for it: public welfare, the public good, the common weal – as the overall more desirable state of affairs, and injustice as greater or lesser negations of those states of affairs, remains intact. Hobbes provides detailed counsel to the sovereign, seeking to perfect sovereignty and the sovereign into something supremely unified,[95] without which citizens are doomed to return to faction so absolute as to threaten the 'war of every one against every one'.[96] Hobbes's all-or-nothing vision, always hovering ominously between total unity or total chaos, God or Satan, dramatises the so-called 'Hobbesian baroque'.[97]

Hobbes's abstract, institutionally directed unity, diametrically opposed to Aristotle's polis-based unity of diverse but active citizens, lays the groundwork for the modern doctrine of *raison d'état*,[98] national interest, which will culminate in the heyday of nation-state positivism, the modern institutionalisation of *rex non potest peccare*, whereby state action, irrespective of its detrimental or abusive character, becomes legitimate precisely because it is state action. Through the doctrine of *raison d'état*, that of *might makes right* becomes elevated from a supposedly necessary evil, a sheer expedient, to a formally, doctrinally legitimate principle of state and government. It becomes supreme justice. Pierre Corneille's astute masterpiece *Cinna*, written a decade before *Leviathan*, will recall the figure of Caesar Augustus as embodiment of the modern nation state and vindication of *raison d'état* – avowedly brutal in the consolidation of his imperial rule (*'Après tant d'ennemis à mes pieds abattus . . .'*), yet suddenly

---

92 See this chapter, text accompanying n. 32.
93 Lev ch. 18.
94 Lev ch. 6.
95 Lev chs 22–30.
96 Lev ch. 13.
97 Schmitt, 1982, p. 150.
98 See, e.g., Lev ch 18.

magnanimous once that absolute power is secure (*'Depuis vingt ans je règne, et j'en sais les vertus'*).[99]

The 17th century will have no illusions about that potentially brutal aspect of unity through absolute sovereignty. Supreme justice will manifest as supreme injustice in a work like Racine's *Britannicus*. The emperor Nero, a *monstre naissant*,[100] a bourgeoning monster, will trace precisely the opposite trajectory to that of Corneille's Augustus in a narrative un-doing or reversal. Nero's rule, like that of the emerging European nation state, having shown promises of peace and prosperity in its inception, will degenerate into, or rather was always all along, arbitrary despotism: *'Enfin Néron naissant/A toutes les vertus d'Auguste vieillissant.'*[101] Those opposed visions of the *raison d'état*, from Hobbes's and *Cinna's* optimism to the bleakness of works like Racine's *La Thébaïde* and *Britannicus*, or Corneille's later *Rodogune*, or *Suréna*[102] display the increasing volatility, if not bankruptcy, of unity as an ideal of justice in the modern nation state, even while fierce justifications remain for invoking it. Rising nationalisms will, over time, often display unity's horrific side, as the Hobbesian paradigm of justice through coerced unity and the Racinian counter-paradigm of injustice through coerced unity[103] each attach equally, indifferently, to the ideal of unity. (Foucault's theory of the surveillance state will present unity in a new light, as something not proclaimed in a pseudo-ethical vein, but rather engineered through a dissemination of power as institutionalised regimentation and routine. That unacknowledged yet hegemonic unity, deployed as a strategy of sheer control, differs, then, from the sense of unity I am examining for the moment, namely, as a declared ideal.)

Locke challenges Hobbes, renouncing the absolute sovereign in favour of a legal order structured on principles of limited, popular sovereignty, secured through individual rights. That difference between Locke and Hobbes, set on a stage from which God, Biblical references again notwithstanding, continues to abscond, inaugurates a dialectic of unity and individuality that will surface in later thinkers, such as Rousseau, Hegel and Marx. When Hobbes introduces the war of all against all as the paradigm of injustice, whereby absolute freedom looms as absolute chaos, which no individual could desire, a strange, glaringly modern, irony emerges. The utmost real, practicable, desirable freedom becomes that which is secured by the utmost, absolute sovereign power

---

99 Cin 4.3.1247–8. Cf. Prigent, 1986, pp. 138–48; cf. Heinze, 2009a, pp. 99–100. ('I've seen endless rivals, dead at my will,/I've had twenty years' rule: I know well the skill.' (reading *vertus* in the early modern sense)).
100 Brt, *Préface de 1670*, JR-OC 372.
101 Brt 1.1.29–30. ('And young Nero's surge/boasts all the skills of Augustus's old age.') On the influence of Seneca's comparison of Augustus's old-age with Nero's youth, see JR-OC 378, n. 2.
102 See, e.g., Heinze, 2010b, pp. 96–101.
103 See, e.g., Heinze, 2009b, 2010a.

watching over it. On a casual reading, Hobbes's transition from the war of all against all into civil society is an utter shedding of individual freedom. In a dialectically subtler, more Hegelian, although not necessarily more appealing sense, Hobbesean unity is presented not as the effacement of individual freedom, but as the best context within which individuals can achieve and preserve it with the security that it requires – unity under the absolute sovereign not as negation, but as pre-condition for individual freedom. A century later, Voltaire will praise the absolute monarchy of Louis XIV for having achieved precisely that synthesis, a total control, which, far from repressing individual humanity, will allow it to flourish with cultural advances equal, in Voltaire's view, to those of ancient Athens and Rome, and of Renaissance Florence.[104]

Lockean liberalism, in a move recalling Aristotle's objection to the *Republic*'s centralisation of power, will re-configure that dialectic of unity and individuality. Locke does not altogether eliminate unity as a socio-political value, although he surely diminishes it. Liberalism generally values unity only insofar as it arises from free choices, which, for some critics, suffices to destroy it altogether. To be sure, from our post-colonial perspective, Locke's Eurocentrism, his century's distinction between the European as civilised and the non-European as primitive,[105] taints any elements of unity in his theory with socio-political exclusion, rich with the possibilities of exploitation witnessed through the appropriation of Lockean ideas in the period of colonialism and imperialism. When Locke does nevertheless set limits to individual rights within the context of the recognised political entity, it is the necessity of civic unity that emerges. Among qualifying members of the political community, for example, he bars the exercise of the property right to an extent that would cause either waste[106] through one's own use or destitution within the political community. He therefore admits private property 'where there is enough and as good left in common for others'.[107] Similarly, his *Letter on Toleration*, be it only insofar as it applies among European peoples, must be read not as a philosophy of indifference towards individual religious choices, but as a call to harmonise them, albeit in a way that is 'free and voluntary'[108] – a diluted but not absent ideal of unity.

In shifting sovereignty from absolute to popular, and shifting the fundamental source of law from the will of the absolute sovereign to the interests of individual rights holders, Lockean theory anticipates limits on *raison d'état*, heralding a perpetual ambiguity, a vicious circle, between individual rights designed to limit state power, and assertions of state power constantly invoked for the supposed purpose of securing those individual rights, which is nothing

---

104 L14 616–20.
105 See, e.g., STCG 5:43–46, 49.
106 STCG 5:38.
107 STCG 5:27.
108 LT 509.

other than the perpetual re-emergence of *raison d'état* even within such liberal theories designed to limit it. Insofar as *raison d'état* embodies a Hobbesean ideal of justice as unity, its weakening moves society further towards injustice, which is indeed the fear of many critics of liberalism, while its strengthening moves equally towards injustice, which is the cry of liberals. Lockean liberalism becomes a surpassing, *Aufhebung*, of *raison d'état* in Hegel's sense of maintaining through incorporation – in other words, for some, not a surpassing at all. Critics of liberalism, like Marx, then see individual liberties not as the weapon against, but as the justification *par excellence* for strong assertions of state power and national interest, as the unity promised by *raison d'état* merely entrenches privileged individual interests.

Locke's emphasis on individual rights within a modern, constitutional order is attacked by Rousseau, who will once again reconfigure the dialectic between unity and individuality. Rousseau radically re-thinks unity as a prime condition for justice, impossible to achieve under the inherently alienating socio-politics of large, modern states built upon the preservation of existing power monopolies and privileged individual interests, and instead realisable only in a *cité* more resembling the ancient Greek polis or early Roman republic,[109] for example, through, in comparison to emerging modern states and empires, small territories and populations, in which each voice counts and citizens can achieve unity through self-government, because they know one another, and gaping inequalities of wealth, status or power are precluded.[110]

Rousseau launches his political project by writing his *Discours sur les sciences et les arts*, followed by his *Discours sur l'origine et les fondements de l'inégalité parmi les hommes*. Both essays decry the disunity, the social fragmentation and individual alienation, wrought by seeming advances in knowledge, technology and so-called 'civilisation', under the aegis of large, powerful sovereigns. Such circumstances generate only individuals becoming ever more estranged from their communities, their neighbours, and themselves.[111] We have misunderstood the modern state, as Rousseau understands it, if we view it merely as a neutral, background arena within which injustices occur as sheer happenstance, with injustice amounting to the sheer sum-total of isolated injustices. Rather, as Marx too will insist, the state is inherently, systemically unjust. It is not a fundamentally just or indifferently neutral place in which injustices randomly occur, but a structurally unjust one, in which it is justice that is at best partial and quixotic, and injustice pervasive and inevitable. Rousseau repudiates both the individual disempowerment represented by Hobbesian absolutism,[112] and the alienation and fragmentation represented

---

109 CS 1.6 361–62.
110 CS 2.9–10 386–91; GP 970. Cf. CS 3.1 397.
111 See this book, Chapter 6, Section 6.10.
112 See, e.g., CS 1.4 355–58.

by Lockean liberalism and individualism,[113] arguably hinting that those are two sides of the same coin.

In his *Du Contrat social*, Rousseau rejects the Hobbesian idea of unity as something to which individuals must be subordinated. Rousseau, in part reminiscent of Aristotle, theorises political unity not as the negation of, but as the creation of, an active, participatory citizenry, which does not sacrifice, but rather cultivates, individual freedom through political unity. Recalling Plato's many kinds of illness all negating only one kind of health, Rousseau speculates, 'There are thousands of ways of assembling people, but only one way of uniting them.'[114] Indeed, 'falsehood is subject to an infinity of permutations; but truth has only one way of being'.[115] Politics as such, as opposed to the sheer coercion that might just as easily be imposed on sheep, is nothing but an overcoming of the schism between unity and individuality. Society must create an 'association that, through its collective strength, defends and protects the person and the goods of each member, such that each is simultaneously united with all while still obeying himself and remaining as free as he was before'.[116] Rousseau will depict justice as the opposite of the alienated and fragmented society of the 'civilised', overweening state, something achieved through a united or 'general will'[117] (*volonté générale*), contrary to the disparate and discordant 'will of all' (*volonté de tous*),[118] although the precise meanings of and differences between those two concepts have long prompted debate.

If justice is 'obedience to the law that one', as member of the body politic, 'has prescribed for himself',[119] then injustice, ideally, would consist only in the violation of that kind of law. But since few if any such laws exist either in 18th-century Europe, or throughout much of the rest of history, injustice consists, above all, in coerced obedience to laws that are not made by and for the citizenry – a citizenry which, in pursuit of justice, would act not in the divisive, factional vein of majoritarianism,[120] but in the unified spirit of the general will.[121] '[W]hat renders the will general is not so much the number of voices, as the common interest which unites them . . . each one submits necessarily to the conditions that he imposes upon the others, an admirable accord of interest and justice.'[122] Under properly constituted popular sovereignty, 'it no longer becomes necessary to ask who maintains the prerogative

---

113 See, e.g., OI 164.
114 CS *Manuscrit de Genève*, 360 n. 5.
115 SA 18.
116 See CS 1.6 360. Cf. CS 1.4 355–58.
117 CS 1.4 355–58. Cf. GP 247–48.
118 CS 2.3 371.
119 CS 1.8 365.
120 CS 2.3 372.
121 CS 2.4 373–74.
122 CS 2.4 374.

to make laws, since they are products (*des actes*) of the general will . . . nor whether the law can be unjust, since no one is unjust towards himself.'[123]

Where the general will prevails, then, there can be no systemic injustice at all. Injustice, for Rousseau, is only what violates it. No major theorist since Plato, not until Marx, will have restored unity to such a central role in the theory of justice and injustice. Nor will Rousseau, theorist of popular democracy, escape some of the same criticisms waged against Plato's antidemocratic rule of the elite guardian class, particularly in the eyes of liberals vigilant about aspirations of overarching unity.[124] Readers' perennial doubts about the concept of the general will serve only to underscore the suggestion that, even while disunity continues to be recognised as a great source of injustice, unity seems to remain an essential and yet a highly problematical condition of justice, arguably an equally potent source of injustice.

Writing at a time when the model of the sovereign, European nation state is nearing its zenith, and the universal Christian kingdom, as imagined by Dante, is almost as distant a memory as the Greek polis, Kant proposes a secular, universalist model of legal unity through the global federalist regime proposed in *Zum ewigen Frieden*,[125] an elaborate structure as distant as one can imagine from Rousseau's model revival of unity in the *cité* of the type found in antiquity, despite Kant's well-known admiration for Rousseau. Kant's revolution in metaphysics, anchoring cosmic order neither in nature nor in God, but in the *a priori* properties of reason as such, introduces a universalist alternative to Christianity, hence a further unifying element, namely, humans' universally shared capacity not only to reason, but to discover within reason the fundamental structure of ethics in the categorical imperative, and the truths that necessarily flow from it and from its application.[126]

Yet both of those unifying drifts in Kant continue, ever since he proposed them, to be seen as unduly abstract. The 'metaphysics of morals' which he proposes as a foundation for social and legal norms retains a highly individualist character, bereft of the overtly communal elements characteristic of the ethical, political and legal thought of Plato, Aristotle or Rousseau. That will become Hegel's criticism. As a condition for the very possibility of substantive ethical reasoning, and therefore as a faculty universally shared by any reasoning being, the categorical imperative unifies reasoning beings indifferently. The historical or cultural specificity of the political community becomes almost arbitrary. As with Locke, Kant's potential for loosening the doctrine of *raison d'état* remains purely theoretical, not least through his own injunction of obedience to the sovereign, an injunction not altogether consistent with the foundations for ethics which, with the categorical imperative, he proposes. But, also as

---

123 CS 2.6 379.
124 See, e.g., Russell, 2000, pp. 660–74. Cf. Heinze, 2007b, p. 343.
125 EF, 'Zweiter Definitivartikel zum ewigen Frieden', 208–13.
126 See this book, Chapter 2, Section 2.3.

with Locke, the contested status of the *raison d'état* as a force for unity means that challenges to it in liberal theory remain equally uncertain.

Hegel's political and legal theory heralds yet another swing back towards justice through stronger unity within the political community, albeit a moderate swing, avoiding Rousseau's citizen-based democracy. Against Locke and particularly against Kant, Hegel's *Grundlinien* renounces the overly rule-bound legalism that would risk demoting socio-political unity to the status of a secondary or residual value. Yet, along with Hobbes and Locke, and against Rousseau, the *Grundlinien* re-affirms the modern state. Hegel renounces the immediate unity that is to be found among the citizens of Aristotle's or Rousseau's societies. Hegel replaces that immediate unity with the symbolic unity incarnated by the monarch exercising sovereign power,[127] transmitted through mediated rather than directly democratic channels, that is, through intermediate levels of social cooperation, within the political and economic layers of a multi-tiered society.

Hegel's intermediate position between Rousseau's strong, polis-like unity and Kant's abstract individualism will come in for searing criticism in Marx's reading, which views it not as a historical, let alone dialectical progression, but as a regression back to the feudal orders of the Middle Ages.[128] From Marx's teleological perspective of post-statist, communist society, which entails the abolition of private property and collective ownership and control of the means of production, the history of the world still continues as one of injustice, in the sense that even moments of qualified or relative justice, which emerged through history to surpass anterior forms of injustice, must themselves be surpassed until unqualified justice in communism is achieved.[129] For Marx, Hegel in the *Grundlinien* merely recapitulates the ontological reification of arbitrary and reactionary class difference – adopted overtly in Hobbesian absolutism, and through the inevitable inequalities, notwithstanding claims of formal equality, inherent within the bourgeois liberalism of the Lockean or Kantian regimes. After only prospective or theoretical re-configurations of the doctrine of *raison d'état* in Locke, Rousseau or Kant, it re-emerges in Hegel largely intact from its Hobbesian form, as the re-affirmation of unity as justice in the absolutist state.

Marxism remains suspicious of the classical vocabulary of 'justice', 'unity' or 'harmony', contemplated in historical abstraction from material conditions of production and property distribution.[130] Marx resists the classical idealist temptation of theorising in any detail the structure or content of future communist society. *Das Kapital*, in Engels's words, explains not 'what the thousand year reign of communism will look like', as an ideal type, but, above

---

127 GPR §§ 275–86.
128 KHR §§ 275–86.
129 See this book, Chapter 2, Section 2.7.
130 See, e.g., Löw, 2001, pp. 182–84.

all, 'what things will not be like',[131] in terms of historically unjust practices or institutions that are to be overcome. What primes is what communism will *not* include, yet those absences do entail determinate content, tantamount to a surpassing of the prime conditions of injustice. Communism must admit no private property, but rather property of which the substance and yields are held, worked and shared in common; no entrenched class structure, but rather universal inclusion and participation; and no imperial militarism, which would turn unwilling or ignorant workers into unwilling soldier-murderers, but only, at most, willing, enlightened, necessary self-defence, against hostile, counter-revolutionary or otherwise expansionist or imperial powers. Each of those values effectively recapitulates justice as unity – as a triumph over exclusive, individual pursuit of self-interest; as inclusion, cooperation, and non-alienation. It is in the terms of an entire human history of deviation from, of negation of, that communist model that injustice acquires unequivocal meaning and substance within Marxism.[132]

Despite much in Marxism that seeks to break with Western tradition, the Marxist notion of an ultimate communist society stands strongly within the tradition of theorising a model of justice along the lines of unity, with injustice expressly or effectively theorised as its opposite. At least in that sense, Marxism, too, counts as a classical justice theory, with the mutual exclusion of justice and injustice rigorously upheld. The interest of Marx or Rousseau lies not in speculating about the precise degree to which they knowingly or inadvertently fall under the influence of Platonic ideas woven into the fabric of Western intellectual history. What is salient is how they underscore the ways in which a long history of theorists otherwise sharing little, from Plato through to Augustine, Aquinas, Dante, Hobbes, Rousseau and Marx, nevertheless promulgate strong theories of justice as unity, with injustice defined as one or another form, and usually as a variety of forms, of the opposite, of disunity.

When Plato claims 'we aren't aiming to make any one group outstandingly happy but to make the whole city so, as far as possible',[133] it might at first be thought to suggest a loose utilitarianism, a calculus whereby a diminution of benefits accruing either to individuals or to numerical minorities is justified with reference to the overall good of the community or of the majority – the greatest happiness of the greatest number. That characteristic might be said to resemble not the earlier utilitarianism of Bentham, which reduces relevant goods to measurable, largely material goods, but rather the later utilitarianism

---

131 Marx's *Das Kapital*, writes Friedrich Engels, does not explain 'wie es denn eigentlich im kommunistischen Tausendjährigen Reich aussehen werde' 'wie die Dinge nicht sein sollen, but only'. Kap, MEW 16: 216.
132 See this book, Chapter 2, Section 2.7.
133 See this chapter, text accompanying n. 41.

of Mill, which emphasises 'higher', intellectual, cultural or spiritual goods.[134] If that modified utilitarianism appears superficially common to Plato and Mill, the means by which they respectively seek it remain too different to warrant linking them much further.

Mill's liberal ideal in *On Liberty* remains committed to individualist politics rooted in the presumption of personal autonomy. Insofar as utilitarianism *does*, even in Mill, involve some scheme for the accumulation and distribution of wealth, it warrants a freer market than can be found in Plato's model society. Recall that, for Plato, even if the working class enjoys whatever freedom the rulers permit, the origin, pursuit, and character of wealth, like all other features of life, remain subject to those guardians' control. Mill's utilitarianism, of course, clashes *prima facie* with his liberalism; limiting individual choice only when it causes harm, or only when it causes harm to one who fails to consent, differs from limiting it to augment the material, let alone spiritual goods of others. While scholars have proposed ways of reconciling those two principles,[135] suffice it to observe that the principle of socio-political unity through balancing or harmonising of interests resurges in new guises, even as concepts and lexicons used to designate it continue to change. As I believe that those patterns continue along similar lines through to our own time, I shall present the remainder of this discussion in outline only.

Mill's 'soft' utilitarianism is also occasionally linked to Aristotle, who identifies happiness as the greatest human good.[136] To be sure, Aristotle's 'happiness' (*eudaimonía*), as distinguished from sheer pleasure (*hēdonē*), envisages the 'complete life'[137] of the citizen active within the civic life of the polis.[138] It differs strongly from the Benthamite calculus of measurable goods. Mill certainly strays closer, but the bourgeoning Europe of free-market, industrial, nation-state modernity sets a stage too different from the ideal of the Greek polis to extend the analogy much further. Aristotelian eudaimonism assumes a far greater degree of socio-political unity than Mill's modern statist context can ever do. Meanwhile, Aristotle, like Plato, envisages restrictions on wealth presumably incompatible with that material side of utilitarianism which urges the maximising of wealth.

From antiquity well into early modernity, the closest one could easily come to anything like an institutionally universal ethics was a universally non-universal one, along the lines of *autres pays, autres moeurs*, 'different countries, different mores'. Even as universalist belief systems emerged, from Stoicism through to Christianity or Islam, the pre-modern and early modern worlds were too loosely bound for the idea of a global belief system to emerge with

---

134 Ut ch. 2.
135 See, e.g., Kelly, 2003.
136 NE 1.7.
137 NE 1.7.1097ª28.
138 NE 1.7.1097ᵇ12.

much reality, except insofar as it was imposed by force, through conquest, colonialism or imperialism. Only since the emergence of an international human rights movement after the Second World War can universalist aspirations of justice and injustice be said to have gained some degree of credence – and even then, of course, with bad-faith adherence on the part of states, as well as good-faith resistance on the part of those who, while committed to justice, question whether the movement's origins or assumptions, or actual institutional arrangements, can plausibly amount to a universalist justice.

Without entering those debates, it is nevertheless worth noting how, in a globalised context that could not be more different from the Aristotelian polis, an ideal of unity, however vast or impressionistic, is nevertheless retained. The first words of the Universal Declaration of Human Rights, a founding instrument of the modern international human rights movement, and a document generally framing rights and interests in individual terms, nevertheless speak of the 'inherent dignity and of the equal and inalienable rights of all members of *the human family*',[139] a phrase repeated in other leading instruments, cryptically introducing that paradoxical notion, or myth, of universal kinship as an ultimate ideal to be served or realised through law or politics.[140] We are again reminded of Hegel's critique of the Roman empire, which simultaneously inflates unity through facile, that is, effectively nominal universalism, and deflates it through the necessary collapse of individuals into juridical abstractions. Concurrent movements, such as the Western European social-welfare state, or international notions of 'solidarity rights' make a similar move, as they can only translate political unity across enormous populations into the language of 'minimum standards'.[141]

Also important for modern, and rather subtler approaches to unity, is the work of Lévinas. Among 20th-century thinkers, Lévinas arguably comes nearest to Plato's and Rousseau's ideals of unity, albeit in a transformed way. Lévinas rejects the Western tradition of recognising metaphysics or ontology as primary sciences in a pre-ethical intellectual moment, as a neutral framework within which ethics then becomes a subordinated or secondary project. Lévinas reverses that priority, identifying ethical relationships as our primordial relationships to humans and to the world, hence a presumption of existential unity, and of ethical consciousness as a fully authentic mode of human existence – the loss of which manifests in distancing and 'othering', modes of disunity, from which ethical failures, injustice, emerge. It is difficult to examine that theory in much greater detail as a traditional theory of socio-political injustice, insofar as Lévinas avoids programmatic theory. It is nevertheless difficult to escape the impression that a well-functioning regime of justice for

---

139 Universal Declaration of Human Rights, G.A. res. 217A (III), U.N. Doc A/810 at 71 (1948), preambular para. 1.
140 See, e.g., Heinze, 1999, p. 35.
141 See, e.g., Goyard-Fabre, 1998, pp. 184–88.

Lévinas would manifest as unity at the most primordial level of human experience, as would injustice as that primordial fragmenting, that is, disunity.

These successive mutations of the ideal of unity from Plato through to postindustrial modernity become not only the object of positive law or programmatic theory, but also of more pervasively critical reflection. In 'La Pharmacie de Platon' and *De la Grammatologie*, Derrida examines, respectively, Plato's and Rousseau's suspicions towards writing as a betrayal or corruption of meaning, and therefore of authentic being. It is unsurprising that, for that particular analysis, Derrida chooses precisely the two justice theorists who make unity their almost exclusive aim, with criteria of measurement, where discussed at all, strongly subordinated to that unity ideal (even more than Marx: Marx's programmatics focus on overcoming capitalism; his final-stage communist society is only surmised and never explained,[142] as Plato and Rousseau do, in programmatic detail).

From Derrida's perspective, that unity emerges as a quest for purity (and indeed Plato's and Rousseau's puritanical moralities have long been noted), whereby injustice would stand always as the product of some contamination seeped into the body politic.[143] Also more prominent for Plato and Rousseau than for other leading theorists is their obsession with physical health, and, in particular, their constant analogies between it and the health of the community, again underscoring the sense that injustice emerges from some impure human agent introduced into society, like some impure organic agent introduced into the body to generate disease. From that notion of pure and impure states of being, of ethics, and of politics, Plato and Rousseau, from Derrida's perspective, generate a series of oppositions – we and them, self and other, insider and outsider, healthy and diseased, chaste and debauched, all of which amount to facets of justice and injustice. Carl Schmitt's 'friend' and 'foe'[144] also assimilate him to that unity model of insider and outsider, pure and impure. Those brief observations will be borne in mind when, in Chapter 5, I return to the problem of unity, examining it not, along traditional lines, as the negation of disunity, but as its cause.

---

142 See this chapter, text accompanying n. 131
143 See generally Derrida, 1967a, 1972.
144 See this book, Chapter 2, text accompanying n. 65.

Chapter 4
Injustice as mismeasurement

Nur jedem das Seine!
Muß Obrigkeit haben
Zoll, Steuern und Gaben
Man weigre sich nicht
Der schuldigen Pflicht![1]

4.1 Introduction

Plato's *Republic* remains the arch-embodiment of the ideal of justice through unity. In the last chapter, it became clear that Aristotle preserves the value of unity, but only insofar as it accommodates other values, including the diversity of the citizenry. The aim of this chapter will be to examine the more prominent role that Aristotle, followed by other, including liberal thinkers, accords to measurement. The traditional binarism qualifies injustice as mismeasurement – application of the wrong measure, or misapplication of the right one. With those two concepts, unity and measurement, ancient Greek thought already identifies the two core elements of the classical model of injustice as the opposite of justice. Every subsequent, programmatic theory will accord a place to one or both of those elements, presenting injustice as some version either of disunity, or mismeasurement, or both. For modernity in particular, proto-liberal or liberal theories from Locke, Kant and Mill through to Rawls and Dworkin, place less emphasis on unity, instead overwhelmingly defining injustice as mismeasurement.

4.2 *Suum cuique* as an empty formalism

Book I of the *Republic* begins Plato's exploration of justice when the wealthy arms merchant Cephalus,[2] who lacks philosophical training or aptitude, quips,

---

1 Bach, 2000b, p. 175. ('Do justice to all men!/So pay what thou owest/To highest or lowest/To duty be true/Give Caesar his due!' (unattributed traditional translation in Bach, 2000b, p. 174).)
2 See, e.g., Zehnpfennig, 2001, pp. 29–36; Annas, 1981, pp. 23–24.

'Wealth can do a lot to save us from having to cheat or deceive someone against our will.'[3] Cephalus contemplates not a critical concept of justice, but a pragmatic avoidance of injustice. Socrates asks whether that remark can be carried further, whether it entails a general principle of justice: '[A]re we to say unconditionally that [justice] is speaking the truth and paying whatever debts one has incurred?'[4] Quickly out of his depth, Cephalus hands the discussion to his son Polemarchus, who defends his father's view in more systematic terms. Polemarchus cites the Athenian poet Simonides, who says 'it is just to give to each what is owed to him'[5] or 'to render each his due'.[6] That definition would later be captured in countless familiar maxims: *suum cuique tribuere*, 'to each his own', 'to each his due', *à chacun le sien, jedem das Seine*.

The proliferation of familiar maxims to express that idea is no accident. Nor is it surprising that that is the first reply offered in the *Republic* to the question about justice, confirming its status as the common-sense view, at least in the commercially vibrant Athens in which Polemarchus has been raised. Polemarchus's simple reply, which Socrates seems at first to refute, is neither naïve nor easy to challenge. It would be hard to find another reply that so pithily characterises the variety of things that law is and does. Whole areas of our own law – contract, tort, property, criminal law, commercial law, tax law, zoning law, employment law, insurance law, human rights law, law governing social services and benefits – still serve to ascertain *who gets what*, often in monetary forms, but also in the sense of services due, appropriate criminal penalties, or other routine regulations of conduct. The task of justice in that sense is to perform the appropriate measurement. Injustice, on the binary model, becomes application of the wrong measure, or misapplication of the right one. Both of those mismeasurements include not only unjust official responses, but also the initial wrongs themselves. For example, to steal from or to wound an innocent person, or to miscalculate the social benefits due to an eligible person, is *prima facie* to apply a wrong measure. Either act leaves the victim with something other than what is that victim's 'own', such as the victim's physical integrity or monetary entitlement.

Legislation and adjudication both risk the appearance of illegitimacy if they fail to execute the principle of *suum cuique* at some decisive level. Yet performing some version of it is never hard to do, even for the most unjust of governments, indeed even if, or precisely when, it is done deceptively or cynically. *Suum cuique* is the sophist's feast. The most unfair law can lay claim to it, just as easily as can the fairest. Tax cuts for the wealthiest can be justified on the free-market grounds that they stimulate economic growth across the board, thereby benefiting the poor, increasing the poor's share of 'what is due' to them. Yet

---

3 R 1.331a–b.
4 R 1.331b–c.
5 R. 1.331e. Cf. Annas, 1981, pp. 24–26.
6 R [HC] 1.331e.

one can just as easily oppose the cuts on social-welfarist grounds, arguing that the poor's share of 'what is due' to them is most justly achieved through some system of redistribution. *Suum cuique* indifferently executes any scheme of law or justice. It contains no inherent ethics, but rather only implements the ethics, good or bad, of whatever system is adopted to determine who gets what. *Suum cuique* exhausts the substance of what most judges, lawyers and public officials actually do throughout their entire lives. They are deemed to have performed their essential social role if they have spent their careers sitting at their desks, giving to each their due, regardless of whether they are executing the will of Cicero or Caesar, Louis XVI or Robespierre, Nicholas II or Lenin. Justice then becomes by definition *suum cuique*, and injustice its opposite, insofar as any scheme of positive law purports to do justice. Kelsen writes,

> It is easy to see that the decisive question for the application of that norm [*suum cuique*], namely what counts as 'one's own', due to each individual, is not determined by that norm itself. The notion that to each is due that which ought to be appropriated to him means that *suum cuique* rests upon the tautology that each ought to receive what each ought to receive. The application of that norm of justice (*Gerechtigkeitsnorm*) presupposes the validity of a normative order, which determines what, for each, 'his own' is, i.e., what is due to him, what he has a right to. . . . That means, however, that any [normative] order, whatever it may adopt as duties and rights, and in particular any system of positive law, entails the norm of justice (*Gerechtigkeitsnorm*) of *suum cuique* and can in that sense be called just.[7]

As a purely formal matter, for example, the anti-discrimination norm[8] represents no more nor less giving 'to each his due' than does *apartheid*; nor does Swedish law any more than did that of Kim Jong Il's North Korea. They simply present different schemes of what is due to each. The maxim *suum cuique* remains intact regardless of its benign or brutal applications. If an underlying norm is just, then the application to it of *suum cuique* adds justice only in the obvious sense of assuring that a just norm is executed according to its own terms. An inscription of *suum cuique tribuere* today adorns the walls of the Harvard Law School Library[9], just as *Jedem das Seine* once drummed inmates into the Buchenwald Concentration camp.[10] When we read in St Paul's Epistle to the Romans, 'Give everyone what you owe him: If you owe taxes, pay taxes; if revenue, then revenue; if respect, then respect; if honour, then honour',[11] the

---

7 Kelsen, 1960, p. 366.
8 See generally, e.g., Heinze, 2003b.
9 See *Quotations from the Langdell Reading Room* (n.d.) (citing Justinian, *Institutes*, Book 1, Title 1, Sec. 3).
10 See, e.g., Brunssen, 2010.
11 Ep Rom 13:7, NIV-UK.

references to 'respect' and 'honour' underscore the conventional obligations inherent in birth, rank and status throughout the ancient world, now endowed with divine sanction: '[H]e who rebels against the authority is rebelling against what God has instituted.'[12] Small wonder that Socrates maligns Simonides: 'It seems that Simonides was speaking in riddles – just like a poet![13] – when he said what justice is, for he thought it just to give to each what is appropriate (προσῆκον) to him, and this is what he called giving him what is owed to him.'[14]

The *Republic's* legal regime can, of course, no more dispense with *suum cuique* than can any other. The whole of the *Republic's* ideal society, like that of the *Laws*, is concerned with discovering what is 'appropriate' for each individual, what each individual should, in justice, have, do, or expect – and what, in that sense, is 'owed' by each to each, and to or from society as a whole.[15] For the incapable to rule, and the more capable to obey is injustice; for those who have proved their conscience and character to join the guardian class, and those better at production or commerce to join the working class, is justice. While unity remains the *Republic's* criterion of justice, a principle of correct appropriation, which is a principle of comparison and measurement, becomes its tool, and injustice is the opposite.

Why, then, does Plato's Socrates summarily refute Polemarchus's reply, when Socrates himself will apply *suum cuique* as a core criterion throughout the *Republic*? Again, whether Polemarchus's unqualified formulation of justice itself as 'to each his due' actually represents justice or injustice depends upon the justice of the sum of background norms to which it is applied. If a despot were, *de jure* or *de facto*, to seize as personal possession all property in the realm – and, for that matter, all individuals resident in the realm as *de jure* or *de facto* slaves, hence as *de jure* or *de facto* property – then *suum cuique* in all subsequent situations would mean disposing of all persons and property such that it either accrued directly to that ruler or otherwise executed the ruler's will. *Suum cuique* would be the very recipe for injustice. That is not to say that *suum cuique* as a maxim of justice assumes a strictly conventionalist stance, to the effect of 'to each his own under prevailing law'. In itself, it leaves undecided whether 'one's own' ought to be construed under existing, positive law or under other criteria.

Polemarchus construes 'give to each what is owed to him', just as many of us construe it, in the everyday sense of performing contracts, paying debts, punishing crimes, indifferent to any possible critical assessment, of the kind Plato's Socrates demands, of underlying economic, political and legal circumstances. Unsurprisingly, 'to each his own' entails, for Polemarchus, 'to

---

12 Ep Rom 13:2, NIV-UK.
13 Cf. Prt 339a–48a.
14 R 1.332b.
15 R. 4.433b, e.

benefit one's friends and harm one's enemies'.[16] That formulation, too, mirrors any number of views in our own time. Under our law, justice certainly includes, for example, violently repelling sudden, unprovoked and overwhelming physical attacks, if necessary to defend oneself, hence 'harming enemies'; or feeding one's family, or paying debts and performing contracts to business associates, hence benefiting – of one or another description – friends. Socrates nevertheless rejects both branches of that 'friends *versus* enemies' formula. On the one hand, we can err about our friends,[17] since a seeming friend can be a covert enemy, as former clients of fraudulent financial advisers could attest. On the other hand, we can err about enemies, since pain or distress *qua* physical or emotional suffering, does not altogether equate with harm *qua* injustice.[18] Those who cause pain or distress, such as devoted parents refusing to fund their minor or adult child's substance addiction, are not necessarily enemies to that child. In that example, to use Socrates' words, 'to benefit one's friends and harm one's enemies' would entail, from the child's viewpoint, the absurd result that 'it's just to do bad things to those', in this case, to the parents, 'who do no injustice at all'.[19]

Justice, on Plato's view, is always inconsistent with harm, but not always inconsistent with pain.[20] It would be self-contradictory to claim that justice can have the aim of causing harm as an end in itself. Justice can, however, use pain as a means to a just end. One example would be physical self-defence, inflicting pain solely to the degree necessary to protect oneself, without any further aim to cause harm to the assailant as an end in itself. Or, again, another example is inflicting the pain caused by a refusal to provide to a loved one a harmful drug or other addictive substance – causing pain in order to help and not to harm the other. Plato draws an analogy to 'surgical burning',[21] which is a form of pain used not to cause harm, but to cure it. That is why Plato, contrary to Polemarchus, insists that justice, although it may cause pain or discomfort, can never have harm to anyone as an ultimate goal of justice. That distinction mirrors Plato's differentiation between sheer feelings of pleasure and goodness or rightness: '[F]eeling enjoyment isn't the same as doing well, and being in pain isn't the same as doing badly.'[22]

The problem Socrates elicits with 'give to each what is owed to him', as Kelsen observes, is not its falsehood, but its vacuous formalism. Polemarchus, lacking any critical approach to the background socio-political regime within which the maxim is applied, implies isolated contexts as adequate for achieving justice. He takes no account of the problem of the justice or injustice of

---

16 R 1.334b.
17 R 1.334c.
18 See generally, e.g., Heinze, 2012a.
19 R 1.334d.
20 See, e.g., R 1.335b–e.
21 Grg 476c.
22 See, e.g., Grg 497a. See also, e.g., Grg 499e–500a.

society's overall norms and institutions. He draws no distinction between 'to each his own' in a tyranny or in a democracy, perhaps understandably since, for purposes of the discussion among those present, he may simply be assuming Athens's democratic context. But he also draws no distinction between 'to each his own' as applied either to the just or to the unjust norms or acts that democracies, too, can sanction,[23] such as the imperial ambition[24] that would later lead to Athens's downfall, or indeed the death sentence that an Athenian jury would pronounce on Socrates.[25] Polemarchus tacitly treats systemic contexts as neutral and therefore irrelevant. That is what our own legal practitioners must generally do.

Given that unity remains Plato's overriding concern, *suum cuique* applies only insofar as it furthers unity. Polemarchus disregards that aim. Cast only in the context of individual pursuit of personal affairs and interests, indifferent as to whether the background norms forge social unity, Polemarchus's *suum cuique* becomes a recipe not for unity but for fragmentation. By contrast, when it serves the dual aim of unity of soul and of society, then, on Plato's view, *suum cuique* serves justice.

> [J]ustice isn't concerned with someone's doing his own externally, but with what is inside him, with what is truly himself and his own. One who is just . . . regulates well what is really his own and rules himself. [. . .] He puts himself in order, is his own friend, and harmonizes the . . . parts of himself. [. . .] He binds together those parts . . . and from having been many things he becomes entirely one, moderate and harmonious. Only then does he act.[26]

The mutual exclusion of justice and injustice fall symmetrically into place.

> And when he does anything, whether acquiring wealth, taking care of his body, engaging in politics, or in private contracts – in all of these, he believes that the action is just (δικαίαν) and fine that preserves this inner harmony and helps achieve it, and calls it so, and regards as wisdom the knowledge that oversees such actions. And he believes that the action that destroys this harmony is unjust (ἄδικον), and calls it so, and regards the belief that oversees it as ignorance.[27]

That fragmentation which results from Polemarchus's application of 'to each his own' divorced from the value of unity means that there is no obvious

---

23 Cf., e.g., Grg 466b. Cf. also, e.g., Pol 4.4.1292ª10–12. Shklar, 1990, p. 22.
24 Cf., e.g., R 1.372e–373e.
25 Ap *passim*.
26 R 4.443c–e.
27 R 4.443e.

limit, within the bounds of positive law, to the individual pursuit of personal affairs and interests, as witnessed also by incentives to litigation – a manifestation of social fragmentation, and of individual alienation from others, once it becomes entrenched and commonplace – whenever it serves those affairs or interests through its sheer likelihood of success. 'To each his own' becomes, recalling Derrida's reading, law's own *phármakon*, law's medicine or poison, depending upon the notion of justice it is called upon to administer.[28] Where unity remains the dominant value, faction and litigiousness remain alien.

> [Socrates:] [W]hat about market business, such as the private contracts people make with one another . . . or contracts with manual laborers, cases of insult or injury, the bringing of lawsuits, the establishing of juries, the payment and assessment of whatever dues are necessary in markets and harbors, the regulation of market, city, harbor, and the rest – should we bring ourselves to legislate about any of these?
> [Adeimantus:] It isn't appropriate to dictate to men who are fine and good [καλοῖς κἀγαθοῖς]. They'll easily find out for themselves whatever needs to be legislated about such things.
> [Socrates:] Yes, provided that a god grants [good laws and their preservation].
> [Adeimantus:] If not, they'll spend their lives enacting a lot of other laws and then amending them, believing that in this way they'll attain the best.[29]

That standard Greek virtue of being 'fine and good' equates, for Plato, with a life of socio-political unity, as emerges from the analogy to medicine that immediately follows, which recalls good health as the one desirable state, and departure from it as the endless undesirable states.

> [Socrates:] You mean they'll live like those sick people who, through licentiousness, aren't willing to abandon their harmful way of life?
> [Adeimantus:] That's right.
> [Socrates:] And such people carry on in an altogether amusing fashion, don't they? Their medical treatment achieves nothing, except that their illness becomes worse and more complicated, and they're always hoping that someone will recommend some new medicine to cure them. [. . .] And isn't it also amusing that they consider their worst enemy to be the person who tells them the truth, namely, that until they give up drunkenness, overeating, lechery, and idleness, no medicine, cautery, or surgery . . . will do them any good?[30]

---

28 Derrida, 1972.
29 R 4.425c–e; cf. L 3.679d–80a, 5.743c–d. Cf. Heinze, 2007a, pp. 100–5.
30 R 4.425e–426b.

The analogy is then drawn back to law, as we witness compulsive and pathological legislation added to the culture of litigation, insofar as the relentless making, amending, un-doing, and remaking of law comes to resemble 'cutting off a Hydra's head': one is cut off, only for two to grow in its place.

> [Socrates:] The person who is honored and considered clever and wise in important matters by such badly governed cities is the one who serves them most pleasantly, indulges them, flatters them, anticipates their wishes, and is clever at fulfilling them. [. . .] [Such] people pass laws . . . and then amend them, and always think they'll find a way to put a stop to cheating on contracts and the other things I mentioned, not realizing that they're really just cutting off a Hydra's head.[31]

The contrast we can draw between Plato's condemnation of Athenian democracy and common criticisms of our own liberal models of justice, is worth considering. Although liberals today worry about excessive litigation, and ponder ways to reduce it, they can only postulate such changes in limited, pragmatic terms, for example, through such a 'Hydra's head' as creating financial incentives for alternative dispute resolution. They cannot draw upon any core values of liberalism to curb litigation, as the core values of liberalism place no obvious limit on it. Liberalism keeps litigation profitable precisely insofar as it offers, in any given situation, some sufficiently alluring likelihood of material gain for interested parties and legal professionals alike.[32] Even judges on the benches can only half-heartedly bite the hand that feeds them. Plato's rejection of Athenian, market-driven democracy shines nowhere more brightly than in his view of rectificatory justice[33] as working best not when, as within liberal contexts, it 'correctly' resolves dispute, after dispute, after dispute, with no stopping point in principle, but when the need for it is itself diminished.[34]

4.3 *Suum cuique* as a decisive element

In one sense, then, *suum cuique* represents the obvious idea that a legal system entails some scheme of deciding who gets what, irrespective of the substantive justice of that determination. Under a centralised and despotic regime, that determination may indeed trace ultimately to the sheer will of the despot: private parties may retain a residual autonomy to determine contractual or other private rights and obligations, but with the caveat that government can interfere in any way, at any time. A benevolent but absolute monarchy

---

31 R 4.426c–e.
32 Cf., e.g., Grg 502e.
33 See this chapter, text accompanying nn. 43 and 45.
34 See, e.g., R 4.425d; Grg 478c–e.

would be, structurally, little different, except that such determinations would supposedly exhibit greater substantive justice.[35] In another sense, the more that choices concerning civic and commercial life are left to citizens, as Plato witnessed in Athens, and as we experience today in free-market democracies, the less the norms governing them are left to the centralised control of governing officials, the more they fall under the direction of abstract legal norms and institutions charged with those norms' application, as articulated in the everyday law of contract, property, commercial transactions, and other predominantly private-law areas. In our own time, that transition from a centralised view of law towards one supporting the autonomous choices of private actors has been invoked to explain, for example, H. L. A. Hart's shift from the sovereignty-based theory of John Austin's so-called 'command theory'[36] to a theory focused on law's facilitation of individual choices.[37]

Aristotle does retain unifying values as central to justice in a 'general' sense,[38] calling it 'complete virtue (ἀρετή) in relation to another',[39] inevitably entailing law's embeddedness in broader social systems of ethics and politics.[40] His scepticism towards overarching unity nevertheless underscores his political ideal of citizen-directed government, which assigns a prominent role to 'special justice',[41] taking the forms of 'distributive' justice[42] and 'rectificatory' (or 'corrective') justice.[43] Under 'distributive' justice, although its principles can apply in some private-law areas, such as intestate succession, Aristotle envisages above all distributions of resources that are publicly held: 'anything ... that can be divided among members of a community who share in a political system',[44] including wealth or resources. In our day, decisions about the spending of tax revenue would represent a typical example. By 'rectificatory' justice, Aristotle denotes a core principle, little changed since his time, namely that, for example, a failure to fulfil a legal obligation, such as violation of the terms of a lawful contract, or breach of a duty in tort, requires some adequate compensation or remedy. Rectificatory justice encompasses transactions that are both voluntary and, in some cases, involuntary (our traditional principles of contract and tort providing some close analogies). The aim is, through an

---

35 See, e.g., Stm 294e, 301b, 302e, 305e. Cf., e.g., Lev chs 22–30.
36 See, e.g., Austin, 1998, pp. 132–34.
37 See, e.g., Hart, 1994, pp. 35–38. Cf., e.g., Cotterrell, 1992, pp. 49–112; Morrison, 1997, chs 9, 13.
38 NE 5.1.1129^{b}26–1130^{a}14.
39 NE 5.1.1129^{b}27.
40 See, e.g., Bostock, 2000, pp. 54–58; Kraut, 2002, pp. 118–25; Heinze, 2009d, pp. 25–30.
41 NE 5.2.1130^{b}30.
42 NE 5.2.1130^{b}31; NE 5.3.
43 NE 5.2.1131^{a}1; NE 5.4.
44 NE [Ir] 5.3.1130^{b}1–2.

assessment of total damages, 'to restore . . . to equality' a harm done by one party and suffered by another.[45]

In Aristotle's ideal polis, abstract norms to which full-fledged citizens can appeal to regulate their affairs endow society with a rule of law character.[46] In Plato's ideal regime, distributive and rectificatory justice arguably operate in opaque ways. A small number of philosopher-rulers guide justice for a population of, metaphorically, 'cave dwellers' – workers nurtured in their early years on myths that teach justice and civic virtue,[47] but lacking the rigour of dialectical reason,[48] and unschooled in grasping justice for the polis as a whole. That justice-behind-the-opacity, in Plato's case, remains difficult for readers to assess. Although we have seen that the *Republic's* class structure entails, by definition, an unmistakable instance of *suum cuique*, the application of that maxim to the minutiae of everyday law remains under the control of the rulers, inscrutable to onlookers.

It makes sense, by contrast, that Aristotle, in view of his citizen-directed 'polity',[49] would pay detailed attention to distributive and rectificatory justice, which proceed according to principles that can immediately be recognised and implemented, case-by-case, by citizens as a whole and as individuals, exercising ordinary powers of judgment (φρόνησις).[50] As a formal matter, then, *suum cuique* applies equally and indifferently to any regime, subsumed utterly by the substantive norms it serves. However, unlike the model society of the *Republic*, 'to each his own' does now emerge as a distinct, central, quasi-autonomous value, a value with some intrinsic meaning in a citizen-based regime, in which great numbers of people, for example, through relatively greater civic activism, as well as comparatively more broadly contractual, privatised relationships, are constantly involved in negotiating the criteria through which whatever is 'due' to each individual remains at the centre of attention.[51] Aristotle provides a critical, theoretical underpinning that the conventionally minded Polemarchus lacked.

At variance with modern justice theories, Aristotle's account of distributive justice excludes from the ranks of society's 'members' women and slaves.[52] His general account of distributive justice nevertheless confirms that an act still counts as a distribution despite any disagreements on the criteria used to decide what makes it just, for example, regarding those who participate or benefit, such that distributive justice, as a formal matter, as a species of 'to

---

45 NE [Ir] 5.3.1132^{a}4–7.
46 See, e.g., Pol 4.5.1292^{a}32–34.
47 R 2.376d–3.392c.
48 R 7.531d–532b.
49 See, e.g., Pol 3.1.1275^{a}20–22, 31–34, 1275^{b}2–5, 3.7.1279^{a}36–38.
50 See NE 3.2–3, 6.5–13.
51 See, e.g., Pol 3.15.1286^{a}32–86^{b}7.
52 Pol 1.3–7; 12–13.

each his own', applies just as straightforwardly in a society that has rejected slavery or women's legal subordination to men. Aristotle claims that 'if the people involved are not equal, they will not [justly] receive equal shares'.[53] That formula can indeed apply such that two citizens receive equal shares of a distribution from which slaves, as unequals, are excluded. But it can just as accurately mean, in modern contexts of taxation and redistribution, that, for example, all adult nationals and legal aliens count for the sake of the distribution, but not dependent minors or illegal aliens; or all adult nationals and legal aliens earning below, but not those earning above, some specified annual income.

If we consider recent liberal theory, we see how those two elements of law, distributions and rectifications, still define programmatic justice theories. Theories in today's liberal democratic contexts retain two core Aristotelian elements, however far they may stray from Aristotle on other points. We find two standard liberal theorists, John Rawls and Ronald Dworkin, who, between them, emphasise precisely those two components of special justice. Rawls devises his 'theory of justice' focused precisely upon the problem of distribution of resources throughout society as a whole.[54] Dworkin's inaugural texts focus on adjudication, justice through the framework of lawsuits, precisely along the familiar, bipolar model of rectificatory justice.[55]

We can certainly examine or postulate positive legal systems lacking satisfactory or effective regimes of distributive or rectificatory justice in practice. We cannot, however, easily imagine programmatic justice theories that would lack foundations for distributive or rectificatory justice. Western programmatic justice theories largely reflect Aristotle in prescribing just distributions and rectifications, diverging only in how that justice is determined. Even writers making no extensive reference to Aristotle seem to work out the institutional details of justice in ways that render just distributions and rectifications decisive for their projects. Rousseau's and Kant's, Bentham's and Hegel's otherwise different theories of law all aim to provide procedural contexts within which distributions and rectifications are ascertained and provided.

What distinguishes other programmatic theorists from Aristotle, then, is not that they reject distributive or rectificatory justice, but that they propose different criteria for the distributions and rectifications. Marx provides a comparator, as Marxism purports to surpass the methods and lexicon of the classical philosophical tradition,[56] yet recapitulates Aristotelian distributive and rectificatory justice. Although Marxism describes perfected communism only in general terms, it can hardly forego fundamental distributive and rectificatory justice, even if it would radically re-define them, having overthrown

---

53 NE [Ir] 5.3.1131^{a}22–3.
54 See, e.g., Rawls, 1999, ch. 5.
55 Dworkin, 1977, 1986.
56 See, e.g., KGP 15–24; Löw, 2001, pp. 182, 192.

capitalist means of achieving them. When Marx cites Louis Blanc's maxim, 'From each according to his ability, to each according to his need!',[57] he adopts a rule for justice in distributive language. How Marx would approach rectificatory justice is less clear, as he provides insufficient precision about what remains as individual interests once property and means of production are collectivised (although it is difficult to escape the impression that communism's ideal, at least with regard to rectificatory justice, would largely recapitulate Plato's in the *Republic*, namely, that strong socio-political justice through unity across society would vastly reduce such litigation[58]). Yet the idea that we would be left utterly bereft of any kind of individual justice (even one, for example, that would use education or rehabilitation instead of penalties as remedies) would seem implausible, and too utopian for a thinker who otherwise ridicules utopian theories.

Aristotle, on Blanc's formula, would impute the less valued 'ability' to a slave, while Marx, at the other extreme, would abolish slavery outright. Aristotle would distribute much of the city's land into the private holdings of male, citizen, heads of household; Marx would abolish private property, male-citizen privilege, and even private families, altogether, subjecting land instead to universal distribution, not through private ownership, but through communal use, according to individuals' needs and to their abilities to keep the land productive. Marx, and *a fortiori* less radical theorists, may change the terms of distribution and correction, but in no way eliminate them; they remain guiding principles for Marx's views of justice and injustice, that is, of domination and oppression.

4.4 Injustice as failure of reciprocity

In Chapter 5.5 of the *Nicomachean Ethics*, Aristotle introduces a further concept of justice, called 'reciprocity' in the exchange of goods and services.[59] Reciprocal justice is embodied, albeit not exclusively, by money: '[A]ll things that are exchanged must somehow be commensurable. It is for this end that money (νόμισμ[α]) has been introduced, and it becomes in a sense an intermediate (μέσον); for it measures (μετρεῖ) all things.'[60] Aristotle does not merely recognise, but positively praises reciprocal justice, and money as its exemplary tool, indeed as a crucial means by which 'the city holds together'.[61]

In the *Republic*, Plato admits currency and trade, for purposes of meeting basic needs.[62] However, he condemns commerce that extends further, to sheer

---

57 KGP 21 ('Jeder nach seinen Fähigkeiten, jedem nach seinen Bedürfnissen!').
58 See this chapter, text accompanying n. 29.
59 NE 5.5.1132^{b}32.
60 NE 5.5.1133^{a}18–20. Cf. NE 5.5.1133^{b}13–28; Pol 1.9.
61 NE 5.5.1132^{b}34.
62 R 2.371b.

accumulation or consumption of ever more material goods.[63] The *Republic* is pervasively constructed to avoid a legal regime primarily driven by, and engineered to support, the dictates of the market.[64] Aristotle certainly does not favour unlimited accumulation of property or wealth.[65] But he sees management of wealth more as a skill to be cultivated[66] than as a necessary evil. The problem with Polemarchus's maxim 'to each his own' is not that Plato imagines no role whatsoever for distributions or rectifications. The problem is that Polemarchus has cited a formula steeped in values determined not by collective, social welfare, but only, indifferently, by profit-driven commerce and private gain. Socrates' rejection of Polemarchus's uncritical *suum cuique* becomes a swipe at Cephalus and his family, whose conception of justice is based fundamentally on values generated by markets and profit – profit derived indeed from one of the effects of unbridled consumerism, namely Athenian commercially imperial warfare and their family's concomitant arms trade. The *Republic* explains offensive warfare as something fundamentally pathological, undertaken for purposes of accumulating more property than we need to live well or justly.[67]

For Aristotle, more hospitable to a moderate market ethos, and therefore of great interest in our own liberal, market democracies, currency (νόμισμα) arises from usage and custom, as part and parcel of, indeed as a paradigmatic embodiment of, law (νόμος) itself.[68] Money, not merely or primarily as accumulated private wealth, but above all as the tool of assigning value and exchanging things accordingly, becomes not, as for Plato, a problem for society. As long as we adhere to distributive and rectificatory justice, consisting of measurement (μέτρον) of value, money becomes essential to society as community or 'association' (κοινωνία): 'Money (νόμισμα), then, acting as a measure (μέτρον), makes goods commensurate and equates them; for neither would there have been association (κοινωνία) if there were not exchange, nor exchange if there were not equality, nor equality if there were not commensurability.'[69]

Law, then, achieves justice through the currency of measurement, as that without which there would be no functioning associations or communities. Throughout modern European, and many other jurisdictions, the comparable principle of 'proportionality' is ubiquitous, a lexicon of either precise or at least theoretical measurement, even where, as in human rights jurisprudence, the interests involved often have little to do with monetary or material loss.

---

63 R 2.372e–373c, cf. 4.416d, 5.464b–c. Cf. Heinze, 2007a, pp. 100–2.
64 R 4.425c–426a; 426e.
65 Pol 1.9, 4.11.1295^{b}1–17.
66 NE 4.1.
67 R 2.373d–e.
68 NE 5.5.1133^{b}14–15.
69 NE 5.5.1133^{b}15–18.

'The just, then, is the proportionate, and the unjust is the counter-proportionate.'[70] Injustice must be the binary opposite, the mismeasurement by which community would ultimately break down altogether. Measurement or 'the measure' defines not only reciprocal, but also distributive and rectificatory jusitce: 'in any kind of action in which there is a more and a less there is also what is equal (ἴσον). [. . .] And since the equal is intermediate (μέσον), the just will be an intermediate.'[71] By implication, injustice then becomes anything which interferes with the mediating function of money or of measurement, such as, for example, duress exerted to coerce a party into an unfavourable transaction.

It is at this point, however, that we approach the limit of what the classical, binary model can teach about injustice. As I shall argue in Chapter 5, unity implodes so as to generate, precisely through those forces aimed to forge it, its own disunity. However, as the societies in which many of us live approach nothing like the strong unity models of Plato, Rousseau or Marx, that insight is of limited value. It is above all the implosion of the Aristotelian model, unity balanced with autonomy, securing justice through measurement, which will be of central interest, as I shall argue in Chapters 6 and 7.

It would be easy at this stage in the analysis to make a familiar move. It would be tempting to chastise Aristotle for making measurement essential to law, and money essential to measurement. Aristotle could then be charged, as Plato charges democracy, with collapsing too much of human life into sheer commodity, abandoning those selfsame community values that Aristotle's notion of general justice would claim to foster. Chapters 6 and 7 could then become another study of the decline of values into valueless and soulless materialism. To be sure, that materialist problematic will play an important role in my attempt to ponder a post-classical concept of injustice. The crucial train of reasoning, however, is *not* that Aristotle identifies measurement as essential to law, and then money as essential to measurement. Rather, he deems measurement essential to law, as specially exemplified, but by no means exhausted, through money as a tool of measurement. In other words, it is not money as such, but measurement as such that drives the norms and procedures of 'special justice', and that undergirds those programmatic theories, as well as those actual legal regimes, which focus fundamentally on measurement as the tool of justice. To make that point more bluntly: Marx will serve the critique, but will not escape it.

Money certainly stands as an exemplary way in which measurement is performed. However, money *qua* money (abstracted from any inherent value of a piece's face value as sheer metal) serves no function other than measurement. It is not measurement that exists for the sake of money, but money that exists

---

70 NE [Ir] 5.3.1131^{b}16–17.
71 NE 5.3.1131^{a}13–14. Cf. Irwin's 'fair' (ἴσον).

for the sake of measurement. Measurement, for Aristotle, comes to underlie not only positive law, but all of justice, all of ethics, all of *phronēsis*.

> There are three kinds of disposition, then, two of them vices, involving excess and deficiency and one an excellence, viz. the mean (μεσότητος), and all are in a sense opposed to each other; for the extreme states are contrary both to the intermediate state and to each other, and the intermediate to the extremes; as the equal is greater relatively to the less, less relatively to the greater, so the middle states (μέσαι) are excessive relatively to the deficiencies, deficient relatively to the excesses, both in passions and in actions.[72]

Even matters rarely subject to formal legal procedures accord with justice through a principle of correct measurement, or proportion ('sym-metry', σύμμετρία, that is, σύμ-μετρία, in the etymological sense of 'measuring together'), represented by the 'mean', which is 'intermediate' (μέσος) between extremes of excess and defect.

> [A]s we see in the case of strength and of health . . . both excessive and defective exercise destroys the strength, and similarly drink or food which is above or below a certain amount destroys the health, while that which is proportionate (σύμμετρος) both produces and increases and preserves it. So too is it, then, in the case of temperance and courage and the other excellences.[73]

4.5 Transition to a post-classical concept of justice

In contemplating a post-classical understanding of injustice, I shall challenge Aristotle's understanding of justice, not because he may be wrong about measurement as essential to it, but because he overwhelmingly appears right about it, as testified by almost any regime that most of us would recognise as a legal system, and by the fact that every programmatic justice theorist, even Plato and Marx, in one way or another, assign a crucial role to measurement. If Aristotle is right, measurement will indeed exemplify justice, *once we are settled* on what justice is. My point, in challenging Aristotle and the binarist tradition, is not that injustice disappears once we reach that agreement, as that point simply re-states the presupposition of all classical, binarist justice theory. I shall instead suggest that, no less than criteria of unity, criteria of measurement must inevitably generate injustice, measurement as such must inevitably generate injustice, however much agreement any given criterion

---

72 NE 2.8.1108^{b}12–19.
73 NE 2.2.1104^{a}12–19.

may command. Measurement, the single salient ingredient of justice, becomes the single salient ingredient of injustice – not because, as the classical model would have it, we apply the wrong measure or misapply the right one, as if finding some other or doing it differently would end the problem (although, obviously, in some cases that remedy will diminish it), but again because, as will be argued in Chapters 6 and 7, measurement as such, the necessary element of justice, is itself the premier cause of injustice.

It is not merely wealth as an object of legal regulation that is key, but measurement itself, as illustrated not only in Aristotle's depiction of money, to which he attaches clear warnings,[74] but, more importantly, as the inevitable meaning of his descriptions of distributive, rectificatory and reciprocal justice, such that all things can be translated into numerical values, rendering them infinitely, indifferently, interchangeable. That notion can be grasped with reference to the concept of 'being as presence', '*Sein als* παρουσία, *Anwesenheit*', which Heidegger will trace back to Aristotle, and will deem altogether foundational to the worldview later associated with European modernity.[75] Descartes, as Heidegger reminds us, will theorise time, space and matter as measurable precisely in terms of universally fungible, interchangeable points, by which the uniqueness – the irreducibility of any thing in space, or of any moment in time, or of any material object – Duns Scotus' *haecceitas*,[76] can be bypassed, and can be rendered superfluous for practical purposes.[77] All essential and determinative elements of being are such insofar as they are measureable. We are again reminded of the famous frontispiece to Hobbes's *Leviathan*, in which the monarch's body is composed of countless, faceless and interchangeable points, each one an anonymised human being.[78] Such images of human beings and affairs reduced to indifferently interchangeable and empty shells will continue to haunt Western modernity into our own time. Recall, for example, George Grosz's *Metropolis*[79] or *Republican Automatons*.[80]

Those Cartesian points in space and time eerily perform the same function as does money for Aristotle. One point on graph X equals, *qua* sheer abstract point, any other point. Within that Cartesian scheme, what reduces space and time to their supposed essence, and simultaneously makes them technologically useful, is that process of abstracting them from their uniqueness, and rendering them into equivalent, infinitely interchangeable 'points'. Justice, like space, time and matter – ultimately everything we can experience in the universe – all fall under our apprehension and control by becoming objects of

---

74 See, e.g., Pol 1.9, 4.11.1295^{b}1–17.
75 Heidegger, 1979, p. 25.
76 I was helped to view that link by Kristeva, 2011.
77 See, e.g., Heidegger, 1979, pp. 89–101.
78 Cf. Schmitt, 1982, pp. 150–51.
79 Grosz, 1917.
80 Grosz, 1920a. See also Grosz, 1920b.

measurement. They function as money does. The Higgs boson, the so-called 'God' particle, performs its explanatory task in the physics of modernity precisely because it can become the universal currency. Money is valuable not primarily in itself (particularly today, when it is a sheer token of credit, bearing little inherent worth through the paper or metal used to make it), but through its ability to render any two sets of things, however distinct, functionally comparable and interchangeable. Justice is achieved through precise but fungible, universally indifferent, measurements of value. '[A]ll goods must have a price set on them; for then there will always be exchange, and, if so, association (κοινωνία).'[81] Not only in Aristotle's slave-holding society, but also in our own globalised world – understood as beginning in its present form with the emerging, colonial nation-states of early European modernity, as witnessed by Shakespeare or Milton, Hobbes or Locke, Corneille or Racine – human beings themselves are not beyond being either literally or functionally bought and sold.

---

81 NE 5.5.1133ª29–30.

Part 2

Post-classical understandings

Chapter 5

Injustice as unity

> ... right and wrong,
> Between whose endless jar justice resides,
> Should lose their names, and so should justice too.
> Shakespeare, *Troilus and Cressida* 1.3.116–18

5.1 Introduction

Some role for measurement as such becomes indispensable, not only within any actual legal system, but within any programmatic theory. Our dominant legal thought has largely emphasised measurement, seen as a tangible and precise criterion, and not unity. Beyond the offhand or rhetorical tributes paid to unity for political purposes, it is seen, for example, among many liberal thinkers as mystical or dangerous.[1] I shall nevertheless look briefly at unity in the present chapter. The suggestion that ideals of political unity either contain contradictions, or are based on mythicised ideals often coercively imposed, is nothing new. In this chapter, a small number of examples will be cited mostly to recall that idea. The problem of unity is worth that brief glance, as it will lurk in the background of the examination of measurement in Chapters 6 and 7.

The law and literature movement has shown that works of fiction illuminate law in the critical, re-contextualised ways that are limited within the filtered contexts of traditional, bipolar litigation. In some cases, of course, literary texts merely recapitulate conflicts arising within the bounds of established law, for example, in the form of isolated disputes within conventional frameworks.[2] In other cases, texts are treated as models for specific styles of legal, particularly judicial, reasoning and writing, again within conventional institutional structures.[3] Yet within the context of the legal theory at issue in this book, the advantage of fictional texts will not be

---

1 See generally, e.g., Popper, 2002a & b; Russell, 2000, pp. 660–74.
2 For a typical, popular work, see, e.g., Dubus III, 2001.
3 See, e.g., Dworkin, 1986.

to serve either of those aims, but will lie above all in their ability to capture political, ethical or legal problems within broader, systemic frameworks, liberated from the formal or effective institutional constraints of legislatures or courtrooms.

5.2 *Antigone*: conventional versus critical contexts

The Antigone story has long been read as representing a standoff between positive and natural law.[4] The action assumes a prior history, related in Sophocles' other Theban plays. Oedipus, after unwittingly killing his father, the Theban King Laius, rescues Thebes from the plague of the Sphinx by solving her famous riddle. Still unaware of his own identity, Oedipus is rewarded by the Thebans with their throne and with marriage to their widowed Queen, his mother Jocasta. The royal couple incestuously beget three children – the two brothers Eteocles and Polynices, and their sister Antigone. After Oedipus's discovery of his fate, and his subsequent exile and death, it is decided that Eteocles and Polynices shall take turns exercising Thebes's royal power. Once Eteocles' term expires, he refuses to hand the crown to Polynices. In retaliation, Polynices musters foreign Greek troops, from Argos, against the Theban homeland. The brothers kill each other, leaving Jocasta's brother, their uncle Creon, on the throne. It is at that point that *Antigone* opens. As Eteocles was the brother who defended the polis, his body receives full interment rites.[5] Antigone insists on a ceremonial burial for Polynices, too, in accordance with religious requirements of honour due to the deceased. Creon forbids it, on grounds of Polynices' treasonous war.[6] Antigone disobeys. Creon imprisons her, and she hangs herself.

The conflict allows various interpretations. It is possible, on the one hand, to see Antigone as accepting the prevailing legal order in general, dissenting only on that one point. It is often in that light that the problem of civil disobedience is presented.[7] That approach can be called 'limited civil disobedience'. Beyond the bounds of the dispute, on that one point of conscience, the prevailing legal order is not further challenged. By analogy, conscientious objectors to military service sometimes present themselves in that light, as dissenting only against certain elements of military policy, and not against the whole of the legal order. As limited civil disobedience, Antigone's predicament resembles a familiar 'hard case', a dispute taken essentially in isolation from its broader socio-legal context, and identified as revolving around one or a small number of rules or principles. On that traditional reading, Creon's ban

---

4 See, e.g., Ant sc. 2. Cf., e.g., Äs I, 3.B.II.3.a., Werke 13:285–91. See also, e.g., Goyard-Fabre, 1992, p. 36; Morrison, 1997, pp. 19–25.
5 Ant 218–21.
6 Ant 222–31.
7 See, e.g., Cri 50d–e.

on burial rites for Polynices represents a positive law injunction,[8] while Antigone's insistence on them expresses a higher-order normative claim that would override even a monarchical decree.[9]

From another point of view, the legitimacy of the background political and legal order can be seen as altogether challenged. To be sure, that is patently what Polynices does in waging war on Thebes. Whether Antigone, too, ought to be viewed as a rebel against the whole of the prevailing order is, on the surface, less apparent. We have seen that Antigone's dilemma arises out of the more complex web of Theban myths, including in particular that of Oedipus. Those stories are adapted in various renditions, by various poets, not only in Greece, but in Rome, and again in early modern Europe.[10] By the 17th century, the revived Theban cycle comes to symbolise ever-looming questions of political legitimacy, a crisis perpetuated when the crown passes within the blood line to Creon – Oedipus's uncle through his mother Jocasta, and then brother-in-law after his mother becomes his wife. That looming incest taboo, leaving aside its interpretations from religious, sociological or psychological viewpoints, can also be read as expressing ongoing doubts haunting the legitimacy of power inherited and exercised through dynastic rule, in antiquity as well as early modernity.[11]

The incest myth looms as a symbol of impurity, pollution, entering not, like Polynices and his Argive legions, from the outside as an intrusion into a supposedly pristine unity, but rather emerging at the monarchy's very heart, from Antigone, as the seed of the mythically generated unity required for the legitimacy of dynastic rule. Antigone, on that reading, represents more than limited civil disobedience, more than sheer disagreement on one issue. If the Argive forces, the impurities from without, are defeated, Antigone persists as the impurity from within, not in the sense of introducing into Thebes a heretofore absent impurity, but in the sense of exposing an impurity, a congenital illegitimacy, always inherent in dynastic patriarchy. By the time of Sophocles, which is also the age of Socrates and the Sophists, ongoing debates about the foundations and legitimacy of *any* political power – the nagging question throughout Plato's *Republic* and *Laws* or Aristotle's *Politics* – and about whether democracy indeed claims greater legitimacy, provide a context within which the problem of legitimacy can be seen as represented symbolically by a congenital curse, a spectre of illegitimacy, haunting a power that rules by lineal descent.[12]

---

8 Ant 825, 834.
9 Ant 499–508, 833, 834–35.
10 See generally Biet, 1994.
11 Symbolic references to royal or imperial incest as means of casting doubt on the legitimacy of a regime are not infrequent in ancient and early modern history and literature. See, e.g., His 3:31; Ham 1.2.157 (cf. 1.4.65); Per 1.21–30.
12 Cf., e.g., the theme of the plague at Oed 31–38.

Antigone, then, undertakes more than limited disobedience.[13] Beyond the confines of her dissent against Creon's decree, she defies, more broadly, kings' 'ruthless power to do and say whatever pleases *them*'.[14] By opening the door to disobedience based on that more fundamental political principle, Antigone heralds the possibility of thoroughgoing challenges to the legitimacy of the regime as a whole. The familiar conflict of natural *versus* positive law, concerning a specific dispute, serves not so much as the focus, but merely as the pretext and prelude to a more fundamental question about the source and exercise of all power in the realm. Creon's proceeding against Antigone for her disobedience, leaving aside the positive-law or natural-law justice of the substantive norms regarding the disposition of the dead (and, after all, that specific dispute, taken in isolation, is a 'hard case' insofar as the denial of burial to a violent traitor, if problematical in *Antigone's* context, is not altogether outrageous as a general proposition[15]), relies for its legitimacy on the legitimacy of Creon's own entitlement to rule. Creon's status as king, as emblem and guardian of political unity, becomes challenged by the rupture, the corrosion, the disunity from within, not at some dissident, peripheral core, but at the core of his own family.

The curse of Laius's line is the curse of law, producing injustice in its self-legitimating pursuit of justice. If Antigone's imprisonment is an injustice, it is not primarily because of the illegitimacy of Creon's edict concerning Polynices. It is not because of that isolated dispute, even if the showdown does bring the latent systemic tensions to a head, but because of the questionable legitimacy of the regime as such. Sophocles' text never tires of repeating that Creon's authority is challenged insofar as it binds Antigone, who, even as a royal woman, retains a diminished political status. Antigone's sister Ismene certainly seeks to admonish her.

> [T]hink what a death we'll die, the worst of all
> if we violate the laws and override
> the fixed decree of the throne, its power –
> we must be sensible. Remember we are women,
> we're not born to contend with men. Then too,
> we're underlings, ruled by much stronger hands,
> so we must submit in this, and things still worse.[16]

Antigone resists a regime that gives her no say, not only because it is monarchical, but because she is not a male subject of it. The anthropologist

---

13 Cf. Pol 5.4.1303^{b}18–19.
14 Ant 567 (translator's emphasis).
15 See, e.g., Knox, 1984, pp. 38, 40.
16 Ant 74–77. Cf. Ant 593, 652, 757–61.

Françoise Héritier has recently recalled that 'the hierarchy between the sexes is the foundation of all hierarchy'.[17]

Antigone might appear to leave us with nothing more than an aporetic hard case along half-legal, half-moral lines – natural law *versus* positive law, as the familiar view runs – insofar as we uncritically accept the background regime as fixed or unconstested, and, within it, Creon's legal and Antigone's moral claims as equally weighed. Above all, however, injustice in *Antigone* arises from the incommensurability of Creon's regime with its own, with any regime's own, need for legitimacy, the inevitable twin to all myths of national unity. Creon fabricates Thebes' unity myth, crucial to his rule precisely insofar as he inherits so contested a throne, in deceptively appointing the deceased Eteocles as the unequivocal hero of Theban unity and Polynices as its unequivocal foe, both questionable myths, given Eteocles' usurpation of Polynices' share of rule. That mythicised unity is imposed by force, as national unity myths often are, resulting in Antigone's punishment. Injustice is not merely, as the classical binarism would generally have it, the result of this or that wrong norm, or of this or that wrong application of a right norm. Injustice arises from the crisis of legal legitimacy itself, from the need to secure a legitimacy that is mythically founded. There would indeed be a problem in proclaiming Antigone altogether right, in view of the real harm Polynices has caused to Thebes. The injustice of Antigone's death nevertheless remains as anything but the sheer negation of some discretely identifiable norm or concept of justice.

5.3 *Macbeth*: unity as the source of disunity

Clashes in conceptions of justice emerge conspicuously within societies confronting sudden or rapid change. Emblematic of Attica in the age of Plato and Aristotle is the decline from its so-called 'golden' 5th century. Athens had risen meteorically as an economic, military and maritime power.[18] Her legal system had required fundamental shifts to accommodate an increasingly robust, trade-based, consumerist economy, with its inevitable shifts towards increased, and more complex, contractual and financial transactions. From Plato's perspective, it is the legal system's pervasive support for transactions in pursuit of individual enrichment, at the expense of community cohesion, that leads to Athens's social and political undoing.[19] Notwithstanding historical differences over great stretches of time and culture, we cannot overlook similar upheavals that herald the West's transition from medieval

---

17 Héritier, 2012. Despite the 1949 publication of Simone de Beauvoir's *Le Deuxiéme Sexe*, Albert Camus's *L'Homme révolté*, not uncharacteristically, overlooks Antigone's disobedience as a rebellion against patriarchy, interpreting her appeal to custom as a purely 'reactionary revolt'. Camus, 1951, p. 47.
18 See, e.g., Martin, 1996, pp. 116–21.
19 See, e.g., R 8.562b. Cf. Heinze, 2007a, pp. 100–5.

feudalism into political, commercial and legal modernity. That transition certainly emerges in philosophical writings of early modernity, but also in art, often inspired by the revival of ancient Greek and Roman thought.[20] Shakespeare is born into that European Renaissance. Scarcely a play in the corpus fails to record those historical shifts, and the crises of law and justice that they entail.[21]

In *Macbeth*, Shakespeare re-visits a character type explored earlier, particularly in a figure such as the aristocratic Henry Bolingbroke, in *Richard II*, *Henry IV, Part One* and *Henry IV, Part Two*, but also in the Bastard of Faulconbridge in *King John*, or in Edmund, Bastard son of the Duke of Gloucester in *King Lear*. Such characters have long been seen as embodying the emerging politics of modernity. They possess an acumen that spurs them simultaneously to challenge, yet to rise within the prevailing political order.[22] Plays such as *Richard II* and *King John* are overshadowed by their memories of a strategically mythologised golden age of justice as national unity, represented, respectively, by the earlier reigns of Edward III[23] and Richard the Lionheart.[24] *Macbeth's* murdered, 'virtuous' King Duncan[25] joins those ranks. He does so with pointed ambiguity, arguably inviting us to return to, and to scrutinise more closely, the legends shrouding Edward III or Richard the Lionheart in the earlier plays. Unlike those plays, Duncan's golden age is not a distant memory, but still present at the start of the action. Its reality still appears before it can be altogether mythologised. It presents an almost textbook example of Benjamin's and Derrida's, and indeed Schmitt's,[26] model of domestic, socio-legal unity forged through armed conflict waged against the outsider, the foreign enemy,[27] who has, moreover, infested the realm through collusion with traitors from within.[28]

On a surface reading, Macbeth's brutal murders appear as manifest injustices. Like Antigone's disobedience, they certainly breach existing norms of positive law. The question traditionally posed has been, 'Why does Macbeth commit them?', with the tacit assumption that the question means, 'Why does he commit those injustices?', 'Why does he violate norms of the existing

---

20 For insight into the ways in which the revival of ancient thought responds to early modern conditions, see generally, e.g., Copenhaver and Schmitt, 1992.
21 See, e.g., Ward, 1999, 20–69.
22 Rackin and Ward, for example, examine such characters with reference to Renaissance Machiavellianism. Ward, 1999, pp. 35, 39–44; Rackin, 1990, pp. 54–55, 62, 66–8, 72–6. See also, e.g., Eagleton, 1986, pp. 1–17; Dollimore, 2004, pp. 197–201.
23 R2 1.2.17; 2.1.40–66.
24 Jn 1.1.85–90, 134–47, 159–62, 167.
25 Mac 1.7.18.
26 The difference, of course, being that what is critically observed by Benjamin or Derrida is enthusiastically endorsed by Schmitt.
27 Mac 1.2.31, 48–63.
28 Mac 1.3.112–17.

legal order, to wage injustice?' When the question is framed in those terms, the explanations often amount to Christian-metaphysical references to evil in the world, or to psychological diagnoses of Macbeth's or his wife's pathologies. Such answers might also include references to the fallen state of man, or to the supernatural powers of the 'weird sisters', or to customary dramatic portrayals of political ambition.[29] The risk of those readings, as recent post-structuralist and cultural materialist scholars have suggested, is that, as with *Antigone*, they may avert our gaze from the background socio-legal order, which we then uncritically take to be unproblematical. Such approaches seek to evaluate justice only on the given society's 'own terms'. The point of any theory of injustice, however, as Hamlet discovers and discovers anew, is that it is precisely the established order that must be examined, as a systemic context within which injustice emerges, and not merely taken for granted as an uncontested background, within which purely isolated instances of injustice appear as conceptually unproblematical opposites or negations of justice. Literary theory has increasingly observed that we cannot meaningfully put the apparent injustice, or 'evil', of a character like Macbeth on trial without scrutinising the justice or injustice of that background regime.[30]

As *Macbeth* opens, the regime suggests a conventional legitimacy. The nobles, including Macbeth, proclaim their loyalty.[31] That loyalty marks them out as internally unified, 'pure', precisely as they have just completed battle against the enemy, the impurity, from without and from within. Macbeth, like Richard III, far from committing injustice by attacking the existing order, draws the society's own socio-political premises to their own logical conclusion.[32] Those premises are clear enough: (a) King Duncan rules, as does Creon, through lineal descent and aristocratic privilege (even if other aristocrats do ratify such succession by election); and (b) that privilege of monarchy through descent is necessarily maintained, as are indeed other regimes, through brute force, however 'virtuous' may appear to be those who gain power through it. Macbeth acts not, so to speak, as an anti-Duncanian, but as an arch-Duncanian, not as an anti-monarchist, but by drawing the logic of monarchy's origin and purported legitimacy to its strict conclusion. Macbeth's exercises of brute force (and which legal regime does not rest on brute force?) are Duncan's, enrolled in Duncan's service, akin to those of any of the other

---

29 For a recent example of what is still an analysis of Macbeth in essentially 'private', de-politicised terms, see, e.g., Brown, 2001, pp. 290–303.
30 See generally, e.g., Dollimore, 2004; Drakakis, 2002; Holderness, 2000; Pugliatti, 1996; Dollimore and Sinfield, 1994; Wilson, 1993; Rackin, 1990; Greenblatt, 1988; Eagleton, 1986; Tennenhouse, 1986.
31 Mac 1.4.22–7.
32 That element of *Richard III* emerges within the context of the first tetralogy taken as a whole, particularly as a successor to *Henry VI, Part Two* and *Henry VI, Part Three*. See, e.g., Heinze, 2009c.

noblemen who hold the regime in place. No sooner has Duncan's world labelled its enemy from without than does the great bulwark of its own internal unity, Macbeth, emerge as its self-generated enemy, its self-generated injustice, not by overturning that society's own principles of justice, but by applying them, indeed on grounds – applied in law from antiquity through to our own day – of no less necessity than 'national security', *raison d'état*. In Stephen Geenblatt's words, 'actions that should have the effect of radically undermining authority turn out to be the props of that authority. [. . .] [M]oral values – justice, order, civility – are secured through the apparent generation of their subversive contraries.'[33]

Like *Antigone*, *Macbeth* begins after the outside enemy, the impurity from without, has been defeated, only to witness Macbeth arising as the impurity within, Derrida's *phármakon*, which, applying the remedy, the militarism, without which Duncan's rule has no existence, becomes that regime's own poison, undoing that selfsame unity. The play may conventionally seduce us to believe otherwise, namely that the unjust Macbeth attacks the just king, and therewith the unity and harmony of the realm. That schoolbook reading elicits our inclination to notice, and to respond more forcefully to, Macbeth's immediate and personalised waging of injustice, rather than to the systemic, institutionalised injustice pervading the established order, but wearing the benign face of its perpetual self-legitimation. If that naïve reading suggests that Duncan is simply just, and Macbeth simply unjust, a critical reading indicates that Duncan's injustice merely benefits from that selfsame official legitimacy which condemns Macbeth's injustice. Macbeth, in that sense, embodies Benjamin's view of violence not as the opposite of, and thing negated by law, but as the very product and mechanism of law.[34]

As *Antigone* suggests, that socio-critical reading is not an entirely modern innovation. Augustine, too, recalls the complaint of the pirate captured and punished by Alexander the Great. Alexander asks, 'What is your idea, in infesting the seas?' The pirate replies, 'The same as yours, in infesting the earth! But because I do it with a tiny craft, I'm called a pirate: because you have a mighty navy, you're called an emperor.'[35] That story's irony, which asks whether we mean anything more by 'justice' than unthinking acceptance of existing power relationships, had already dominated discussions about justice in Plato's *Republic* and *Gorgias*.[36] One of the great Shakespearean questions is indeed, 'What drives Macbeth?' That question assumes Macbeth to be distinctly pathological, not because he commits violence against a peaceful, harmonious world, but because his failure to use violence to uphold the pre-existing violence necessarily pre-supposed by Duncan's rule makes Macbeth,

33 Greenblatt, 1988, p. 53.
34 Benjamin, 1965; Derrida, 1992, pp. 29–57.
35 CD 4.4.
36 R 1.338b–2.368b; Grg 466b–527e.

superficially, seem violent in a way that the others are not. Some writers examine – again, the distinct capacities of literature in illuminating law become apparent here – the imbalance between our attention to the random event and our attention to the systemic forces underlying it. Those forces reveal more about injustice than we can learn from events treated in isolation. My aim is not simply to urge that we examine broader social and political forces. That suggestion is old, beginning in antiquity, with political theory itself, and augmenting with the 'sociological turn' of the 19th century.[37] Rather, my point has been that any such broad-based examination of law, politics and society defeats the misleading intuition that justice and injustice can satisfactorily be grasped in that intellectual isolation which makes them appear as mutually exclusive opposites.

A Marxist, dialectical-materialist reading could go further, proclaiming Macbeth neither a political villain nor a political exemplar, but nevertheless a political hero. Macbeth may admittedly show no sign of establishing a better regime, but lays bare the contradictions of power and hierarchy upon which the existing one rests. Admittedly, questions still remain about the 'weird sisters', and their relationship to Macbeth's seeming lack of control over his ambition. Yet it is precisely law's origins in, and continued reliance upon, violence which becomes obscured through the mythologising processes required for it to appear as legitimate, as part of the normal and natural way of things. Its violent underbelly then suddenly appears in paranormal, unnatural forms, 'unnatural hags', muffled voices – from the outside? Or from within? – murmuring only from sidelines and peripheries. The sisters' peripheral and obscure existence recalls the cave to which Creon sentences Antigone. Law's self-mythologising exiles Aleithia to Lethe. As to Macbeth's ambition, just as Shakespeare's ubiquitous notion of ambition constantly betokens more broadly the emerging, market-driven world of fierce competition,[38] Macbeth, on a dialectical-materialist reading, symbolically anticipates a historical movement out of feudalism, by exposing the contradiction between monarchy's mythologised, divine-right legitimacy and the brute force upon which it, like all law, leans. On that view, Macbeth's – like, on Marx's view, capitalism's – failure to create a better regime is unsurprising. The transition replaces one set of contradictions with another.[39] Competition may replace divine right, but without overcoming the system's reliance upon brute force.

Such ongoing crises of legitimacy remain acute in 17th-century thought. As modern states emerge, the doubts raised by Shakespeare are echoed by such poets as Middleton, Milton, Corneille and Racine.[40] Justice may remain

---

37 Understanding law and politics with reference to broader social forces becomes central, e.g., in Weber, 1972.
38 See this chapter, text accompanying nn. 20–21.
39 Cf Maus, 2008, p. 977.
40 Cf., e.g., Heinze, 2009a.

ineffable and controversial in the human world. On conventional readings, however, if God exists, perfect and omnipotent, then God's justice must be definitive and eternal. In *Paradise Lost*, Satan, rebellious against that order, must, by standard binary logic, 'incarnate' injustice.[41] But is Satan unjust because he has rebelled against God's order, or does he rebel against God's order because he is unjust? Plato had long ago put, effectively, the same question, 'Is what is holy holy because the gods approve it, or do they approve it because it is holy?'[42] However we phrase the question, if, on either of those two formulations, it is the latter of their options that is true, then justice becomes autonomous, and God superfluous.

The former option amounts to straightforward autocracy. The just is just solely through the imposed will of the figure who holds the ultimate power, which we commonly see not only as anathema to legitimacy, but as crucial to what we reject in absolute monarchy. God's divine order, on the second option – Satan rebels because he is unjust – constructs injustice as nothing other than disobedience *per se*. More Antigone than Macbeth, Milton's Satan at the Fall kills no one. His trespass, inducing Adam and Eve to disobey God, becomes injustice in the question-begging sense that leaves God's authority still unclear. In our workaday world, we look for independent harms, or positive goods, as evidence of a norm's legitimacy. We view as despotic the notion of a legal prohibition that serves the purpose not of protecting persons or preventing harms, but merely of punishing, or preventing, nothing other than the breach of a prohibition itself, for its own sake. If I, as King, forbid the playing of hopscotch for no reason *other* than that I forbid it, we might say that breaches of the rule do not merely punish injustice so much as they fabricate it *ab initio*. Those who believe in God's justice may, of course, explain the absence of rational explanation through God's mystery. *Was Gott beschlossen hat,/Kann die Vernunft doch nicht ergründen* – 'Reason cannot fathom what God has decreed'.[43] However, since human justice, particularly within any programmatic concept, cannot so easily bypass reason, that view renders God's justice not essential to, but irrelevant to, human justice.

Milton's Satan, as has long been observed, is not a comic-book villain with pitchfork, but a dissident within a political community. He exhorts the heavenly hosts,

> Will ye submit your necks, and choose to bend
> The supple knee? Ye will not, if I trust
> To know ye right, or if ye know yourselves
> Natives and sons of heaven possessed before
> By none, and if not equal all, yet free,

---

41 PL 9.166.
42 Euthphr [HC]10a.
43 Bach, 2000a, p. 149.

> Equally free; for orders and degrees
> Jar not with liberty, but well consist [with liberty].[44]

That protest is answered not with a rational, let alone legitimate, explanation, but with a rebuke.[45] Taking a step further than Antigone or Macbeth, Satan sets forth a political vision with which many in liberal modernity would agree,

> Who can in reason then or right assume
> Monarchy over such as live by right
> [as] equals, if in power and splendour less,
> In freedom equal? or can introduce
> Law and edict on us, who without law
> Err not.[46]

No such alternative order can emerge when unity is fixed by insuperable coercion. A naïve reading of that passage may see Satan damning himself, undoing his own argument, when he refers to 'us . . . without law', as an admission of his affinity to injustice. If we read 'without law' as 'without justice', then Satan speaks an absurdity – surely if one lacks justice, then one 'errs'. However, it is precisely that reduction of justice to imposed law that Satan questions in that passage. If we read 'without law' as 'without imposed law', then we are faced with incommensurable justice theories. God's punishment of Satan then becomes not the redress of injustice, but God's own fabrication of injustice for the sake of constructing his order as justice. Now it is for Satan to emerge as God's *phármakon*, both the remedy of existence, which guarantees the justice, through freedom, of God's universe, by according us freewill, and its own, internally generated poison, when that free will is exercised to challenge that regime of justice. One man's Satan is another man's freedom fighter.

5.4 Talbot: merit and myth

Stock Shakespearean portrayals of feudalism's decline include the conflict between the older, feudal order of status-based privilege, and the modern meritocratic ethos. That conflict can be construed, in loosely (that is, as mentioned earlier, not assuming any historical teleology) Hegelian-dialectical terms, as a system producing precisely the forces that undermine it. In Western Europe, early modern monarchies centralise and consolidate power at the

---

44 PL 5.787–93.
45 PL 5.809–48.
46 PL 5.794–99.

expense of the broader, old aristocratic class.[47] The path to power increasingly lies less in privileged birth, and more in the acquisition of the knowledge and expertise required to achieve political office.[48] By the end of his career, in collaboration with John Fletcher, Shakespeare makes that theme of precarious meritocracy dominant, through the downfall of Cardinal Woolsey depicted in *Henry VIII*.[49] The conspicuous, increasingly anachronistic exception to that rule becomes the monarchy itself, as Marx will later detect in lampooning what he sees as the arch-meritocratic, arch-bureaucratised nation state, albeit under the tutelage of a residual, hereditary monarch, as proposed by Hegel in the *Grundlinien*.[50] In order to monopolise power, early modern monarchy steadily replaces the once powerful medieval aristocracy with a meritocracy, in the form of appointed officials under its own control, the historical transition from *noblesse d'épée* to *noblesse de robe*. The monarchy ends up in the ironic position of relying, to maintain its peremptory control, upon precisely that meritocratic principle, which, on its own logic, renders monarchy itself superfluous.

Meritocracy, no less than monarchy or democracy, prevails only insofar as some brute power keeps it, too, in place. Merit and brute force are, of course, not the same thing. We ordinarily see them as opposites. Bolingbroke's superior political savvy is, however, nothing without his and his allies' armed troops.[51] Those soldiers' task is to follow orders, to obey power, regardless of their leader's merit. Merit stands not on its own, but only insofar as it is backed by the very principle of force that it is supposed to overcome. As Rousseau would later suggest, the world of meritocratic competition serves not to abolish, but merely to re-configure, socio-political coercion. It serves not to eliminate state coercion, but rather adds ever-spiralling rivalries among individuals,[52] whose hallmark is the ever-more legalistic world. It serves not to reduce coercive relationships, but to proliferate them,[53] merely replacing the sword with the lawsuit.[54]

The meritocratic order does not overcome recourse to brute force, but requires it more and more, anticipating that Foucauldian modernity, in which the freedom of liberal societies emerges in tandem with ever expanding surveillance and covert control.[55] Throughout the corpus, Shakespeare, far

---

47 See, e.g., Holderness, 2000, p. 29. See also, generally, Tennenhouse, 1986; Rackin, 1990; Prigent, 1986.
48 See, e.g., Holderness, 2000, pp. 24–9.
49 H8 3.2.436–45.
50 See this book, Chapter 2, Section 2.7 and Chapter 3, Section 3.5.
51 R2 2.3, 1–67, 3.2.200, 3.3. Cf. Rackin, 1990, p. 124 (discussing Holinshed).
52 See this book, Chapter 6, Section 6.10.
53 Cf. Rousseau's famous dictum, 'Man is born free, but is everywhere in chains', CS 1.1, JJR-OC 351.
54 Cf., e.g., commenting on 1H6 2.4, Heinze, 2009c, pp. 143–49.
55 See, e.g., Dollimore, 1994; Greenblatt, 1994.

from naively welcoming the new meritocratic principle, repeatedly presents it through the ethically ambiguous lens of 'ambition',[56] which, as *Macbeth* suggests, is pressed as indifferently into the service of injustice as justice. Constant cynical and often quasi-obsessive remarks about who is 'in' or 'out', 'up' or 'down',[57] the hallmark not of static feudalism but of socially mobile modernity, cast the same dim light upon modernity's emerging ethos of meritocracy. In Chapter 6, I shall argue that meritocracy becomes typical of injustice arising not as the negation of justice, but as its very embodiment.

Emblematic of idealised, 'golden age' justice is the myth of pervasive harmony, quasi-mystically shared among the members of the political community. Such a legend is evoked in *Henry VI, Part One*, in the character of Sir John Talbot,[58] whom Shakespeare's audiences nostalgically recognised as a chivalrous hero of a bygone age.[59] On a first encounter, the Countess of Auvergne mocks the warrior, seeing him more as a weakling 'dwarf' than a Titan.

> Is this the scourge of France?
> Is this the Talbot, so much feared abroad [. . .] ?
> I see report is fabulous and false.
> I thought I should have seen some Hercules,
> A second Hector, for his grim aspect
> And large proportion of his strong-knit limbs.
> Alas, this is a child, a silly dwarf.
> It cannot be this weak and writhled shrimp
> Should strike such terror to his enemies.[60]

As Talbot's soldiers have secretly besieged the Countess's castle, he replies with a riddle,

> . . . I am but shadow of myself.
> You are deceived, my substance is not here;
> For what you see is but the smallest part
> And least proportion of humanity.
> I tell you, madam, were the whole frame here,
> It is of such a spacious lofty pitch,
> Your roof were not sufficient to contain't.[61]

---

56 See, e.g., JC 1.2.314, 2.1.22, 3.1.82; 3.1.25–6, 3.2.74–96, 110. Cf. R2 1.3.130; H8 3.2.441.
57 See, e.g., Lr 24.15; R2 3.3.177, 192. See also this book, Chapter 7, text accompanying n. 19.
58 See this book, Chapter 2, Section 2.3.
59 See, e.g., Holderness, 2000, pp. 116–24; Leggatt, 1988, p. 6; Rackin, 1990, pp. 150–56.
60 1H6 2.3.14–23.
61 1H6 2.3.50–6.

112 The Concept of Injustice

The enigma becomes clear when Talbot's men burst in, taking the Countess as their prisoner: 'Talbot is but shadow of himself.../These are his substance, sinews, arms, and strength.'[62] That supposed harmony, 'fabulous and false' after all, will soon be shattered, as the more banal English nobles, the power structure behind the myth, fail through internecine power struggles to deliver Talbot's reinforcements, leading to his slaughter by the French. The myth, the unity, laboriously contrived, is demolished in a dash. The play's power-mongering nobles signify not the destruction of some earlier harmony, so much as its self-realisation. Talbot and his men, like *Macbeth's* King Duncan, never innocently stand aside from that broader regime of violence. They presuppose and perpetuate it, however 'virtuously' they may appear to do so. As in *Macbeth*, what collapses along with the myth of harmony is a foundation for justice. And the collapse of that foundation is something very different from what it is too easily taken to be, namely the active commission of injustice. The commission of injustice assumes, on the conventional, binary model, some conceptually prior justice, as more than sheer myth. Systemic injustice arises not only from breaches of just norms, but also from the fact that a supposed system of norms was only ever mythicised as justice in the first place. The mythic harmony of Edward III's reign, depicted in the comically sentimental fantasy of John of Gaunt's famous 'sceptered isle' speech,[63] will face a similar rude awakening, as Edward's progeny take up generations of mutual cannibalism that will mark the entirety of Shakespeare's English octology.[64] Injustice rages all around us, while justice becomes thinkable only insofar as it is mythicised. The revelation is vividly symbolised when Edward's grandson, Richard II, first pondering his unified image in a mirror, and then smashes it into 'a hundred shivers'.[65] Shakespeare constantly recounts that lost illusion with reference to the West's greatest 'golden age' myth of all, perfect harmony in Eden.[66]

The brief appearance of a recovered unity in the person of Henry V, whose regime Talbot symbolises, being its last, pseudo-heroic vestige,[67] will prove itself to be a sheer illusion.[68] England will slip into a world in which, in Randall Martin's words, 'there is no foreign enemy to demonize, no epic hero to inspire patriotic sacrifice, and little evidence of the human kinship that, paradoxically, war seems sometimes to breed more readily than peace. Instead

62 1H6, 2.3.62–3.
63 R2 2.1.40–66.
64 Cf. Rackin, 1990, p. 30. On the continuities and discontinuities of Shakespeare's two historical 'tetralogies' see, e.g., Holderness, 2000, pp. 1–12.
65 R2 4.1.289.
66 Gen 2.8; R2 2.1.42. Cf. Forker, 2002, pp. 74–78.
67 See, e.g., 1H6 1.1.6–16. Cf. Holderness, 2000, pp. 116–24.
68 H5 epil 11–12. Cf. Holderness, 2000, pp. 111–14.

a nation turns on itself in epidemic savagery, dissolving its own foundations.'[69] (*Henry V* famously shows how the illusion of justice relies, above all, upon effective myth-making, indeed overt propaganda. The most unjust actions become painted in the colours of justice though the control of people's perceptions.[70])

Meritocracy is, by definition, a system of measurement. But so is feudal aristocracy. Only their criteria differ. Shakespeare avoids portraying one as justice and the other as injustice. Injustice in Shakespeare arises not out of the 'failure' of one set of political forces (feudal, aristocratic, monarchical) to fulfil ideas of the other (meritocratic, republican, communist[71]), which we would certainly expect from a straightforwardly binary failure of injustice to fulfil the ends of some justice theory. Meritocracy and republicanism are undermined just as surely as feudalism or monarchy. Again, the point is not a nihilist one, which would render meaningless any search for justice, although it might hint at reasons why the familiar, programmatic theories invariably end up more problematical than their authors would have wished. The point, rather, is that gross injustice should be seen less as the right concept of justice 'gone wrong', and more as the perpetual crises surrounding any purportedly 'right' theory of justice. As in *Antigone*, injustice abounds in *Macbeth* or in Shakespeare's political dramas, but not principally as the application of a 'wrong measure'. There is no obvious concept, no theory or regime of justice that produces any such measure in an uncontroversial way.

---

69 Martin, 2001, p. 1. Cf. Leggatt, 1988, pp. 1–31.
70 See, e.g., Rackin, *supra* n. 22, at 30, 72, 80, 82, 114–15. See also Pugliatti, 1996, pp. 137–53.
71 England's history of peasant uprisings had long generated proto-Marxist discourses of abolition of private property and class hierarchy, which Shakespeare famously dramatises in Cade's rebellion, 2H6 4.2–7. See, e.g., Ward, 1999, pp. 138–40; Pugliatti, 1996, pp. 154–73.

Chapter 6

Injustice as measurement

La moitié de ma vie a mis l'autre au tombeau.[1]

Pierre Corneille

6.1 Introduction

Despite the modernity of themes in *Macbeth* or in Shakespeare's other political dramas, their nominally ancient or feudal settings keep a foot in the past. Heralding new worlds, they trace the demise of old ones. Of all the plays in the corpus, the society of *The Merchant of Venice* remains least anchored in any such traditional order. It presents the shift from feudalism to modernity not as a transition, but as a *fait accompli*. Shakespeare's outstandingly modern play offers fertile ground for the study of measurement as the criterion of justice in our own time. *The Merchant of Venice* may lack *Macbeth's* gorily medieval apparel. No Duncan, no personal will controls Venice's suit-and-tie world. Power instead remains diffused through modernity's Kafkaesque machinery of credit records and law reports. Beneath its jovially businesslike veneer – isn't joviality always the veneer of the modern business world? – Shakespeare's Venice matches *Macbeth's* brutality point for point, maintaining indeed the power to snuff out, from its inception, any modern Antigone, any modern Macbeth. Modernity does not improve upon, but merely replaces the terror of feudal swords with that of writs, decrees and lawsuits.[2]

The psychology of the dominant Venetian class, I shall argue in this chapter, is so drenched in the vocabulary of measurement, its elite so compulsively generates and re-generates that mindset anew, that no other order, no ethical or political alternative, becomes imaginable. Every human relationship, friendly or hostile, reduces to measurement. Human value collapses into the

---

1 'Half my life's a grave dug for the other.' Cid 3.3.810.
2 Also replacing armed coercion is the rise of the surveillance state, as displayed by characters such as the King in *Henry V*, Claudius and Polonius in *Hamlet*, the Duke in *Measure for Measure*, Polixines in *The Winter's Tale*, or Propsero in *The Tempest*. See, e.g., Dollimore, 1994; Greenblatt, 1994; Wilson, 1993, pp. 153–57.

lexicon of fungible comparison, monetary terms being typical, but by no means sole examples, as measurement reaches further, into non-monetary domains. By the end, the play's socio-legal order has altogether confirmed itself, altogether closed in on itself, unlike other Shakespearean comedies, which provide more open endings, richer in alternative paths for their characters. The point is not that feudalism had known a more humane world, nor that its hierarchy lacked measurement as both a requisite of justice and origin or injustice. In *Troilus and Cressida*, Ulysses' praise for 'degree, priority and place'[3] harks back, after all, to a feudal mythology; he pays homage also to the internal 'unity . . . of states'.[4] Modernity proliferates justice-as-measurement as the displacement of unity. If Shakespeare depicts feudalism as the inscription of the human within both brutal and mythicised worlds, he shows also that what we affectionately call 'humanism' emerges precisely as Western history is headed towards its steady de-humanisation of humanity.

To make such claims is to invite the retort: 'Would justice be better served without measurement?' or 'Should we not simply replace bad criteria of measurement with better ones? Perhaps we simply need measurement 'with a human face', or 'socially responsible' measurement?' Yet those queries continue to presuppose the traditional binarism, according to which justice is achieved by eliminating that which opposes or negates it. The problem is not that justice ought to be achieved without measurement, but rather that justice does indeed require precisely that practice of measurement which necessarily entails injustice.

6.2 'Will much impeach the justice of the state'

Measurement surfaces as the hallmark of justice in modernity in various ways. Venice's nominally monarchical figure, the Duke, for example, confronts limits on his powers, through the operation of bureaucratised law, far more overtly than his counterparts in the other plays.[5] To be sure, one characteristic of political modernity is the strengthening of national sovereignty along Hobbesian lines,[6] with the increasing concentration of power at the centre, and subordination of competing exercises of jurisdiction, as displayed in the culmination of the second tetralogy in *Henry V*, with its hyper-personalised, iconicised sovereign monarch.[7] Another characteristic, however, runs, at least on surface appearances, in the opposite direction. Power is disseminated

---

3 Tro 1.3.85. As noted, Shakespeare lineation follows OXF4.
4 Tro 1.3.99.
5 On the role of the common law as the merchant class's weapon against the power of the monarchy and aristocracy, see, e.g., Raffield, 2010, pp. 25–29; Wilson, 1993, pp. 131–37; Ward, 1993, p. 131.
6 See, e.g., Ward, 1999, pp. 20–21; Wilson, 1993, pp. 136–37.
7 See, e.g., Dollimore and Sinfield, 2002, p. 218; Greenblatt, 1994, p. 33; Rackin, 1990, pp. 29–30; Tennenhouse, 1986, p. 84.

through law in de-personalised ways, as enacted nowhere more forcefully than in *The Merchant of Venice.*

Shakespearean drama is replete with monarchical or ducal figures confronting tenuous holds on power, such as, to name only the two most directly comparable to Venice's Duke, in view of their temporarily abridged power, the Duke Senior of *As You Like It* or *The Tempest*'s Prospero. The limits those men face are of a more traditional, power-political character, and not of the quasi-constitutionalised, formal-legal character that Shakespeare presents in Venice. Similarly, any formal-legal circumscriptions of ducal authority in *The Two Gentlemen of Verona, The Comedy of Errors, A Midsummer Night's Dream, Romeo and Juliet, Measure for Measure* or *Othello*, are certainly never emphasised, and may be conspicuously overridden.[8] The Duke in *The Merchant of Venice* is the only such figure in Shakespeare who seriously confronts the express legal constraint of having to avoid taking, or being seen to take, action *ultra vires*. None of his counterparts in the other plays have so expressly laid down upon their offices the kinds of boundaries prescribed by a quasi-autonomous *corpus juris*. That configuration of law and power underscores the peremptory emphasis on the play's proto-liberal modernity.[9] Nowhere in Shakespeare do we find the kind of rule-of-law explanations that are still invoked by states and businesses today to assess the risks of investment and trade in foreign jurisdictions, indeed on an embryonically global scale, with *rex non potest peccare* far from sight.

> The Duke cannot deny the course of law,
> For the commodity that strangers have
> With us in Venice, if it be denied,
> Will much impeach the justice of the state,
> Since that the trade and profit of the city
> Consisteth of all nations.[10]

The only possible analogies to such formal-legal limitations might be found in the Roman Republican settings of *Julius Caesar* or *Coriolanus*. Those storylines, however, maintain a root in antiquity, evoking less immediately a proto-liberal, proto-capitalist modernity as stark as that portrayed in *The Merchant of Venice*. Venice follows not any individual leader, but rather the ubiquitous yet faceless operation of a law stewarded, like H. L. A. Hart's bourgeois legal subjects, by market actors,[11] and by the independent,

---

8 See, e.g., Err 5.1.392; MND 4.1.178.
9 See, e.g., Drakakis, 2010, p. 3 (noting Venice's reputation for democratic institutions in Shakespeare's time).
10 MV 3.3.26–31; cf. MV 4.1.103–6, 215–16. On the Duke's official limitations, see, e.g., Mahood, 2003, p. 16.
11 See this book, Chapter 4, text accompanying nn. 37. See also, e.g., Holland, 2005, pp. xxiv–xxxi; Cerasano, 2003a, pp. 7–15; Ward, 1999, pp. 127–28; Bruster, 1992, pp. 12–19.

professionalised and technocratic judiciary, who emerge as motors of the modern state.

If *Henry V* provides an 'Austinian', 'top-down' power structure, *The Merchant of Venice* ushers in Hart's world of citizen-participatory, 'facilitative' law, followed, right on cue, by Dworkin's world of the 'hard case'. The play's famous dispute incarnates that clash of norms lacking any obvious priority *inter se*, therefore requiring professional, expert appraisal of a quasi-autonomous body of legal norms, institutions and procedures,[12] indeed as part of the progressive development of the entirety of the legal regime. That kind of Dworkinian hard case in *The Merchant of Venice* knows no parallel in Shakespeare. Other such petty (not in the sense of 'unimportant', but in the sense of being focused on discrete individuals, taking the form of actually or potentially bipolar litigation, as opposed, say, to large-scale constitutional or public law matters) or private-law controversies[13] mostly present factual difficulties – Who did what and why? They include, for example, the accusations against Egeon in *The Comedy of Errors*,[14] against Hero in *Much Ado about Nothing*,[15] against Romeo in *Romeo and Juliet*,[16] against Falstaff in *Henry IV, Part Two*[17] or *The Merry Wives of Windsor*,[18] against Desdemona[19] or Iago[20] in *Othello*, against Angelo in *Measure for Measure*,[21] or against Hermione in *A Winter's Tale*.[22] Those problems are not necessarily simple or straightforward. They are not, however, so emphatically displayed as indeterminate conflicts of norms, requiring any such elaborate, professionalised, self-contained and self-directing legal apparatus.

That proto-liberal modernity of *The Merchant of Venice* provides a context for injustice, not merely, as a Marxist critique might view it, through an ethos of individualised liberty as justice, but more broadly through its ethos of measurement as justice. This society dominated by formal, individual liberties may elicit its dependence upon measurement in a particularly overt way, but, as we have seen, measurement is not the sole province of liberal theories. Marxism's 'from each according to his abilities, to each according to his needs' is also a maxim of measurement, no less immune to producing injustice than

---

12 MV 4.1.103–06.
13 More overtly political cases, as in the dispute between Bolingbroke and Mowbray in *Richard II*, or concerning the law of war, as in *Henry V*, or the conflicts in *Titus Andronicus*, *Julius Caesar* or *Coriolanus*, also cannot be said to stand as typical of Dworkin's hard cases.
14 Err 1.1.13–22.
15 Ado 4.1.32–42.
16 Rom 3.1.181.
17 2H4 2.1.71–72, 84–101.
18 Wiv 1.1.93–94.
19 Oth 5.2.74–76.
20 Oth 5.2.238, 307–28.
21 MM 5.1.39–42.
22 WT 3.2.12–19.

are the liberal models. Measurement in Marxism is, admittedly, not identical to that of liberalism, as Marx, like Plato or Rousseau, places strong emphasis on unity. As we saw in the preceding chapter, however, unity theories entail their own production of injustice, not through the sheer failure or negation of unity, but precisely through its realisation.[23]

6.3 'Pageants of the sea'

A risk for modern viewers is to view the overall economic life in *The Merchant of Venice* as ordinary, requiring no more scrutiny than any other play that might feature commercial transactions. The play's famous loan for 3,000 ducats means little to us. In many of today's currencies, that number triggers at most an idea of a solid, not an exceptional amount. Shakespeare's public would have recognised the sum as vast, expecting no less from Venice's reputation for wealth and decadent excess.[24] That oversight can distort our view of the plot, making the play's financial context appear mundane. Shylock's incredulity at the news that his daughter had spent 'fourscore ducats' in one night,[25] tantamount to as many as thousands of euros today, reminds us that his society does not deal in trifles. Even modernising performances on today's stages tend to present Shakespeare's Venetians through an idiom of upper-class bourgeoisie, and not of the arrant, *Dallas*-style excess that the play suggests. If today's performers were, for example, to substitute '3 million ducats' for dramatic effect, our audiences might more readily grasp the prominence and pervasiveness of the play's economics, emblematic of the pervasive ethos of justice-as-measurement, dominating and structuring the characters and plot.

The only wealth generally at issue in Shakespeare's medieval historical dramas is land and its associated titles. By contrast, no play in the corpus more insistently refers to moveable property and transient ownership, wealth or credit literally in motion, than *The Merchant of Venice*: Antonio's far-flung ships, the valuables stolen from Shylock and smuggled away, Bassanio's volatile credit flow, the impending transfer of Portia's wealth, the rush to Venice to secure Antonio's debt and the sequence of ring transfers. Another sign of the play's modernity is that wealth in the old, aristocratic form of land ownership is never mentioned.[26] When Antonio has his four 'argosies'[27]

---

23 Cf. this chapter, Section 6.10.
24 See PEN2 113. See also CAM4 83. Holland, 2005, pp. xxvi–xxviii.
25 MV 3.1.101–5.
26 Here too, the Roman plays, albeit staging an earlier period of history, also hint at an incipient modernity: pre-modern, in the sense that it is still land, as an object of political and military conquest, which is the important property; yet modern in the sense that the associated titles of nobility which would later emerge in medieval Europe are, so to speak, already dispensed with in Rome's formally or functionally republican polity.
27 MV 1.1.9. See this chapter, Section 6.4.

abroad, when Portia attracts noble suitors from far and wide[28] (despite lacking any noble title of her own), it becomes obvious that, in our day, they would occupy the positions of multi-millionaires. They exude the free-market extremes not of a moderately, but of an embarrassingly wealthy Antonio and Portia, an abysmally indebted Bassanio, a meteorically ambitious Lorenzo. Neither Venice nor Belmont are places of thrift. Nowhere in the corpus are money, and its manifold legal trappings – finance, credit, interest, debt – regurgitated with such excess, such psychological fixation, on its purely measureable character: 'Take thrice thy money';[29] 'Pay him six thousand . . . double six thousand, and then treble that';[30] 'If every ducat in six thousand ducats/Were in six parts, and every part a ducat'[31]. Money and measurement live, breathe and reproduce on their own.[32]

The merchant Antonio opens the play, announcing his cryptic sadness.[33] Antonio's de-individualised cronies, indistinguishably a 'Salarino' and a 'Salanio',[34] spontaneously reduce Antonio's psychological state, his gloom, to measureable quantities, namely, Antonio's commercial risks.[35] Salarino opens the explanation with reference to Antonio's mind, which is assumed to be 'tossing on the ocean',[36] a mind indeed immersed in socio-economic forces reduced to terms of measurement.

> There where your argosies with portly[37] sail,
> Like signors and rich burghers on the flood,
> Or as it were the pageants of the sea,
> Do overpeer[38] the petty traffickers
> That curtsy to them, do them reverence,
> As they fly by them with their woven wings.[39]

The play, here too, opens by announcing a completed, proto-capitalist displacement of feudalism. It is no longer kings and counts, but now 'rich burghers' who receive the 'curtsy' of a 'petty' entourage, indeed appropriating that 'pageant' of social difference that had once served to display aristocratic

---

28 MV 1.1.167–72.
29 MV 4.1.224, 231.
30 MV 3.2.297–98.
31 MV 4.1.84–5.
32 See MV 1.3.93. Cf. Pol 1.9.1257^{b}1–1258^{a}19. Cf. also Drakakis, 2010, p. 55.
33 MV 1.1.1. See, e.g. ARD3 392; PEN2 105–6.
34 Further compounded with a third character, the messenger 'Salerio'. On these roles and their spellings, see, e.g., ARD3 163, 428–30.
35 MV 1.1.8–40.
36 MV 1.1.8.
37 'Portly' is glossed as, 'stately; but the next line suggests big-bellied corpulence, i.e. wind in the ships' sails billowing them out'. OXF4 103.
38 Cf. ARD3 171, noting ARD2's suggestion of a pun on 'peer of the realm'.
39 MV 1.1.9–14.

privilege. Not only do wealth, and, in the market world, concomitant power distinguish those social classes. Rather, the distance between the high, 'portly' and 'overpeering' vessel and the low, 'petty' one reduces the comparison to terms of literal, physical measurement – yes, partly in monetary terms, but also in the crudest terms of measurement *as such*.

Throughout Europe, terms like *Your Highness*, *Votre Altesse* and *Ihre Hoheit*, had long emerged as almost literal measurements between sovereign and subject. In the busy harbours of the market-driven world, any large and wealthy vessel can sail along to exact curtsies from lowlier ships. The powerful craft 'flying by' the weak ones again translates power as a measured and compared quantity of speed. That passage's nautical imagery, in conjunction with Salarino's first, instinctive reply to Antonio, all join to underscore modernity's figurative inundation by the law of markets and measures, reaching beyond our pockets, into our brains. Salanio further underscores the suggestion of psychological immersion in the consciousness of wealth, reminding his friends that 'the better part' of his 'affections', too, would lay with such commercial 'ventures':[40] 'And every object that might make me fear/Misfortune to my ventures, out of doubt,/Would make me sad.'[41]

6.4 'Like a golden fleece'

An 'argosy' is the name for a 'large merchant ship',[42] which, according to Mahood, was privately owned, and 'replaced the state-owned trading galleys of Venice. The name derives from Ragusa (now Dubrovnik) where many of them were built.'[43] Drakakis meanwhile observes Alexander Pope's 'suggestion . . . that the word derives its origin from the famous ship *Argo*, since there are two further references in the play to the story of Jason'.[44] Those two interpretations in no way exclude each other. The dramatist could easily have had both in mind. Pope's idea deserves attention. Shakespeare's educated viewers would have recognised allusions to the well-known legends of the Argonauts, which appear, for example, in Ovid. To compare: with conspicuously feminist insight – not his last – Pierre Corneille's *Médée* (1635) will present Jason as a brash, Machiavellian social climber, coarsely boasting about his manipulation of Medea and of other women for the sole sake of his personal advancement.

In the opening scene of *The Merchant of Venice*, Bassanio's seeming verses of love thinly veil more prosaic ends. His first reference to Portia concerns her

40 MV 1.1.15–16.
41 MV 1.1.21–22.
42 Crystal and Crystal, 2002, p. 21.
43 CAM4 69. Cf. PEN2 106. Drakakis adds, 'The earliest form was *ragusye* but it appears in English in the 16th century as *Aragouse*, *Arragouese* or *Arragosa*.' ARD3 170.
44 ARD3 170. Cf. PEN2 106.

wealth:[45] 'In Belmont is a lady richly left.'[46] The play's obsessive language of measurement and comparison hovers close by.

> Her name is Portia, nothing undervalued
> To Cato's daughter, Brutus' Portia;
> Nor is the whole wide world ignorant of her worth.[47]

At that point, Bassanio's identification with Jason emerges,

> For the four winds blow in from every coast
> Renownèd suitors, and her sunny locks
> Hang on her temples like a golden fleece,
> Which makes her seat of Belmont Colchis' strand,
> And many Jasons come in quest of her.[48]

Drakakis recalls the golden fleece as 'the prize' sought by the Argonauts. 'Portia's hair is likened to the *golden fleece* because she is the possessor of a rich inheritance, but the idea of the *golden fleece* has a wider commercial resonance.'[49] Bassanio's value, assessed via comparison – 'rivalry' – with those 'many Jasons', must measure up to Portia's.

> O my Antonio, had I but the means
> To hold a rival place with one of them,
> I have a mind presages me such thrift.[50]

'In its two meanings of "profit" and "success",' observes Mahood, 'thrift' will count as 'another important word in the play's language'.[51] I shall further argue, however, that even the financially precarious debtor Bassanio nevertheless, and more importantly, remains within the socially safe, privileged ranks of the Venetian economic elite, with little regard for the brutality, the injustice, always generated through Venice's norms and institutions of justice, through which that superior class maintains power.

6.5 'Mine own teaching'

Portia's entrance does not accidentally parallel Antonio's, he being her counterpart at the highest echelons of the play's socio-economic class structure.

---

45 ARD3 186; CAM4 77; OXF4 111.
46 MV 1.1.161.
47 MV 1.1.165–7.
48 MV 1.1.168–72.
49 ARD3 186 (original italics). Cf. Girard, 2004, p. 354.
50 MV 1.1.172–75.
51 CAM2 77. Cf. ARD3 187; OXF4 111; PEN2 110.

Portia, too, declares herself melancholic, 'aweary of this great world'.[52] She hears a reply different from those bandied about by Antonio's toadies. Portia's confidante Nerissa, both a woman and, albeit still a gentlewoman, lower born than Portia, and therefore excluded from Venice's highest ranks, stands at a critical distance[53] from Venice's mercantile hierarchy. If, as some scholars suggest, 'Nerissa' derives from the Italian *nero*,[54] then Nerissa may indeed, as will become apparent, elicit the darker side of a seemingly 'golden' Portia. Unlike Antonio's companions, Nerissa finds no cause, aside from the needless excess of Portia's wealth, which, unlike Antonio's, is now depicted as something ethically questionable.

Nerissa questions whether Portia is indeed 'weary' at all: 'You would be [weary], sweet madam, if your miseries were in the same abundance as your good fortunes are.'[55] Nerissa all but quotes the *Nicomachean Ethics*[56] *verbatim*: '[F]or aught I see, they are as sick that surfeit with too much as they that starve with nothing. It is no mean happiness therefore, to be seated in the mean.'[57] Portia's posture as 'seated', like Antonio's assurance, '[m]y ventures are not in one bottom trusted',[58] nag us to peer beneath those 'bottoms' on which each is 'seated', in search of a darker underbelly. By recalling the plight of the poor – those at the other end of the culture of wealth and markets from which Portia so 'richly'[59] benefits – Nerissa thrusts Portia's uncritically apolitical lament into an ethical and political context. She does so in the Aristotelian language of comparison and measurement. Nerissa applies a classical standard of measurement in order to call a modern regime of measurement into question.

In Shakespeare's feudal plays, mythical ideals of justice may be constructed around figures like Edward III, Henry V, Talbot or Duncan, but those figures nevertheless represent the flesh-and-blood of a commemorated past. Again reinforcing the play's modernity, any such ideals in *The Merchant of Venice* have been utterly collapsed into such packaged maxims, obscurely retrieved from classical or Biblical antiquity, but lacking any comparable presence as a

---

52 MV 1.2.1–2.
53 According to Drakakis, the name 'Nerissa' may suggest a 'contrast . . . between the mistress, Portia, who is "fair" (1.1.162), and Nerissa who is "dark"'. ARD3 164. On that reading, Nerissa's role can more broadly be construed as providing contrast and counterpoint with regard to Portia, reflecting Portia's shadowed sides, contrary to Salarino's and Salario's fawning replies. Cf. PEN2 110.
54 See, e.g., ARD3 164.
55 MV 1.2.3–5.
56 Shakespeare's familiarity with Plato and Aristotle reflects that of educated Renaissance authors. See generally, e.g., Copenhaver and Schmitt, 1992. Platonic and Aristotelian ideals emerge in *The Merchant of Venice* not in their usual Renaissance posture of a living antiquity, but as bygone, unrecoverable memories in Venice's modern market world. See, e.g., MV 5.1.56–57, 63.
57 MV 1.2.5–8. Cf. NE 2. 2, 8–9.
58 MV 1.1.42.
59 MV 1.1.161.

deeply felt point of reference. Similarly, Lorenzo will invoke a Platonic image of cosmic unity or harmony only late in the play, and then as an afterthought, something peripheral and distant,[60] devoid of ethical meaning in modernity. Jessica declares herself 'never merry', she is never brought into harmony, into internal unity, by its 'sweet' sounds.[61] A disunited modernity is 'out of joint'.[62]

Portia's socio-legal status is more complex than Macbeth's. Even this heiress of high economic rank, as a woman, is legally subject first to her father's, then to her husband's, will.[63] Portia's dead father controls her destiny beyond the grave through his — written and legally binding — will,[64] emblematic of women's entrenched legal subordination. If the more conventional bar to women's choices in Shakespeare is the living father's authority,[65] *The Merchant of Venice* underscores its modernity by reducing that authority to an instrument binding in law, and therefore no longer needing the father whose will it expresses. That same political society which secures Portia's privilege simultaneously assures that the will of a dead man overpowers the will of a living woman.[66] Portia will pursue justice for herself, securing as much power as possible within this man's world, by simultaneously upholding yet manipulating the very legal system that subordinates not only others, like the 'alien' Shylock,[67] a subordination in which she will vigorously participate, but also subordinates her as a woman. Portia ends up doing nothing in this regime without drawing personal gain, as the only available path to her own empowerment, and most so when her conduct appears altruistic — just. I shall shortly argue that Portia, as a woman, pursues whatever justice she can — optimising and securing her status within Venice's socio-ethnic power structure, which even the debtor Bassanio can provide for her — by participating in the injustice which that power structure, to preserve its identity and hierarchical privilege, must do to others.

The murky area between the extent to which a woman may, and the limit beyond which she may not, exercise her liberty, is no oddity in the world of well-bred Shakespearean women. In *The Comedy of Errors*, Adriana, on the one hand, deplores men's domination,[68] yet, on the other, benefits from a

---

60 MV 5.1.56–57, 63.
61 MV 5.1.69. Cf. Drakakis, 2010, pp. 106–12; Raffield, 2010, pp. 22, 29–33.
62 Ham 1.5.196.
63 Cf. Sokol and Sokol, 2003, p. 126; Wilson, 1993, p. 214 *et passim*. Other options, such as entry into chaste religious orders, impose their own limitations on women's choices. See, e.g., MND 1.1.65–6; Ado 4.1.240–43; MM 1.4.10–13.
64 MV 1.2.89–91, 2.1.15–19.
65 See, e.g., MND 1.1.22–121; Rom 3.5.124–5, 142–95; Ham 1.3.88–136.
66 MV 1.2.23–24. Cf. Tennenhouse, 1986, p. 53.
67 MV 4.1.345. Much has been written about the status of Jews in Venice as legal aliens, and against a broader English and European historical backdrop. See, e.g., Drakakis, 2010, pp. 17–48; Shapiro, 1996; Halio, 1993, pp. 1–13; Mahood, 2003, pp. 2–22.
68 Err. 2.1.10–29.

socio-legal order that authorises her to command and indeed to beat her household servant Dromio, precisely as her husband does.[69] Portia half-protests her subordination to her father's will, but never shuns that wealth and privilege which offer her upward mobility within the bounds of the prevailing order. She both falls victim to her society's injustice within the context of existing law and politics, yet will also, precisely in availing herself of the means to overcome that injustice, to rise above it, actively perpetuate the same injustice against other socio-legal subordinates, in rising and remaining above them, which her liberalised society's socio-legal regime requires.

If we uncritically accept Venice's prevailing socio-legal order 'on its own terms', then Nerissa's counsel amounts to nothing more than a prim, moralistic injunction that we should be more attentive to the poor when we enjoy our own good fortune. The more important question concerns those 'terms' of Venetian law and society. The injustices in which Portia and the other Venetians will participate will not merely be the application of wrong measures, or the misapplication of right ones – injustice as habitually understood on the binary model. Measurement itself is in crisis, constantly promising characters the only means of achieving the justice they, we, seek at the expense of justice for others, with injustice the constant result – invisible injustice when justice is viewed, as we habitually do, as a sheer sum-total of isolated ethical contexts, yet immediately rendered visible when we renounce our conventionally convenient amnesia of justice's broader, systemic contexts. Contrary to the bright-eyed formulas of the binarist models (that is, to get more justice, we simply need to negate more injustice), justice shows itself to be a more strictly zero-sum game. The privileged members of this hierarchical society, a slaveholding society,[70] cannot easily be rendered 'just' when they benefit from the socio-legal hierarchy. Nerissa might, then, on a conventional understanding of justice, within the immediately isolated context, be charging Portia with applying the wrong measure. However, her retort can also be read in more critical, systemically socio-political terms, as a challenge to the entire unequal order from which Portia benefits (and from which Nerissa, too, must benefit: can we really expect her to find some other, somehow 'better', employment?).

Portia's reply to Nerissa avoids taking up any challenge that would require her to measure her conduct according to those same ethical principles which she will invoke not only to justify the socio-legal order, but to turn that order against Shylock, who is rendered by law an inferior, a non-citizen, being a Jew.[71] For the time being, she pointedly dismisses the suggestion of scrutinising her own conduct in view of any such principles: 'It is a good divine [clergyman] that follows his own instructions.'[72] Prophetic of her later, hypocritical

69 Err. 2.1.79–81. Cf. Heinze, 2009e, pp. 258–62.
70 MV 4.1.89.
71 MV 4.1.345.
72 MV 1.2.14–15.

role as advocate of justice, in which she will impose law, and its ethical values, upon Shylock, her socio-legal inferior, that disdain in her first scene indeed announces a conveniently jocular confession of hypocrisy, 'I can easier teach twenty what were good to be done' – as she will indeed later do – 'than to be one of the twenty to follow mine own teaching.'[73] Although moral hypocrisy is a common theme in literature and in Shakespeare, it emerges specifically in *The Merchant of Venice* such that it is precisely the socio-ethnically privileged characters' pursuit of justice that will constantly result in injustice. The avowedly Christian Portia can pummel Shylock within the safe framework of the legal order, and will do it with panache, as modernity's writs and decrees always apparel violence with decorous legitimacy. What she can never do, without contradiction, is to defeat Shylock while challenging that socio-legal order. Although money constantly exemplifies measurement-as-injustice in the play, measurement, at the most foundational level, proves pervasive beyond the play's sheer commercial framework. Portia will measure Shylock according to the most fundamental principles of law and ethics from which she will exempt both herself and the full-fledged, privileged Venetian males.

Portia's predicament, like ours, is not that she lives within a clear ethos of justice, whose criteria she either altogether fulfils or altogether betrays. She instead either passively suffers the injustice of patriarchy, or actively causes injustice to another socio-legal outsider. Her inherited wealth, not aristocratic in origin, presumably derives from the same source as Antonio's or other wealthy Venetians', that is, from commerce. The ethos of commerce is in principle anti-aristocratic. Anyone with something to buy or to sell can enter the marketplace, society's *pro forma* equaliser, regardless of rank or (non-aristocratic) class. Marketplace equality measures out marketplace justice. Yet that same justice, not contradicting but consistent with its own principles, undermines marketplace equality. As an equal participant in the marketplace, Portia's father has accumulated wealth, and then exercises the socio-economic autonomy that it grants him. He attaches his daughter to property interests that leave her bereft of the selfsame autonomy, choice of a husband, that the sheer ethos of the marketplace, that is, liberalised equality would grant. Far from overcoming women's socio-legal dependency, rooted in feudalism, Venice's commercial world merely commodifies it. Portia's father creates a lottery, reducing her to a prize trinket for the arbitrarily lucky suitor, irrespective of her wishes.

The limited autonomy Portia inherits, along with her father's wealth, she will exercise in the same way. The same system of market-based justice that secures her father's, and therefore her own wealth, will also augment the socio-legal autonomy which that wealth nourishes, and which secures her father's will by abrogating hers. The market's ethos of merit and competition translates

---

73 MV 1.2.15–17.

into the lottery designed to measure the man who is best for Portia, granting her to the most eligible bidder. The marketplace values that would perform justice, in securing her father's fortune, equally create a meritocratic competition with Portia as the object of purchase. Contrary to the conventional ethos of the marketplace, which promises increasing prosperity (an increasing 'pie') in lieu of a zero-sum game, Venice's mercantile regime does not even-handedly expand social autonomy for all rational actors. It fiercely expands some people's autonomy at the expense of others' autonomy.

Disguised in court, Portia joins the ranks of privileged Venetian men who will crush the *de jure* alien Shylock, while Christian faith is invoked to legitimate the prevailing socio-legal order. Neither Portia nor, as Shylock points out, the other Venetians, ever demand 'mercy'[74] for Venice's 'many a purchased slave',[75] but only for the play's privileged tycoon Antonio. Any such quest would require more than 'justice' within the principles of the existing legal order, a step that Portia, as she had made clear to Nerissa, and shows in her later actions, has no intention of taking.

6.6 'The complexion of a devil'

Moving on from Portia's weariness, she and Nerissa next discuss the suitors arrived in hope of Portia's 'worth'. As a commodity, the 'golden fleece', Portia is instrumentally valued for that profit motive. Similarly, we will only ever see Bassanio, who describes Antonio, with the obvious pun on 'dear',[76] as his 'dearest friend',[77] interact with Antonio in connection to the loan.[78] Lorenzo, meanwhile, sues for a wealthy wife, eloping with the Jew's daughter without Shylock's consent – an affair of state for Hermia's father in *Midsummernight's Dream*[79] or for Desdemona's father *Othello*,[80] yet for which Jessica's 'alien' father will have no such recourse. In seizing Jessica, Lorenzo will actively conspire in robbing the wealth that Jessica steals from her father.[81] Like Portia, Jessica does greater justice to herself only by committing injustice against another, who indeed turns out to be that same Shylock. Far from any criminal or civil action being brought against Lorenzo, the theft will be ratified and enforced in law.[82] Law transforms that injustice into justice.

Bassanio's privileged social status, even despite his debts, can secure Portia's within the highest ranks of the Venetian hierarchy. In the meantime, contriving

---

74 MV 4.1.179.
75 MV 4.1.89.
76 See, e.g., Crystal and Crystal, 2002, p. 116.
77 MV 3.2.290.
78 Cf. Rackin, 1990, p. 101 (discussing R2 2.1.57).
79 MND 1.1.
80 Oth 1.3.
81 MV 2.4.29–32.
82 MV 4.1.377–80.

a game whereby Nerissa names six of the prior suitors in turn,[83] Portia launches into the Shakespearean corpus's exemplary litany of ethnic slurs,[84] as each man is measured solely in terms of familiar national traits – the Neapolitan is a fool,[85] the German is crude[86] – in a crescendo that culminates with her anticipatory branding of the Moroccan Prince, before he has even arrived, as having 'the complexion of a devil'.[87] In this world of masques,[88] Portia will plead in court disguised as 'Balthasar',[89] traditionally one of the eastern Magi, not only underscoring the play's recurring theme of de-sacralisation of the holy, but subsuming through mockery the image of the kind of oriental prince that the ethnic outsider Morocco represents, at the same time, subsuming the name of her own socio-legal subordinate, her servant Balthasar.

Given the significance of saints in the same Roman Catholicism whose God Portia will invoke to justify the legal system,[90] she strikingly notes her revulsion at marrying the dark-skinned alien, even if he had 'the condition of a saint'.[91] All foreigners, all aliens, will be shunned in favour of the ethnically indigenous Bassanio, who will serve as Portia's ladder from her already-privileged status in backwater Belmont up to the top of Venetian society. The opaque, exogenous Other will be shunned in favour of a reproduction of that which is endogenous, familiar, the copied self, with obvious irony on the characters' constant profession of universalist Christian values. Hence the residual ideal, or shadow, of unity, now the unity of liberal modernity – freely chosen, not in a spirit of Christian universal love, but with a xenophobic zeal to tighten ethnically Venetian-Christian ties within the tightest of exclusive socio-economic communities, defined all the more sharply in contradistinction to Portia's, and the Venetians', lists of excluded, socio-ethnic and socio-legal outsiders.

Shylock, too, like the foreign suitors, will be loathed by the elite Venetian power structure, to whose aid the disguised Portia will run as *jurisconsultus ex machina*: less, to express it in modern terms, like one of our own struggling

---

83 MV 1.2.35–37.
84 Portia's roll-call of national stereotypes is not unprecedented. Master and servant play a similar game in *The Comedy of Errors*. See CE 3.2.116–44. Unlike that exchange, however, Portia's remarks more pointedly reduce a series of living individuals to ethnic types.
85 MV 1.2.39. Cf. OXF4 114, glossing 'colt'.
86 MV 1.2.81–96.
87 MV 1.2.127. Cf. MV 2.7.79. Devils were customarily portrayed as black, not red. See, e.g., NOR2 1127, n. 1. Cf. NOR2 444, n. 5; OXF4 117, 152; PEN2 113, 126.
88 MV 2.4.21, 2.5.23, 8.
89 See, e.g., Mahood, 2003, pp. 36–40.
90 MV 4.1.192–3.
91 MV 1.2.126. Cf., on the miscegenation taboo in the play, and Shylock as 'metaphorically "black" and therefore diabolical', see Drakakis, 2010, p. 73. See also, generally, Hall, 1992.

legal aid attorneys who sacrifices a lucrative career to help the poor, and more like Lovells or Baker & MacKenzie rushing to the aid of Shell or Exxon (and indeed appearing to do so *pro bono publico*, as a 'good Christian'!). Portia aiding Antonio is the wealthy and powerful aiding the wealthy and powerful. Aiding him at what? To save his life, and above all to restore him to his *status quo ante* of wealth and power, as our most powerful and prestigious law firms do today. On the threshold of liberal, capitalist modernity, unity forms part of justice only insofar as it is freely chosen. Do the Venetians practice the transition they preach, from the 'old' Jewish law to the 'new' Christian law of universal unity? Not at all. What they practice is the transition from the old, mythical unity of Christian, feudal hierarchy to the new law of the liberal marketplace, in which they can self-select their group unity along ethnic and socio-economic lines, seceding from Venice's cosmopolitan and purportedly Christian humanity, to take refuge in the elective unity of the economic power elite.

Just as Portia's father has made her a coveted commodity, so does Portia, in her game with Nerissa, pluck the foreign suitors, one by one, like goods from a shelf, mocking them as knockoff imports, not fully human; about the Frenchman, for example, 'God made him, and therefore let him pass for a man.'[92] For Lynda Boose, 'it may well be Portia ... who can best lay claim to being the signified "merchant" of the play's ambiguous title'.[93] Shylock, too, will be merely another alien for disposal. Relentlessly throughout the play, Shylock will be addressed or referred to not by name, but only by his generic status: 'Jew', 'Jew', 'Jew'. Portia, this most socio-economically successful of Shakespearean women, will emerge as Shakespeare's premier racist,[94] outdoing even Iago precisely in her nonchalance.[95] Although Othello, and certainly Aaron in *Titus Andonicus*, become targets of racism, it is in *The Merchant of Venice* that racism becomes tied deeply into the world of liberalised markets, through their ethos, their psychology, of fiercely competitive, inter-personal measurement. Some performances soften the embarrassment by playing the Prince of Morocco as a comically flamboyant warrior-type, and the – also ethnically distinct – Prince of Aragon as foolish and effete, eliciting comical effects which were arguably pursued on Shakespeare's stage. Dignified performances of both roles, as has been done for Shylock for over a century, would nevertheless be altogether consistent with the text, and could highlight the

---

92 MV 1.2.54–55. Cf. MV 1.2.84–86, 96.
93 Boose, 1988, p. 249.
94 Some scholars cast doubt upon the distinction long drawn between a stark, male and competitive Venice and a supposedly soft, nurturing Belmont. See, e.g., Tennenhouse, 1991.
95 The Nurse's racism in *Titus Andronicus* is facially cruder (Tit 4.2.59–68), lacking Portia's refined, linguistic dissimulation, yet cannot match Portia's, in view of Portia's paramount role. Similarly, if Gratiano's anti-Semitism is more immediate and overt, Antonio's, as I shall argue, is more methodically, albeit covertly, calculated, and brews within the mind of someone whose wealth has emerged out of the selfsame credit-driven economy for which he reviles Shylock.

suggestion that the repulsiveness of these various socio-ethnic outsiders lies above all in Portia's and the Venetians' minds.

No play in the corpus so successfully as *The Merchant of Venice* displays the transformation of the unity ideal within the measurement world. A self-chosen internal community, in the form of socio-economic unity and ethnic purity, emerges among the Christians, who must both profit from and despise the impure outsiders – Morocco, Aragon, Shylock – who threaten contamination. Shylock is Antonio's *phármakon*, created by the Christian Venetians as the necessary remedy and their self-inflicted poison. Scotland's *phármakon* Macbeth is not so much Duncan's nemesis as Duncan's own creation, and Shylock not so much Antonio's nemesis as Antonio's own creation. Each is the agent necessary for their regime's respective schemes of justice, the means by which their societies generate their own legitimated injustices.

Commodification as measurement reduces the human to a checklist, an inventory, to which fungible and indeed cheap values can be ascribed: the Duke of Saxony's nephew is a German; a German is vile when sober, and viler when drunk.[96] Needless to say, such men appear manifestly inferior when measured against the native Bassanio's – at this point, wholly presumed, through sheer appearances, but untested – refinement. Money and markets provide a backdrop that would satisfy Marxist analysis to a considerable degree. It would be overstatement, however, to reduce the characters and action to sheer economic activity. Portia's successive slurs certainly arise within, and derive from, a competitive market context that serves as Venice's socio-economic 'superstructure' (*Überbau*). However, it is not economic activity that is at issue in an unqualified sense in such passages. What is directly and immediately occurring is measurement *as such* – measurement that is always especially, but not solely, symbolised through money. Those justice theories that would condemn one system of measurement, merely to replace it with another, which all programmatic theories necessarily do, take too little heed of measurement itself as an origin of injustice.

One might object that Portia's fault is not measurement *per se*, but rather, along traditionally binary lines, mismeasurement, extrapolating from simple appearances and stereotypes, which eclipse the complexity of human beings. The ethics of *The Merchant of Venice* would, on that reading, remain conventionally humanist. The play's injustices and hypocrisies would make sense as *mis*measurements in view of supposedly just, correct measurements in each situation. But do they? If it is unjust for Portia to reduce humans to stock figures, then it is just to refrain from doing so. If it is unjust for Antonio to spit on Shylock, then it is just to refrain from doing so. Those ordinary, isolated, 'micro' binarisms are straightforward enough (even if it has taken centuries for Shakespeare lovers to recognise them). But what, within any

---

96 MV 1.2.83–84.

broader theory of justice, does 'refrain' mean? Should Antonio show, along Christian lines, selfless and unreserved love for Shylock? Or is Antonio, along contemporary liberal lines, entitled to hate Shylock, as long as he commits towards Shylock no unlawful action? Or should Antonio, along Marxist lines, positively join forces with Shylock to overthrow the prevailing regime of socio-political hierarchy and private ownership? The same kinds of questions can be put to Portia. Should she freely exercise her intra-ethnic and economically ambitious preferences, as long as she does so like a good liberal – as long as she obeys the letter of the law, which cannot control such predilections?

Any of those ethical readings can certainly be seen as notionally consistent with the action. The play might just as easily be said to presuppose any or none of them, or indeed to be eliciting precisely the problem of ethical complexity, and theoretical indeterminacy, in situations of socio-political crisis. The play's injustices are not sheer negations of some 'underlying' model of justice, that is, of right measure. There is endless measurement going on in the play, at the root of countless injustices; yet the way in which they are or may be *mis*-measurements, incorrect measurements, which would somehow presuppose some prior model of the correct ones, remains altogether opaque. Justice may indeed consist largely in measurement; the problem is that injustice takes on that same quality. Measurement can be identified at the origin of both justice and injustice, but not merely as mirror-image opposites or straightforward negations of each other.

6.7 'Kindness'

Returning to Antonio's 'weariness', recent interpretations, influenced by gender theory, have persuasively examined Antonio's crisis of homoerotic companionship with Bassanio.[97] Another reading, as already noted, focuses on Antonio's possible anxiety about his commercial expeditions, but which Antonio expressly denies.[98] That denial cannot wholly be dismissed, as the play highlights Antonio's complacency, before his moment of crisis, about his investments.[99]

If, for argument's sake, we take Antonio at his word, and it is not, or not solely, wealth as such, and not, or not solely, love that depress him, could it be some other visceral force? The play reveals little about Antonio's sorrows, but much about his passions. What echoes like a thunderbolt is his compulsive hatred of Shylock. Shylock recalls that history. Antonio, far from challenging it, zealously embraces it. Shylock protests that Antonio calls him 'dog'[100] and

---

97 MV 2.8.50. See, e.g., Sinfeld, 1996.
98 MV 1.1.41–45.
99 See, e.g., MV 1.1.41–45.
100 MV 1.3.107, 124. Cf. MV 2.8.14; 4.1.127.

'cur',[101] invective not far from Portia's measurements of the foreign suitors. Antonio kicks ('spurns'[102]) and spits[103] on Shylock's beard,[104] associated with his faith,[105] and on Shylock's pious garment, his 'Jewish gaberdine'.[106] Antonio relishes those memories with pride and with the fantasy of their renewal: 'I am as like to call thee so again,/To spit on thee again, to spurn thee too.'[107] It is Antonio's position of socio-legal superiority that warrants him to kick and to spit at Shylock publicly, leaving Shylock powerless to reply, much less to retaliate. On Antonio's playground, he can punch a target who may not punch back.

Antonio's passions are not limited to, nor do they principally consist in, spitting, kicking, or verbal abuse. Above all, his efforts have been directed at Shylock's life through an assault on Shylock's limited channels for self-support, in view of the *de jure* or *de facto* exclusion of Jews from land ownership and professions:[108] 'He hath . . . thwarted my bargains',[109] cries Shylock, to the tune of 'half a million'.[110] In an economy in which fourscore ducats are hefty, and 3,000 enormous, the activity here can be nothing less than Antonio's concerted effort, over a long time, effectively, albeit by legal means, to kill Shylock. Is that claim of Shylock's exaggerated? Perhaps it is, although the overall point would seem to be the same, regardless of the numerical figure to be placed on it. Shylock's speech is generally notable not for mendacity, so much as for a deflating candour, in constant contrast to the Christians' dissembling and hyperbole. He stings more with inconvenient truths than with fabrications. Shylock's references to rats infesting a ship[111] or a home,[112] compared also to thieves,[113] hint at his grasp of Antonio's motives – a pestilence gnawing at the foundations of his life: 'You take my house when you do take the prop/That doth sustain my house; you take my life/When you do take the means whereby I live.'[114] They reflect the parasitic quality of Venice's web of socio-economic relationships. In view of the general acceptance of lending at

---

101 MV 1.3.115. Cf. MV 3.3.18.
102 MV 1.3.114.
103 MV 1.3.122.
104 MV 1.3.114.
105 Lvt 19:27.
106 MV 1.3.109. A 'sober' garment that Gratiano, particularly vicious towards Shylock (e.g., MV 4.1.122–37, 360–63), will himself wear (MV 2.2.182), not, as Shylock does, for devotional purposes, but out of self-interest.
107 MV 1.3.126–7.
108 See this chapter, sources cited in n. 67
109 MV 3.1.53–54. Cf. MV 1.3.41–42, 46–47; 3.3.2–3, 22–4.
110 MV 3.1.52.
111 MV 1.3.22–23.
112 MV 4.1.43.
113 MV 1.3.23.
114 Cf. MV 4.1.371–73. Cf. Eccl 34:22.

interest, or through some analogue device, in our own time,[115] it can be difficult to draw any obvious analogy to Shylock's situation. We can nevertheless imagine, for example, a wealthy, ethnically white businessman willingly foregoing profit, and thereby superficially appearing to benefit a poor, white community, by offering cheaper goods, but with the sole intention of undercutting the prices in a black-owned shop. A community value benign in the abstract, providing low prices for poor consumers, becomes repulsive, unjust, in its aims and effects.[116] The opacity of such a motive holds justice and injustice in a precarious copula.

If Shylock will, for the first time, seek Antonio's life grossly, overtly, within the bounds of law, it is because Antonio has incessantly sought Shylock's life, surreptitiously, 'playing the system', within the bounds of law and of legally sanctioned privilege. That unequal measure gives the lie to the Duke's later insistence on a 'difference of . . . spirit'[117] between benign Christians and vengeful Jews.[118] The Duke's bias glares at the start of the trial, in his informal chat with Antonio,[119] which, of course, violates judicial impartiality, as the Venetians continue to seal their clubbish amity. The Jew certainly *is* vengeful – on the assumption, as Portia, Antonio, Bassanio, the Duke, and all privileged Venetians must assume – that the existing order is inherently just. In this legalist, post-feudal, proto-capitalist world, Shylock's bodily self-defence cannot be sought through the heroic-aristocratic drawn swords of Hamlet and Laertes. He seeks it through the legally sanctioned contractual instrument.[120] For Terry Eagleton, those, like Antonio, 'who wield power can afford to dispense with exact justice . . . since they, after all, control the rules of the game. It is less easy or intelligent for outcasts like Shylock, whose sole protection lies in the law, to conjure it away so cavalierly.'[121]

But why Antonio's original loathing of Shylock? '[W]hat's his reason?,' Shylock asks, and answers, 'I am a Jew.'[122] 'He hates our sacred nation'.[123] Why does Antonio feel such hatred? If he and other Venetians hate the practice of lending at interest, why not just avoid it? If avoidance of it were to place him at a competitive disadvantage against other Venetian merchants (although no such suggestion is ever made), then his gripe would have to be directed

---

115 Of course, part of the play's irony lies in the fact that lending at interest was already lawfully practiced by London's Christians, even while they preached against it. See, e.g., Mahood, 2003, pp. 19–22.
116 Cf. Boose, 1988, p. 249.
117 MV 4.1.364.
118 Cf. Wilson, 1993, p. 132; Girard, 2004, p. 356.
119 MV 4.1.2–5. Cf., e.g., Girard, 2004, p. 359.
120 On the common law as a weapon for the merchant class's assertion of political power against the aristocracy, see this chapter, n 5.
121 Eagleton, 1986, p. 41.
122 MV 3.1.55.
123 MV 1.3.45.

against the entirety of his fellow Venetians who benefit from the practice, and not chiefly against those who simply do their bidding. Be that as it may, contemplating the proposed loan, Shylock asks if he may speak to Antonio. Bassanio proposes that all three meet for dinner. Meals and meal invitations are always a precarious affair in Shakespeare. They are often aborted or disrupted, betokening fractured relationships, often with grim links to lawlessness or injustice.[124] In *The Comedy of Errors*, constant references to broken and altered dinner engagements subordinate this social intercourse to the forces of the market.[125] Shylock ironises,[126] 'to smell pork, to eat of the habitation which your prophet the Nazarite conjured the devil into'.[127] In displaying knowledge of Christian Scripture, the standard by which the Venetians measure the Jew, although not themselves, Shylock suggests that his adherence to faith is informed. It is not the 'blind', 'stubborn Jewry'[128] of the 'faithless Jew'.[129] His comment suggests a reason for that choice, namely Christians' hypocritical practice of their own professed principles.[130]

Hypocrisy includes the failure to measure oneself or those whom one prefers to the punitive standard by which one measures someone else. It by definition invites questions about the hypocrite's own failure. But it also raises a question about whether the measure applied by the hypocrite is even the correct one. One of the play's hallmark displays of hypocrisy emerges when Antonio, asking Shylock to lend to him at interest, insists that he never otherwise engages in that practice[131] – always an interesting attitude on the part of an actor who attributes sin to an act – although he shall do so now, and famously imputes sin[132] to Shylock's scriptural defence of it.[133] Antonio and Shylock disagree on the right measure – whether or not it is consistent with biblical law to lend money at a profit (or at 'interest', the term itself being in question;[134] after all, if interest is merely another form of profit,[135] then it is

---

124 See, e.g., Tit 5.3; Mac 3.4; Tim 11; Tmp 3.3.
125 See, e.g., Err. 1.2.22–6, 1.2.44–50, 3.1.62–65. Cf. Candido, 1997, pp. 199–225.
126 MV 1.3.27–32.
127 MV 1.3.31. Cf. Matt 8:28–34. If the passage is an aside (cf. OXF4, differing from ARD3, NOR2, CAM4 and PEN2), then Shylock's response is not necessarily a refusal, but only a hint of Shylock's conflicted feelings. See also MV 2.5.11–15. Cf. Watt, 2008, p. 240.
128 R2 2.1.55. Cf. MV 4.1.31.
129 MV 2.4.37. Cf. MV 1.3.108.
130 Cf. Cerasano, 2003a, pp. 12–13 (noting Venetians' assimilations of Christian belief into their commercial interests).
131 MV 1.3.67.
132 MV 1.3.94–5
133 MV 1.3.68–87.
134 MV 1.3.72–4.
135 See, e.g., Cohen, 1982, pp. 765–89; Drakakis, 1996, pp. 23–53. If Aristotle expresses some doubt about retail trade, he is downright censorious of usury. See Pol 1.10.1258^{b}2–7. Conspicuously, however, Shylock is never accused of having engaged in usury as such at any prior time (that is, charging extortionate, as opposed to usual and reasonable

hardly more sinful than Antonio's gigantic business ventures). In imputing to Shylock a Satanic mis-reading of the Bible, a breach of natural law, Antonio creates a compound hypocrisy, falsely – hypocritically – accusing Shylock of hypocrisy.

Under Christian law of Shakespeare's time, only one ethics can be called absolutely unethical, namely, the code of unqualified sin, or evil. At the very moment of committing his own compound hypocrisy, Antonio compares Shylock to Satan.[136] Shylock never draws any such comparison. He never equates Christianity with evil *per se*. His measure for Christians is not Jewish standards, but their own standards. That is why many commentators' perennial view of Shylock as representing what Hood Phillips calls 'strict justice' as opposed to Portia's 'mercy',[137] or what Ward calls, 'positive and formal' law, as opposed to 'the alternative Aristotelian idea of law legitimated only insofar as it prescribes the good of the community',[138] far from transcending positivism, plunges headlong into the positivist trap of construing law in isolation from ethics or society. Shylock turns strictly legalistic only after having been pushed to the extreme of humiliation, culminating in the Venetians' collusion, with impunity, in the theft of his daughter and his wealth. Re-inserted into his broader, social and ethical context, we find that Shylock in fact constantly tries non-litigious means, challenging the Christians not on the legality, but on the morality of what they say and do, and indeed emphatically appealing for a bond of friendship[139] – Aristotle's paramount civic value[140] – which Antonio vehemently rejects. Meanwhile, as to Portia's Aristotelianism, or even her sense of Christian mercy, we have already glimpsed her commitments to those values, and we shall see more.

If Shylock does indeed 'cite Scripture for his purpose'[141] of making money, the point of the Scripture he cites is to explain the substantive equality of, despite the surface veneer of any *pro forma* difference in ethical measure between, Antonio's and Shylock's equal 'purposes' of earning profit through their respective occupations – businesses equally dependent upon one another, insofar as Antonio's mode of commercial venture, in an increasingly complex and expanding economy, critically relies upon Shylock's mode of finance through loans. In parallel, it is at the moment when Lorenzo learns that he shall collect Jessica, along with the 'gold and jewels' stolen from Shylock, notwithstanding the constant ascription of greed to Jews, that he responds

---

interest rates), nor of any unethical business practice. Under English law in Shakespeare's time, up to 10 per cent interest was permitted. See, e.g., Cerasano, 2003a, p. 15.
136 MV 1.3.94–95. Cf., in parody, MV 2.2.19–22.
137 Hood-Phillips, 1972, p. 91.
138 Ward, 1999, p. 131.
139 MV 1.3.134.
140 See, e.g., NE 8.1.1154^{b}20–29.
141 MV 1.3.95.

with a Christian natural-law reference – 'If e'er the Jew her father come to heaven/It will be for his gentle daughter's sake.'[142] Similarly, it is at the moment that Jessica first throws Lorenzo and Gratiano[143] one casket of stolen valuables, and then promises to return with more, that Gratiano, opportunistically reversing his own stereotypes, exclaims 'a gentile, and no Jew'.[144] But as to the dinner invitation, Shylock continues, 'I will buy with you, sell with you, talk with you, walk with you, and so following, but I will not eat with you, drink with you, nor pray with you.'[145] Trivially enough, in buying, selling, talking and walking, Jews are equal in Venice. It is because of their religion, signified through the laws governing how they eat, drink and pray, that they are consigned to alien, as opposed to citizen, status. Bassanio uses a dinner to seal a financial transaction; for Shylock, meals retain their sacramental character.[146] Pre-Holocaust readings often abstracted the play's action from any such political context, often uncritically accepting the legally enforced class system of the Venetian Christian world by accepting it as a neutral, unproblematical, or at least historically justified, backdrop. From that perspective, as isolated, 'micro' events, Shylock's speech and actions are indeed excessive. But when the background social world is grasped as a set of rigorous, socio-political forces, flourishing through Venetian law, the socio-legally inferior Shylock offers the dominant Venetians precisely what they offer him, the same injustice that they coercively impose to preserve their hierarchy. He offers the Venetians their own injustice back to them on the terms their own laws dictate, precisely equal measure,[147] mirror-imaging the Venetians' insistence, proclaimed by Portia, that it is *they* who are merely meeting out Shylock's own measurement to him.[148] 'Shylock appears most scandalous', writes René Girard, 'when he stops resembling himself to resemble the Venetians even more.'[149]

Antonio has deployed Venice's socio-legal hierarchy against Shylock's life, setting the measure for Shylock's famous bargain. Antonio perpetuates his injustices within, and as an integral part of, his society's legal regime. Shylock's move is not to commit injustice within a just world, but to translate that injustice from the blissfully anonymous and systemic to the crudely immediate and overt. Immediate and overt injustice is a crime; anonymous and systemic injustice merely fade into the neutral background of *the way things are*.

142 MV 2.4.33–34.
143 Adopting spelling in ARD3.
144 MV 2.6.51.
145 MV 1.3.33–35.
146 Although Shylock does later go to dinner, the conditions and motives remain cryptic. MV 2.5.11–21.
147 Cf. MM 5.1.410–13.
148 MV 4.1.301–68.
149 Girard, 2004, p. 356.

Unsurprisingly, post-Holocaust readings risk swinging to the other extreme, stylising Shylock altogether as victim.[150] Yet that simplification fails to explain the injustice of Shylock's scandalous suit. The point of Shylock's character is not that he is exceptionally just, but that his injustice, far from departing from his Venetians' norms, altogether recapitulates them, and never exceeds that practiced, with impunity, by the citizen Venetians. Shylock becomes a *speculum principum* which surpasses any in *Richard II*,[151] precisely because it mirrors not the older model of power ultimately invested in one sovereign, but rather the new, Foucauldian model of power ubiquitously disseminated through social and economic pressures and practices.

Shylock insists on the hypocrisy of Antonio engaging in the activity of money-lending, for which Antonio has long reviled Shylock: '[M]oneys is your suit'.[152] 'Suit' means, of course, 'request',[153] but 'more than a simple request . . . since it implies a legal process'.[154] Yet 'suit' also means 'clothing, dress, garb',[155] contrasting Antonio's exterior with the sacramental understatement of Shylock's 'Jewish gabardine', upon which Antonio has 'spit'. The pernicious comparison and measurement will once again arise between Antonio and Shylock. Shylock asks why he should lend interest to someone who perennially and publicly humiliates him for doing so. A round of contractual negotiation begins. Shylock's dissent against injustice becomes articulated in the *quid pro quo* terms of Venice's only system of justice, the justice of measurement and markets. Shylock faces doom because the only vocabulary available to him to protest against the Venetians' injustice is the vocabulary which enables that injustice in the first place. Each proposed bargain highlights the measure that determines it. Shylock first asks whether he should performatively recapitulate the socio-political hierarchy, whether he should openly, and literally, display his inferior social measurement, like the 'petty' vessels who 'curtsy' to the 'rich burghers': 'Shall I bend low?'. He then continues in the language of formal, legal equality – the contractual consideration, the contractual measure, the *quid pro quo*: 'and for these courtesies',

> Shall I bend low, and in a bondman's key,
> With bated breath and whisp'ring humbleness,
> Say this: 'Fair sir, you spat on me on Wednesday last;
> You spurned me such a day; another time

150 Cerasano writes: '[A] post-Holocaust sensitivity requires that audiences question whether Antonio's "punishments" really fit Shylock's "crimes".' Cerasano, 2003a, p. 2. The pre-Holocaust question, by no means vanished today, was generally the opposite, namely, whether Shylock's desired 'punishments' really fit Antonio's 'crimes'.
151 See this book, Chapter 5, text accompanying n. 65.
152 MV 1.3.116.
153 CAM2 88.
154 ARD3 215.
155 Crystal and Crystal, 2002, p. 430.

You called me dog; and for these courtesies
I'll lend you thus much moneys?[156]

Antonio confirms that past conduct as his fixed measure: 'I am like to call thee so again.'[157] He then opens the negotiation about the contractual terms, recalling conspicuously Schmittian notions of friends and foes.

If thou wilt lend this money, lend it not
As to thy friends . . .
But lend it rather to thine enemy,
Who, if he break, thou mayst with better face
Exact the penalty.[158]

On its own terms, the justice of the marketplace, in which we 'exact the penalty' for a breached contract, may not set the benchmark for close 'friends', but it certainly sets it off from other public and commercial relationships, despite the fact that most are not motivated by enmity in any such overt sense. Antonio adopts the measure of enmity to describe a contractual bargain involving a penalty for breach. Shylock counters by proposing Antonio's own standard of friendship, whereby the legal regime is deployed to help fellow Venetians, other socio-legal insiders, by seeking, through legal means, the ruin of the socio-legal alien.

Shylock will translate that complex web of 'macro', systemic relationships into an immediate, 'micro' one, merged into the four corners of a recorded instrument. As Antonio does with fellow Christians,[159] in order to target Shylock's life, so does Shylock propose a loan without interest, in order to target Antonio's. When Bassanio interjects, 'This were kindness',[160] a triple pun, launched from the first, obvious sense of 'kindness' as amiability, also suggests, as a second meaning, 'to do things as they are done by us, by our own kind, our own kin and kindred'.[161] Coupled with that second meaning, the 'kindness' additionally denotes equal measure, something done 'in kind', *quid pro quo*, and then precisely 'as we do it'. As to *that* 'kindness', *that* application of the Christians' own measures, Shylock explains: 'This kindness will I show.'[162] As Antonio, through his position of socio-legal privilege, does with Shylock, so does Shylock, through Venetian law, seek Antonio's life, 'an equal pound' – 'equal' being glossed as 'precise or just',[163] 'stipulated as

156 MV 1.3.120–25.
157 MV 1.3.126.
158 MV 1.3.128–33.
159 See this chapter, n. 109.
160 MV 1.3.139.
161 Cf., e.g., MV 2.8.35. See, e.g. Halio, 1993, p. 41. Cf. Ham 1.2.65.
162 MV 1.3.140.
163 PEN2 118.

exact'[164] – of Antonio's flesh.[165] Now it is Antonio who confirms with the same, three-tiered layering: '[T]here is much kindness in the Jew.'[166] The Jew now seems like us, acts like us, uses our justice, our measures; he is a gentile, i.e. 'gentle[167] Jew':[168] 'The Hebrew will turn Christian; he grows *kind*.'[169] Of course, when Shylock does 'turn Christian', conforming to the socially enforced standard of measure[170] it will be through that same coercive power structure from which the play's injustices arise in the first place.

6.8 'As swift as yours'

The Prince of Morocco's opening words show him prescient of the power matrix he has entered. He confronts its system of measurement anticipatorily: 'Mislike me not for my complexion',[171] defending himself not in response to a declared aversion, but rather on the expectation of a presumed one – 'I would not change this hue'[172] – justifiably in view of Portia's own anticipatory revulsion. For Aristotle, justice as measurement entails treating like persons or things alike.[173] In feigning to do Morocco justice by comparing him to the other foreign suitors, Portia cynically deploys that language of equal measurement to achieve the arbitrary reduction of Morocco's humanity to his 'hue': 'Yourself, renownèd Prince, then stood as fair/As any comer I have looked on yet/For my affection.'[174] That remark cannot be defended on grounds that Morocco, in choosing the golden casket, will supposedly prove his unworthiness by failing to show good judgment, since not only has that moment not yet occurred, but Morocco's bad judgment in choosing the gold casket, as I shall argue, is itself questionable.

One feature of the play is the way socio-political inferiors assert equality by measuring their humanity against that of the privileged Venetians. They often do so not by immediate reference to refined human qualities, but rather through indirect reference, via an equalising of those same body parts by which baser humans, associated with manual labour, are otherwise measured and shown to be inferior, as anchoring inferiors in their bodies confirms their inferior rank.[175] (Recall the servant Maria in *Twelfth Night*

---

164 NOR2 1130. Cf. CAM4 89.
165 MV 1.3.145–48.
166 MV 1.3.150.
167 Cf. CAM4 90.
168 MV 1.3.174. Cf. MV 2.4.33–4, 4.1.33.
169 MV 1.3.175 (emphasis added).
170 MV 4.1.383, 387.
171 MV 2.1.1.
172 MV 2.1.11.
173 NE 5.3.1131^{a}10–23.
174 MV 2.1.20–2.
175 Cf., e.g., Heinze, 2009e, p. 252.

referring to her mistress: '[W]e can hardly make distinction of our hands.'[176]) Those same inferiors assimilate such characterisations into their tacit rebellions against the arbitrarily unequal measurement. Morocco is not of equal worth *simpliciter*, but of equal worth despite his skin colour. Not merely he, but rather his face or gaze (his 'aspect') has frightened his enemies.[177] He is not merely valorous, but rather need only be measured against 'the fairest creature northward born'[178] in order 'to prove whose blood is reddest'.[179] The point is not that indigenous, high-born characters are never spoken of with reference to their bodies – they certainly are, and particularly when they are being disparaged[180] – but only that aliens or subordinates are often referred to in that way routinely, conspicuously and sometimes relentlessly.[180a] It is not Shylock in particular who measures out human worth in pounds of flesh. His entire Christian society does it through indirection; he does it directly.

Shylock proclaims his equal measure of human qualities, using so-called 'congeries', a rhetorical device of ascending, in this case, from the human body to the human being, measuring himself precisely to the criterion set by the full-fledged humanity of the Venetians: 'Hath not a Jew eyes? Hath not a Jew hands, organs, dimensions, senses, affections, passions?'[181] Throughout the play, Shylock's dictionary of blunt speech, alluding constantly to the organic and material, certainly teases out traditional myths of Christian spirituality and Jewish baseness. Beneath that veneer, however, it equalises surface hypocrisies, measuring Venice's privileged Christians, who preach more justice than they practice, against the common run of humanity. Barred from the measure of socio-legal equality with Antonio, barred from spitting, kicking or insulting Antonio, unable to undermine Antonio's trade as Antonio undermines his, Shylock can only replace equal measure in the socio-legal sphere with equal measure in the organic and physical, as he does in his infamous bargain.[182] It is at the moment of demanding such forfeit that the play's actual scales of justice famously appear,[183] putting to us in age-old imagery the question as to how much justice is achieved, and how much injustice perpetuated, through that ultimate criterion of justice – measurement.

176 TN 2.3.149–50.
177 MV 2.1.8–9.
178 MV 2.1.4.
179 MV 2.1.7.
180 Endless jokes about Falstaff's body throughout *Henry IV, Part One*, *Henry IV, Part Two* and *The Merry Wives of Windsor* are obvious examples, as are countless references to the younger Richard's deformities in *Henry VI, Part III* and *Richard III*. See also, e.g., Lr 4.265–70; 7.380–82.
180a See, e g., Heinze, 2009e p. 152.
181 MV 3.1.55–57. Cf., e.g., Drakakis, 2010, pp. 74–77. Cf. R2, 3.2.175–76.
182 MV 1.3.145–48. Cf. Eagleton, 1986, pp. 42–43, 45; Girard, 2004, p. 354; Watt, 2008, pp. 245–49.
183 Cf. Watt, 2008, pp. 244–45.

Gratiano, privileged as a Venetian, yet not of the highest ranks, assures his master Bassanio of his own equal qualities through reference to an equally capable body part, in a characteristically Shakespearean moment of triviality-*cum*-rebellion: 'My eyes, my lord, can look as swift as yours.'[184] Curiously, in view of his later, vituperative attack on Shylock,[185] Gratiano meticulously measures out his comparison to his master, studiously extrapolating from the body to the human being.

> My eyes, my lord, can look as swift as yours.
> You saw the mistress, I beheld the maid.
> You loved, I loved; for intermission[186]
> No more pertains to me, my lord, than you.[187]

6.9 'As much as he deserves'

Few devices in Shakespeare so dramatically symbolise the precarious link between measurement and justice as the play's casket scenes. The worth of each of the three suitors must be measured, like Lear's measurement of his three daughters.[188] The casket scene displays not Lear's kind of publically decreed will, in the sense of volition, proclaimed by the fading feudal sovereign; but rather the legal will, the recorded, signed and sealed testament, of the emerging bourgeois *paterfamilias*, equally aimed at exercising a posthumous, patriarchal and proprietary power through law. Portia's father is not a deeply individualised Lear. He is the absent, anonymous, fungible, any-old placeholder for the modern, monied, male head of household, just as the loved-before-known Bassanio might just as well be any well born and bred Venetian male. Portia's father deploys law to stage his own ritual, whereby, or so he hopes, his 'largest bounty', his daughter and his fortune, 'may extend/Where nature doth with merit challenge'.[189]

If the prize of *Lear*'s old order is the aristocratic wealth of land, that of the new order is represented by caskets, each cast in metal, the element of money and coinage, infinitely and indifferently transferable wealth. Nerissa's Aristotelian exhortation of embracing the mean between the extremes might well have pointed to the silver casket as the wise choice: cheaper than gold, dearer than lead, and therefore, following Aristotle, neither unduly prizing

---

184 MV 3.2.197.
185 MV 4.1.122–37, 359–96.
186 Glossed as 'delay', sluggishness being stereotypically attributed to lower ranks. Cf. MV 2.4.8–9, 45–6. 'Gratiano has been as swift as Bassanio.' OXF4 173. Cf. CAM4 133. Bassanio had already chided Gratiano for 'wild' conduct unbecoming of the higher classes. MV 2.2.162–69.
187 MV 3.2.197–200.
188 Cf. Wilson, 1993, pp. 222–27.
189 Lr 1.46–47.

nor unduly disparaging wealth.[190] Yet the silver casket turns out to be a wrong choice in the market-driven universe. In nascent modernity, one will not prosper by following some Aristotelian mean, no more than does Cordelia's moderately measured-out 'no more nor less',[191] which would apply only the measure of moderation to wealth and its acquisition. The one who wins is the one willing to play the high-risk games that Antonio plays, exemplified in the marketplace by low investment, worth lead, for a high return, worth gold, and in that sense to 'hazard all he hath'[192] in the modern marketplace, 'in hope of fair advantages'.[193] That means, for Bassanio, who can handily choose the lead casket because he 'hath' nothing at all to 'hazard' aside from debt, being willing to hazard even the life of that supposedly 'dearest friend' and 'kindest man'[194] Antonio, violating the Venetian's own conception of Christianity's supposed anti-interest laws in the process, and without whose gift Bassanio could not court Portia at all.

When Morocco reaches the Aristotelian middle, the silver casket, he casts his entire being in terms of measurement. He, too, mirrors, yet also surpasses the lexicon of sheer money: '[P]ause there, Morocco,/And weigh thy value with an even hand.'[195] Morocco's self-measurement will speak the language of masculine worth. Perhaps his merit does not 'extend so far as to the lady'? And yet to be too 'afeard of my deserving/Were but a weak disabling of myself.'[196] If Morocco chooses wrongly, it is not because he lacks the universal and eternal enlightenment of some storybook wise man. Are we seriously to believe that Bassanio possesses it? Why would we assume that the merchant of Belmont, Portia's father, can boast any existential insights greater than that of knowing how to multiply his wealth; or that his 'virtue'[197] extends beyond Cephalus's and Polemarchus's mercantile concepts of keeping promises and paying debts?

The riddle of the caskets is locked less in universal and eternal 'human' truth, and more in the truths of modern markets. The fault of the Prince of Morocco (and of the Prince of Aragon) is not to choose wrongly in any absolute sense of mistaking some unwavering truth, but only in the relative sense of misapprehending the values of commercial success. Morocco cannot so handily 'hazard all he hath', since he apparently, unlike Bassanio, *has* things. If Shakespeare, through a character like Bassanio, 'created a new ideal: the love marriage',[198] it is because Bassanio has nothing other than love, and debt, to contribute, and will instead play the parasite of his new wife's wealth for some

---

190 NE 4.1.
191 Lr 1.84.
192 MV 2.7.9, 16.
193 MV 2.7.19.
194 MV 3.2.290. Cf. MV 2.8.35.
195 MV 2.7.24–5.
196 MV 2.7.29–30.
197 MV 1.2.27.
198 See Sokol and Sokol, 2003, p. 128 (quoting Dash).

indeterminate future.[199] Nor, as Morocco suggests, can he ever realistically expect 'as much as he deserves' from a society that will always, arbitrarily, define him *a priori* as undeserving on grounds of his skin colour.

By contrast, Morocco, standing before the gold casket, can scarcely be faulted for concluding that 'the lady' is 'what many men desire', since it is the riddle's author who set his daughter up in precisely that commodified role. The rule of marketplace success, as the play exhorts in scene after scene, is to apply a measure precisely opposite to those one preaches. This exotic, and in that same sense seemingly naïve outsider, could not possibly guess correctly. We are beguiled into overlooking the fact that, on all but superficial appearances of ethnicity, Morocco is so clearly the superior of the three main suitors – the only man, a would-be Moor of Venice, who, on all available information, can actually boast both military and political achievements wrought through individual merit. Morocco can presumably bring Portia some of that wealth that she and her world hardly shun, and into which she has been so deftly assimilated. But what matters in the market world is not the static wealth of a feudal aristocrat like Morocco, but the capitalist's tools for increasing wealth as capital-intensive self-reproduction, wealth that can 'breed fast'.[200] The debt-laden yet far from risk-averse Bassanio turns out, in our modern world, to appear as the wiser investment. The three suitors form a sequence, whereby Morocco represents the old, heroic-feudal past; Aragon represents the mercantilist present of commercial markets rising in tandem with centralising monarchies; and Bassanio represents a *laissez-faire* capitalist future.

The suitor who does, by contrast, embrace Nerissa's notion of the Aristotelian mean, the silver casket, is, if only by tradition, the play's pre-eminently foolish character, as witnessed by the prize he will find enclosed. Greek ideals may not be foolish in any eternal scheme, but have no place in free markets. The Prince of Aragon indeed voices the play's only lucid scepticism towards worth and measurement – towards a society where feudal privilege is supposedly to be supplanted by the market-driven meritocracy, yet where merit is acquired, traded and measured as just another commodity. Only a fool would take that Aristotelian course in this market world.[201] The insights of this post-Armada, and therefore invariably laughing-stock Spaniard, collapse into platitudes, inevitably drowned by the howls of an audience who need hardly heed Aragon's intended or inadvertent meaning.

---

199 MV 3.2.157–74.
200 See this chapter, n. 32.
201 Any suggestion, then, that it would be distinctly Shylock, and not the whole of the play's Christian-capitalist money-mongers, who falls short of an Aristotelian ideal of general justice, or who presses the law into unjust outcomes, is problematical. If, in a Marxist sense, Shylock has alienated his humanity within a market-driven world, he is scarcely the only one to do so. Cf. White, 1996, p. 163.

> Why, then to thee, thou silver treasure-house.
> Tell me once more what title thou dost bear.
> 'Who chooseth me shall get as much as he deserves' –
> And well said too, for who shall go about
> To cozen fortune, and be honourable
> Without the stamp of merit? Let none presume
> To wear an undeservèd dignity.[202]

As we saw with Marx, the perils of measurement are perceived, yet are never surpassed.

> O, that estates, degrees, and offices
> Were not derived corruptly, and that clear honour
> Were purchased by the merit of the wearer![203]

Albeit a noble himself, Aragon challenges the existing socio-legal order, imagining arbitrary measurement replaced by meritocratic measurement.

> How many then should cover that stand bare,[204]
> How many be commanded that command?
> How much low peasantry would then be gleaned
> From the true seed of honour, and how much honour
> Picked from the chaff and ruin of the times
> To be new-varnished?[205]

Like the audience roar at the stage-fool Spaniard, the play's socio-legal brutality will present this now-misbegotten fantasy, that there can be just measurement within this market world, with the head of a 'blinking idiot',[206] impressed upon Aragon in no uncertain terms.[207] Aragon, unlike Morocco presents no evidence of achievements to boast of, again raising the play's incessant question about whether one measures up to one's own meritocratic standards. Even if his wealth is purely inherited, it still outweighs Bassanio's, leaving the motto of the lead casket distinctly unattractive. When Aragon despairs, 'Did I deserve no more than a fool's head?',[208] Portia, once again snaps back with stunningly cynical realism. If, as she snorts, '[n]o man ought

---

202 MV 2.9.33–39.
203 MV 2.9.40–42.
204 'Should wear hats who now stand bareheaded (before their social superiors).' NOR2 1144.
205 MV 2.9.43–48.
206 MV 2.9.53.
207 MV 2.9.67, 72, 74, 79.
208 MV 2.7.58.

to be a judge in his own cause'[209] (precisely what Portia will do, feigning the guise of impartial justice to intervene in a case in which her new husband has an immediate financial interest), then Aragon's notion of just measurement has not only 'offended', but done so in a way that surpasses his capacity to scrutinise: 'To offend and judge are distinct offices,/And of opposèd natures.'[210] At the same time, if offending and judging refer to the respective roles of Aragon and Portia, then Portia's response refers to her own capacity to judge, which, as we have seen, she displays all too evidently throughout the play.

In the ring exchange sub-plot, Portia, eminently her father's daughter, will have invented her own device to take, and to enforce, the measure of her husband's worth. When Bassanio arrives, he is measured up as the most 'likely'[211] ... ambassador of love' on sight.[212] Portia then shows how law and justice, whose values she glibly urges upon Aragon or Shylock, are to be manipulated in this new world, as her will trumps her father's after all. With all but a wink and a nod, she drops the hint that, although she will supposedly 'never' be 'foresworn',[213] she nevertheless 'could teach' Bassanio '[h]ow to choose right'.[214] Suddenly, unlike the other suitors, Bassanio's deliberations will be accompanied by well-rehearsed musicians, coaching him to follow not only his 'heart' and 'eyes', but his 'head'. And then for, so to speak, good measure, they will versify that admonition in the rhyming scheme 'bred', 'head', 'nourishèd', which, abracadabra, all rhyme with 'lead'.[215] Bassanio immediately takes the hint: 'So may the outward shows be least themselves.'[216]

Like her high-society counterpart Antonio, Portia has played and won the high-risk game. Instead of flatly defying the law set forth in her father's will, she openly declares obedience to its 'letter', subverting its 'spirit' (as, of course, Shylock is accused of doing), through tricks that might have failed, but have succeeded. Thus is measurement managed in our own socio-legal world. One swears allegiance to law, tricking it covertly within its own legal bounds. In that respect, measurement, the just as the fair and proportionate, can certainly produce justice, yet just as readily produces injustice.

6.10 'Le plus beau, le plus fort'

Within the Western canon, the philosopher who comes closest to identifying measurement as such at the origin of injustice is Jean-Jacques Rousseau, in

209 As glossed in OXF4 157 (citing Tilley).
210 MV 2.7.60–61.
211 Glossed as 'suitable', NOR2 1145; and as both 'handsome' and 'promising', ARD3 279.
212 MV 2.9.91.
213 MV 3.2.11–12.
214 MV 3.2.10–11.
215 MV 3.2.63–72. On Portia's overriding of her father's will, see, e.g., Boose, 1988, pp. 247–48; Watt, 2008, pp. 241–43.
216 MV 3.2.73.

his two famous *Discours*, followed later by the strong unity theory contained in his *Contrat Social*. Not unlike Plato, whom he sometimes quotes on this point, Rousseau argues that much of what we call 'civilisation', and its concomitant advances in commerce, science and technology, far from providing what we mistakenly believe to be fulfilment of our needs, and cures for our ills, in fact actively create needs and ills which people living without such achievements had never felt.

We can draw upon more arguments in our own time to support that view than either Plato or Rousseau could have cited. It is a commonplace that, before the late 20th century, no one 'needed' to start up a personal computer or carry a mobile telephone, let alone engage in those technologies' specific operations, such as locating news, videos, music, games or social networks. Today, people feel distress at the lack of such conveniences. In earlier times, 'needs' for cigarettes, pharmaceuticals, household appliances or other manufactured products were equally unknown. Rousseau does not deny that many such goods bring benefits, but asks whether those benefits outweigh their associated burdens, notably in rendering us ever more dependent upon them, and ever more physically or psychologically sensitive even to their temporary deprivations.

Rousseau perhaps never convinced many readers that 'noble savages' had once wandered the earth, wholly autarchic, neither wanting nor needing either 'civilisation' or its related sciences and technologies. Even less obvious is his theory as to why such people would have abandoned their primordial self-sufficiency, increasingly gathering into social units. He avowedly asks the reader to imagine those people more as means of developing a critique for existing human societies than as a literally accurate world history. What nevertheless remains remarkable is his view of how human groups engender their first social activities, after the basic needs of food and shelter have been met. '[S]ong and dance, true children of love and leisure, became the amusement or rather the occupation of idle men and women gathered together.'[217] Those social activities subsequently *eut un prix*, which might be translated as 'came to be prized', given that Rousseau at this stage has mentioned trade only in passing, as indeed something perhaps sporadic – *le commerce passager*.[218] Gourevitch nevertheless justifiably translates the phrase as 'acquired a price': 'Everyone began to look at everyone else and to be looked at himself, and public esteem acquired a price.'[219]

That translation is fair enough, as long as we recall that Rousseau envisages here not the evils of trade or commerce as such – which he has not yet analysed at that point in any detail, and which, at that stage of social life, have not yet assumed complex forms – but above all *prix*, 'price' or 'prize', not merely as

217 OI-Gour 1997:166 (OI, JJR-OC 3:169).
218 OI, JJR-OC 3:169.
219 OI-Gour 1997:166 (OI, JJR-OC 3:169).

something to be commodified, but, more primordially, as something to be measured – between rival persons, objects or actions. Rousseau stresses the point through the rhetorical device of anaphora, the constant hammering of *le plus* (the most): 'The one who sang or danced *le mieux* (the best)', and then, by extension, '*le plus beau* (the handsomest), *le plus fort* (the strongest), *le plus adroit* (the most skilful) *ou le plus eloquent* (or the most eloquent) *devint le plus consideré* (came to be the most highly regarded)'. For Rousseau, this was 'the first step toward inequality and vice'.[220] Rousseau certainly recognises existing class differences as manifestations of that inequality, yet a Lockean, meritocratic alternative is little better, as it still presupposes the culture of property, trade and competition which would merely turn one regime of vicious inequalities, one scheme of measurements, into another.

Those qualities of being *le plus beau*, *le plus fort*, etc. were not yet full-blown market commodities in early societies as viewed by Rousseau, but were immediately subject to measurement. It is hard for us, children of capitalism, to see anything surprising in the suggestion that talents and skills should be measured to assess desert, to assess justice. Like Antonio and Shylock, Portia and Bassanio, drenched in a world of market standards, all of us are born and bred into meritocratic values, which presuppose such measurement. We deem them to be an obvious and unqualified benefit. We deem it to be justice, indeed positively progressive, for societies with histories of privilege based on the arbitrary criteria of birth, ethnicity, religion or sex. It is meritocracy, however, as a reduction of humans to criteria of measurement, that Rousseau condemns as harshly as any aristocracy determined by standards of birth. The necessary tool of justice – for surely we children of Locke all agree that the *prix*, the prize and the price, should go to the most qualified, the most skilled, the most diligent, in a word, the best – becomes, for Rousseau, the very origin of injustice: '[F]rom these first preferences arose vanity and contempt on the one hand, shame and envy on the other.'[221] It takes little time for attitudes engendered in those social activities to generalise to the group, to the human condition, as such, and for measurement – Eden's serpent, necessary to human justice, yet necessarily producing injustice – to dominate normative thought: 'As soon as men had begun to appreciate one another and the idea of consideration had taken shape in their mind, everyone claimed a right to it, and one could no longer deprive anyone of it without impunity.'[222]

That 'without impunity' already displays measurement and self-measurement as both primordial attitudes and responses. Responses to perceived mismeasurement are themselves measured out, either to be met in kind or to be surpassed in vengeance: 'Thus everyone punishing the contempt

---

220 OI-Gour 1997:166 (OI, JJR-OC 3:169).
221 OI-Gour 1997:166 (OI, JJR-OC 3:170).
222 OI-Gour 1997:166 (OI, JJR-OC 3:170).

shown him in a manner proportionate to the stock he set by himself, vengeances became terrible, and bloodthirsty and cruel.'[223] Non-European 'savages' in fact resemble Europeans to the extent that all are at one or another stage of having left their primordial autarchy: 'This is precisely the stage reached by most Savage People known to us; and it is for want of drawing adequate distinctions between ideas, and noticing how far these Peoples were already from the state of Nature, that many', Rousseau has Hobbes in mind,[224] 'hastened to conclude that man is naturally cruel and that he needs political order in order to be made gentle'.[225] Society now truly begins: '[T]he already established relations among men required in them qualities different from those they derived from their primitive constitution.'[226]

The supposedly primordial human had not needed justice or ethics, nor notions of good and bad, right and wrong, measurement and mismeasurement, except for what was good or bad, right and wrong, for sheer survival. But now 'morality was beginning to enter human Actions and since, before there were Laws, everyone was sole judge and avenger of the offenses he had received, the goodness suited to the pure state of Nature was no longer the goodness suited to nascent Society'.[227] Morals and ethics, law and justice would now become nothing more than the ever more pervasive and fastidious attention to measurement. Civilisation and law become the *phármakon* of injustice, its necessary cure and its inevitable cause. '[P]unishments had to become more severe in proportion as the opportunities to offend became more frequent.'[228] Since leaving the state of nature, 'all subsequent progress has been so many steps in appearance toward the perfection of the individual, and in effect toward the decrepitude of the species'.[229]

Rousseau speculates about the origins of law and society, ironising Locke's view: 'The first man who, having enclosed a piece of ground, to whom it occurred to say *this is mine*, and found people sufficiently simple to believe him, was the true founder of civil society.'[230] Private property is of course, as Plato had observed and as Marx would amplify, commodification *par excellence*. Measurement is its essential tool, operating through a detailed legal regime, a regime of justice as *suum cuique*: 'From the cultivation of land, its division necessarily followed; and from property, once recognized, the first rules of justice necessarily followed: for in order to render to each his own [*rendre à*

---

223 OI-Gour 1997:166 (OI, JJR-OC 3:170).
224 OI-Gour 1997:151 (OI, JJR-OC 3:153–54).
225 OI-Gour 1997:166 (OI, JJR-OC 3:170).
226 OI-Gour 1997:166–7 (OI, JJR-OC 3:170).
227 OI-Gour 1997:167 (OI, JJR-OC 3:170).
228 OI-Gour 1997:167 (OI, JJR-OC 3:170).
229 OI-Gour 1997:167 (OI, JJR-OC 3:171).
230 OI-Gour 1997:161 (OI, JJR-OC 3:164) (Rousseau's emphasis).

chacun le sien], each must be able to have something.'[231] Justice as measurement would perhaps raise no difficulties in a world of equal needs, equal skills, and both equal and ample resources.[232] But that 'proportion' would inevitably be 'upset': '[T]he stronger did more work; the more skilful used his work to better advantage; the more ingenious found ways to reduce his labor; the Plowman had greater need of iron, or the smith greater need of wheat, and by working equally, the one earned much while the other had trouble staying alive.'[233]

For Rousseau, we are 'free' in the state of nature because we are not slaves to ever augmenting needs. Civilisation calls us free while making us slaves.

> [M]an, who had previously been free and independent, is now so to speak subjugated by a multitude of new needs . . . and especially to those of his kind, whose slave he in a sense becomes even by becoming their master; rich, he needs their services; poor, he needs their help, and moderate means do not enable him to do without them. He must therefore constantly try to interest them in his fate and to make them really or apparently find their own profit in working for his: which makes him knavish and artful with some, imperious and harsh with the rest, and places him under the necessity of deceiving all those he needs if he cannot get them to fear him and does not find it in his interest to make himself useful to them. Finally, consuming ambition, the ardent desire to raise one's relative fortune less out of genuine need than in order to place oneself above others, instils in all men a black inclination to harm one another.[234]

That pernicious ambition emerges as rivalry, comparison, competition, all through the necessary instrument of justice – measurement.

> [A] secret jealousy that is all the more dangerous as it often assumes the mask of benevolence in order to strike its blow in greater safety: in a word, competition and rivalry on the one hand, conflict of interests on the other, and always the hidden desire to profit at another's expense. [. . .] Now, once inheritances had increased in number and size to the point where they covered all the land and all adjoined one another, men could no longer aggrandize themselves except at one another's expense. [. . .] Thus, as the most powerful or the most miserable claimed, on the basis of their strength or of their needs, a kind of right to another person's goods, equivalent, according to them, to the right of property, the breakdown of

---

231 OI-Gour 1997:169 (OI, JJR-OC 3:173). Cf. OI-Gour 1997:166 (OI, JJR-OC 3:170).
232 OI-Gour 1997:169 (OI, JJR-OC 3:174).
233 OI-Gour 1997:170 (OI, JJR-OC 3:174).
234 OI-Gour 1997:170–1 (OI, JJR-OC 3:174–5).

equality was followed by the most frightful disorder: thus the usurpations of the rich, the Banditry of the Poor, the unbridled passions of all, stifling natural pity and the still weak voice of justice, made men greedy, ambitious, and wicked.[235]

Justice can now emerge not to triumph over, but to require and to feed upon injustice.

> Lacking valid reasons to justify and sufficient strength to defend himself; easily crushing an individual, but himself crushed by troops of bandits; alone against all, and unable, because of their mutual jealousies, to unite with his equals against enemies united by the common hope of plunder, the rich, under the pressure of necessity, at last conceived the most well-considered project ever to enter the human mind; to use even his attackers' forces in his favor, to make his adversaries his defenders, to instill in them other maxims and to give them different institutions, as favourable to himself as natural Right was contrary to him. [. . .] 'Let us unite,' he told them, 'to protect the weak from oppression, restrain the ambitious, and secure for everyone the possession of what belongs to him: Let us institute rules of Justice and peace to which all are obliged to conform, which favor no one, and which in a way make up for the vagaries of fortune by subjecting the powerful and the weak alike to mutual duties.'[236]

In that imaginary speech pronounced by the rich and powerful to the subjugated to dress up injustices as justice – and Rousseau will indeed add that '[m]uch less than the equivalent of this Discourse was needed to sway crude, easily seduced men'[237] – the brutal reality of justice as measurement will now be cloaked in a myth of justice as unity.

> In a word, instead of turning our forces against one another, let us gather them into a supreme power that might govern us according to wise Laws, protect and defend all the members of the association, repulse common enemies, and preserve us in everlasting concord.[238]

As Thrasymachus would have agreed, the best way to commit injustice is to convince others that it is justice: 'All ran toward their chains in the belief that they were securing their freedom.'[239] Rousseau's *Contrat Social*, a

---

235 OI-Gour 1997:171 (OI, JJR-OC 3:175–6).
236 OI-Gour 1997:172–3 (OI, JJR-OC 3:177).
237 OI-Gour 1997:173 (OI, JJR-OC 3:177).
238 OI-Gour 1997:173 (OI, JJR-OC 3:177).
239 OI-Gour 1997:173 (OI, JJR-OC 3:177).

programmatic justice theory, will seek a more authentic unity; yet we have already seen how that ideal will fare. He will thereby inevitably presuppose 'just' measurements, neglecting his critique in the *Discours*, which casts doubt upon the degree to which measurement can proceed on the assumption of the classical binarism, aiming to achieve justice defined as the sheer subjugation of injustice.

Be that as it may, having examined the origins of existing injustices, Rousseau resumes a language steeped in the terms of measurement, which seems the very recipe for the proto-liberal, quasi-autonomous legal regime of Shakespeare's Venice: '[E]ven without the Government's intervention, inequality of prestige and authority becomes inevitable among Private Individuals as soon as, united in one Society, they are forced to compare themselves to one another and, in the continual use they have to make of one another, to take account of the differences they find.'[240] The ways we measure one another 'are of several kinds'. If we take our own modern and many earlier societies into account, then four principle types of measurement emerge (treating 'nobility and rank' as two variations of the same type). '[W]ealth, nobility or rank, Power and personal merit are generally the principle distinctions by which one is measured in Society.'[241] Rousseau like Shakespeare, and Marx like Plato, can suggest that wealth is nevertheless the ultimate form of measurement 'to which they are finally reduced, because . . . it can readily be used to buy all the rest'.[242] Like Shakespeare's image of our psychological inundation by the ethos of measurement, Rousseau underscores that selfsame psychological immersion, as the means whereby we achieve justice are precisely what turn us all into mutual enemies.

> [T]his universal desire for reputation, honors, and preferment which consumes us all exercises and compares talents and strengths, how much it excites and multiplies the passions and, in making all men competitors, rivals, or rather enemies, how many reverses, how many successes, how many catastrophes of every kind it daily causes by leading so many Contenders to enter the same lists.[243]

The best, the just, becomes indistinguishable from the worst, the unjust.

> [I]t is to this ardour to be talked about, to this frenzy to achieve distinction which almost always keeps us outside ourselves, that we owe what is best and what is worst among men, our virtues and our vices, our Sciences and our errors, our Conquerors and our Philosophers. [. . .] [I]f one sees a

---

240 OI-Gour 1997:183 (OI, JJR-OC 3:188–9).
241 OI-Gour 1997:183 (OI, JJR-OC 3:189).
242 OI-Gour 1997:184 (OI, JJR-OC 3:189).
243 OI-Gour 1997:184 (OI, JJR-OC 3:189).

> handful of powerful and rich men at the pinnacle of greatness and fortune while the masses grovel in obscurity and misery, it is because the former value the things they enjoy only to the extent that the others are deprived of them.[244]

Rousseau's challenge to meritocracy rejects free-market notions that fierce competition promotes the most favourable socio-economic conditions, presumably as the best foundation for just political and legal systems. Marx, too, throws down the gauntlet. Competition, for Marx, takes place neither among persons equal at the starting point nor under neutral rules. It instead forms part of a broader process by which the working population, disadvantaged from the outset, becomes progressively de-humanised in an ever accelerating decline, and in tandem with ever mounting competition, until the workers turn into nothing more than eating, sleeping and working machines. It is wealth, particularly in its privatised form, which produces that injustice, yet wealth as the constant expression of sheer measurement and comparison.

> Through the increase of the solely working class of people, competition among workers grows, so their price decreases. In the factory that position of the worker reaches is zenith. [. . .] [As] competition among capitalists grows, along with the concentration of capital, the large capitalists ruin the small ones [. . .] Insofar as the number of capitalists declines, their competition with respect to workers almost no longer exists at all; and insofar as the number of workers increases, their competition among each other becomes that much more expanded, unnatural and violent.[245]

Measurement becomes competition, competition becomes de-humanisation, and de-humanisation becomes the very model of injustice. That process occurs not only across populations economically governed by principles of measurement and competition, but within the lives of those most subject to that de-humanisation.

> [T]he division of labour renders [the worker] ever more one-dimensional and dependent, bringing about not only competition of people, but also of machines. Once the worker has deteriorated to a machine, the machine can come to bat as his competitor.[246]

---

244 OI-Gour 1997:184 (OI, JJR-OC 3:189).
245 ÖpM-1, MEW 40: 473–74.
246 ÖpM-1, MEW 40: 474.

Marx later continues, describing the justice of a privileged class as itself the injustice of those subordinated to it. Under rigidly capitalist conditions of ownership and production, wealth measures all, and the most grotesque comparisons dominate society.

> Work creates miracles for the wealthy man, but deprivation for the worker. It creates palaces, but caves for the worker. It creates beauty, but deformity for the worker. It replaces [human] labour with machines, thrusting some of the workers back into barbaric [kinds of] work, while turning the others into machines. It creates genius [*Geist*], but also creates idiocy, stupidity for the worker.[247]

---

247 ÖpM-1, MEW 40: 513.

Chapter 7
Measurement and modernity

Hierdurch ist die Verdopplung, welche früher an zwey einzelne, an den Herrn und den Knecht, sich vertheilte, in eines eingekehrt.[1]

G. W. F. Hegel

7.1 Introduction

The notion of 'modernity' captures the view that societies 'guided by Reason [are] destined to become ever more efficient and productive'.[2] Justice, in that context, characteristically takes the form of Benthamite or Rawlsian types of projects, plotted out in comprehensive, programmatic and technocratic steps, despite differences in their aims or means. Legal modernity holds special interest for the analysis of measurement theories, as most modern justice theories, for example, in the utilitarian and liberal traditions, reduce fundamentally to measurement, with unity acknowledged, if at all, in only weak or rhetorical ways. *The Merchant of Venice* has shown us a society immersed in the values of measurement, preaching yet never practicing supposedly higher ethical values, with unity collapsed into a sheer strategy for turning the results of measurement to one's optimal socio-economic advantage.

That play does not stand alone as a sketch of justice-as-injustice in modernity. *The Merry Wives of Windsor* had prompted Friedrich Engels to write to Karl Marx, 'The first act of the *Merry Wives* alone contains more life and reality than all German literature.'[3] Similarly, Marx concluded that Shakespeare had 'depicted the essence (*Wesen*) of money precisely',[4] namely as the reduction of all things to commodified, and in that specific sense measureable, value. According to Marx, Shakespeare in *Timon of Athens*, a play now known to have

---

1 PhG IV.B., Werke 3: 162. 'The duplication, which had been divided between two individuals, the master and the servant, thereby becomes one.'
2 Chevallier, 2004, p. 14 ('les sociétés guidées par la Raison [sont] appelées à devenir toujours plus efficaces et performantes').
3 Quoted in NOR2 1255.
4 ÖpM-3, MEW 40: 564.

been co-authored with the master of urban satire Thomas Middleton, elicits two decisive characteristics of money, or indeed of what I am calling money as measurement. First, money is 'the visible God (*die sichtbare Gottheit*), the transformation of all human and natural qualities into their opposite'.[5] It makes 'destroyers' seem 'courteous', 'wolves' seem 'affable', and 'bears' seem 'meek'.[6] Timon speaks to gold coins, 'Thou sold'rest close impossibilities.'[7] Second, for Marx, money is 'the universal whore, the universal pander of individuals and peoples'.[8] As Aristotle had explained, and Rousseau confirmed, money does those things only through and as measurement. It is only one of the guises assumed by measurement as justice. The aim of this chapter is to deepen the last chapter's observations about justice as measurement under the specific conditions of modernity.

7.2 'I'll counterpoise'

Both the main and the minor plots of *Timon of Athens* count among the simplest in the Shakespearean corpus. Shakespeare and Middleton contemplate two basic dramatic premises, instead of elaborating intricate ones. Unlike *The Merchant of Venice*, which displays a more characteristically Shakespearean web of 'things are not as they seem', expecting the viewer to do considerable thematic excavation, *Timon of Athens* is dramatically straightforward. Its parallel plots reflect, respectively, two spheres of the early modern, mercantile state – a sphere of commerce, which patterns the main story, and a military sphere shadowing that commercial one in the sub-plot, just as the early modern mercantile state links military exploits to financial ones. Timon starts out excessive in his generosity to fawning friends, then – unlike Bassanio, whose friends rescue him within the liberal, freely chosen unity which they forge as an ethnic and socio-economic elite – ends up abandoned by them, when he falls into debt and ruin. Even bonds of unity such as those privileged, xenophobic Venetian ones which had salvaged Bassanio have now utterly disintegrated. Timon's life ends in reclusive, self-imposed exile beyond Athens's walls. Meanwhile, the minor plot centres on the captain Alcibiades. Banished for criticising the corruption of a senate that decides to hang one of his soldiers, Alcibiades' troops wage a successful revenge against Athens.

That theme of banishment unites the two plots. It is forced upon Alcibiades, whose military world is a world of force; and it is freely chosen by Timon, whose commercial world is a world of free choice. The two exiles are linked by the apparent themes of the Athenians' ingratitude: towards Timon's

---

5 ÖpM-3, MEW 40: 564. Cf. Tim 14.387, 14.581.
6 Tim 11.94; cf. 14.28–30.
7 Tim 14.388. Dawson and Minton gloss 'sold'rest' as 'binds'. ARD3 301. Jowett observes, 'Soldering was often a metaphor for sexual union.' OXF4 294.
8 Cf. Tim 14.43; ÖpM-3, MEW 40: 564–65.

generosity and towards Alcibiades' military achievements. The inside and outside of Athens remains clearly demarcated in both plots – for Timon, turning his back on the city walls, and for Alcibiades, penetrating them by military force. Shakespeare's Athens has drawn his Venice to a logical conclusion. Venice's hermetically sealed insiders forge an antiseptically exclusive socio-economic unity through more-or-less successful love and amity. *Timon* lacks any central love story,[9] as its male citizens exist as social automatons. They conspicuously lack spouses, children, families, lovers or female counterparts,[10] and Timon's compulsive references to them as a band of 'friends' will ring hollow indeed.[11] They interact with one another only in either professional or mundane contexts.

Justice and injustice in the play superficially suggest a conventional divide between law and morals. On that reading, even if we concede Timon's spendthrift folly, he nevertheless falls victim to the moral injustice of friends hungry to 'feed' upon that foible.[12] At a legal level, the opposite emerges. It is Timon who commits injustice, having incurred debts he cannot pay, and even created complex chains of debt.[13] Superficially, Athenian justice resembles that suggested by a naïvely humanist reading of *The Merchant of Venice*, namely, that mercy ought to prevail over the 'strictly legal' justice which comes to tyrannise Timon and Alcibiades. That reading would have us pity Timon as we might pity Antonio. We would 'forgive' them their human shortcomings – 'human', and indeed 'universally' so. That universalist-humanist reading requires considerable abstraction from social processes, assuming, as it does, that some fundamental matters of justice arise regardless of politics.

Antonio and Timon must be understood not as individuals whose problems arise in abstraction from social processes, but as integral exponents of those processes, indeed more as architects than as victims of them. As Rousseau and Marx would later suggest, Timon's or Antonio's prosperity depends upon entire regimes of justice that secure it, which nevertheless remain inherently guarantors of injustice. Timon's encounter with injustice leads him to curse humanity, but, like Antonio, Timon displays little grasp of the specific role he had played as premier beneficiary of Athenian justice.[14] His overreaction of cursing all of humanity and its injustices outright may indeed provoke in us a universalist-humanist compassion, averting our gaze from that injustice which persists as a product of the justice upon which Timon, like us, thrives. Doing justice always entails doing injustice, because it entails participation in social processes which require criteria of justice that we want

9 Cf. this chapter, text accompanying nn. 33–36.
10 See, e.g., Jowett, 2004, pp. 36–39.
11 Cf. this chapter, text accompanying nn. 49–54.
12 See, e.g., Tim 2.203, 4.154.
13 Cf. this chapter, text accompanying nn. 55–61.
14 See, e.g., Tim 5.40–42.

and for which we can provide no alternative, mostly criteria of measurement, yet which inevitably do injustice. Timon's tragedy is no more the injustice inflicted by Athenians than it is the justice that he had, until his fall, vigorously pursued.

The first word spoken about Timon, by one of his countless erstwhile flatterers, is 'incomparable'.[15] Comparison and measurement pervade Athens, as they dominate Venice. Like Antonio's friends in the opening scene, Timon's guests set the play's mercenary tone in the language of comparison and measurement. As with Venice's vessels that 'curtsy' to great ships, this opening scene underscores differentials measured between high and low, mighty and humble, rich and poor. Even the nautical imagery of immersion is retained. Timon's Steward Flavius, for example, will later admonish him, 'I have/ Prompted you in the ebb of your estate/And your great flow of debts.'[16] One caller, a Poet, describes a tribute he has composed to Timon. The Lady Fortune, as John Jowett reminds us, is more commonly depicted with a wheel churning up and down individuals who exercise no power over their fates.[17] This poet, to the contrary, has 'throned' Fortune 'upon a high and pleasant hill'.[18] 'In contrast with a wheel,' Jowett writes, 'a hill allows post-Machiavellian human agency, or the appearance of it: people *labour* to climb.'[19] Within that transformed vision, Timon's friends are called 'rivals',[20] whom Fortune, still favouring Timon, transforms into 'slaves and servants'.[21]

Speaking to another artist, who is a Painter, the Poet persists in describing Timon's friends, and therefore rivals, in terms of relative measurements of material worth. 'Some' are 'better' than Timon's 'value',[22] yet have nevertheless 'laboured after him to the mountain's top/Even on their knees and hands'.[23] Seeming to speak about Timon with detachment, the Painter nevertheless shows these artists equally enthralled to the ethos of comparison and measurement. He responds to the Poet with a one-up.

> A thousand moral paintings I can show
> That shall demonstrate these quick blows of Fortune's
> More pregnantly than words.[24]

15 Tim 1.1.10.
16 Tim 4.135–7. Cf. 2.54–5, 9.13.
17 Tim OXF4 40.
18 Tim 1.64–5.
19 Tim OXF4 175–6 (Jowett's emphasis).
20 Tim 1.73.
21 Tim 1.72.
22 Tim 1.80.
23 Tim 1.87–8.
24 Tim 1.91–3. Cf. ARD3 96–97 (commenting on 'the paragone, or competition, current in the Renaissance over the question of whether painting or poetry was the superior art'.).

After Timon's fall, the Painter visits him. Timon guesses that the visit is spurred by rumours that Timon has given away gold, which he had accidentally found buried, to those who visit him in his self-imposed exile. Once his suspicion is confirmed, Timon cynically ironises on flattery through terms of hyperbolic measurement and comparison, thrice employing a superlative. Dawson and Minton observe that 'Timon plays on two meanings of *counterfeit*, "likeness" and "falsely represent", at once flattering the painter and accusing him of hypocrisy'.[25]

> Thou draw'st a counterfeit
> *Best* in all Athens; thou'rt indeed *the best*;
> Thou counterfeit'st most lively.[26]

Class barriers inform every play in Shakespeare, but their treatment is not uniform throughout the corpus. In the earlier plays, they are unequivocal. Characters may betray class tensions and may clash along class lines, but the divisions never blur. There is no confusion about social differences between Proteus and Lance, Petruccio and Grumio, the Antipholi and their Dromios, Biron and Costard, Don Pedro and Dogberry, or indeed the aristocrats and commoners in Cade's rebellion.[27] In the middle and later plays, as Shakespeare focuses more closely on the waxing bourgeois and meritocratic ethos, and its consequences for the waning, aristocratic order, the divides steadily blur. The arbitrariness of class differences is highlighted through the ever fiercer terms of measurement and comparison that are invoked to enforce them. Hamlet is 'a prince out of [Ophelia's] star'[28] who 'with a larger tether may . . . walk'.[29] The measurement and comparison now becomes explicit and necessary, because of Hamlet's and Ophelia's liaison. Bertram is, for Helen, 'a bright particular star/. . . so above me',[30] a measurement and comparison that becomes emphatic precisely insofar as Bertram will stray within Helen's reach. Polixenes inveighs against 'a sceptre's heir,/That . . . affects a sheep-hook',[31] precisely because his son and heir has crossed the boundary of class. Posthumus is, for Cymbeline, a 'basest thing',[32] after his daughter has eloped with that young commoner.

Timon would appear to triumph over that age-old injustice of high talent blighted by low birth. An old, wealthy Athenian, with one daughter as his

---

25 ARD3 317. (Editor's italics).
26 Tim 14.614–16 (emphasis added).
27 See, e.g., Heinze, 2009e, pp. 247–58.
28 Ham 2.2.141.
29 Ham 1.3.124.
30 AWW 1.1.88–89.
31 WT 4.4.416–17.
32 Cym 1.1.126. Particularly ironic, in view of Cymbeline's second, non-aristocratic marriage to his Queen. See Pitcher, 2005, p. 162.

sole heiress, complains that Timon's servant Lucilius ranks too low to continue courting his daughter. In the play's lexicon of measurement, he insists, '[M]y estate deserves an heir more raised/Than one which holds a trencher.'[33] As an isolated ethical dilemma, Timon's remedy, granting Lucilius a fortune precisely measured to the old man's, to turn Lucilius into 'an equal husband',[34] seems, leaving aside the sexual innuendo, perfect justice: 'Give him thy daughter,/What you bestow in him I'll counterpoise,/And make him weigh with her.'[35] But that remedy overcomes no injustice at all. Timon recognises that injustice lies solely in the happenstance of fortune, and that Lucilius ought otherwise to be deemed worthy of the match, having proved loyal to Timon.[36] In doing justice merely by measuring up and paying the difference, however, Timon, far from overcoming, wholly acquiesces in the terms of, and in the injustice of, arbitrary class difference. For a remedy he merely administers more of the disease, the *phármakon* of measured wealth. Timon's social justice operates wholly within the terms of an economic order that generates the injustice which he purports to overcome. Timon actively perpetuates that injustice, which assures that others will eternally suffer it even if Lucilius, through the random happenstance of his master's caprice, evades it.

Even after Timon's dramatic turn against wealth and privilege, he will still fall into a stock aristocratic attitude, which not only assumes class differences, but positively scoffs at low birth.[37] Meanwhile, given the closeness of the name 'Lucilius' to 'Lucullus' – the flattering Lord who had consumed Timon's wealth but will deny Timon any aid, and similar to the 'Salerio' and 'Salanio' of *The Merchant of Venice* – Timon, far from deploying his wealth in a way such as to overcome Athenian injustice, remains part of the machine by which yet another Athenian of Lucullus's mould, or 100 of them, will always be manufactured.

Also a mirror of his master Timon, the servant Flaminius will curse Lord Lucullus for refusing to help with Timon's debts: 'Let molten coin be thy damnation.'[38] Jowett recalls, 'The wicked are by tradition punished in hell by a version of their sins, in this case usurers being boiled in or drinking molten lead.'[39] Dawson and Minton draw an analogy to punishments meted out in Dante's *Inferno*.[40] Like Timon, Flaminius, believing he utters a value

---

33 Tim 1.121–2. The reference is to a domestic servant. 'A *trencher* was a wooden plate.' OXF4 179 (editor's italics).
34 Tim 1.144.
35 Tim 1.148–50.
36 Tim 1.146.
37 Tim 14.251–71.
38 Tim 5.51.
39 OXF4 228. Cf. PEN2 155–6.
40 ARD3 227.

that transcends the measuring-out of *suum cuique* – in law, Lucullus owes Timon nothing – in fact recapitulates it. My point is not to villainise Timon no more than to villainise Antonio, but to understand them as exemplars of all of us, participating in norms necessary for justice yet necessarily productive of injustice. The play's attention to social forces beyond isolated events emerges not only through its constant commentary on the otherwise simple action, but also through the play's tendency to de-individualise and anonymise many of its subordinate characters, reducing them to fungible exponents of their classes.[41] Timon confirms that suggestion when, like Othello, he claims he has acted not 'ignobly', out of bad motives, but only 'unwisely', out of ignorance.[42] The deeply individualised and often nebulous concept of *motive* is of particular concern to injustice within ethically isolated contexts. Within broader social, economic and political processes, it is ignorance and knowledge that determine one's relationship to justice and injustice. Antonio's individual motives against Shylock are anti-Semitic; but it is above all Venice's institutionalised anti-Semitism, and its citizens' ignorance or sheer indifference about it as an active product of their own pursuits of justice, which seat Venetian anti-Semitism as a systemic, hegemonic injustice, as injustice in the most meaningful sense, and not merely as an incidental and wholly personalised happenstance. Timon starts the play as an Antonio and ends up as a Shylock – a Shylock created by his own Antonio.

The captain Alcibiades seeks to save one of his men from the death penalty for killing another in a brawl. Shocked at the state's legalist rigidity, he, like Timon, will rail against the hypocrisy of Athenian senators who mete out such harsh sentences while benefiting from their offices to enrich themselves in corrupt financial practices.[43] The senators' legalism becomes a spoof of law reduced to terms, indeed clichés, of measurement as precisely measured retribution, as if the weightiest cases can be summarised in a formula: 'He forfeits his own blood that spills another.'[44] Like Timon, Alcibiades has himself not altogether transcended those same values, despite seeming to condemn them, when he oddly describes the soldier's prior military valour as 'a sufficient briber for his life'.[45] It is ironic that the senators fear a tempestuous soldier as one liable to promote 'factions',[46] given the deep social disintegration, the frontal assault on unity, constantly represented by a society living and breathing nothing but justice as measurement and its peremptory instrument, money.

---

41 See, e.g., Dawson and Minton, 2008, p. 1.
42 Tim 4.169. Cf. the dichotomy of 'bountiful' and 'wise'. Tim 5.38–39.
43 Tim 10.96–97.
44 Tim 10.87.
45 Tim 10.60.
46 Tim 10.30, 10.71.

7.3 'To set a gloss'

When Timon preaches, 'Faults that are rich are fair',[47] he revisits the perennial theme, recurrent in Shakespeare and early modern literature, that wealth propels notions of justice. It becomes the universal measure, adorning the grossest injustice as justice: '[C]eremony was but devised at first/To set a gloss on faint deeds.'[48] As Rousseau suggests, in analysing measurement as conceptually prior to money, it is not as if some other criterion of measurement becomes a better guarantor of justice. It is not fundamentally money, but fundamentally measurement, albeit with money as its familiar embodiment, that, for Rousseau, spawns inequality and thereby injustice. Greater justice can perhaps be promoted through fairer distribution – which Timon at the outset obsessively performs, even if randomly or in caricature. Any notion of fairer distribution, however, far from triumphing over, still only recapitulates measurement, indeed in monetary terms, as the necessary tool of justice.

Timon announces to his friends, 'More welcome are ye to my fortunes/Than my fortunes to me.'[49] He travesties in the apparel of altruism, as an ideal of universal justice, the algorithm of 'more x than y', which only recapitulates the selfsame worldview of measurement and comparison that will condemn him to injustice, once it becomes his turn to tumble into being more debtor than creditor, more x than y. Far from pursuing values above those of measurement and comparison, which would ultimately oppose him to all other Athenians, Timon frequently reiterates them, not unlike the other flattering Lord Lucius, who, anticipating Timon's immanent request for help, compares his prior gifts from Timon with those accepted by Lucullus: 'I must needs confess I have received some small kindnesses from him, as money, plate, jewels, and suchlike trifles – nothing comparing to his', that is, those given to Lucullus.[50] Dawson and Minton observe that 'Lucius, by referring to the gifts bestowed on him as *trifles* in comparison with what Lucullus customarily received, shrewdly prepares the way for his own imminent denial of Timon.'[51] Again to the gathered Athenians, Timon rejoices, 'I have told more of you to myself than you can with modesty speak in your own behalf',[52] more x than y, as if it were a contest. Invoking the gods to that effect to answer his own rhetorical question, Timon's bogus comparative turns to a hyperbolic superlative: '"O you gods," think I, "what need we have any friends if we should ne'er have need of 'em? They were the most needless creatures living."'[53] Timon's professed aspirations aim to transcend measurement even as his choices of

47 Tim 2.13.
48 Tim 2.15–16.
49 Tim 2.19–20.
50 Tim 6.17–19.
51 ARD3 229 (editors' emphasis).
52 Tim 2.89–91.
53 Tim 2.91–4.

words show him infused with it: 'I weigh my friend's affection with mine own. [. . .] 'tis not enough to give./Methinks I could deal kingdoms to my friends.'[54]

Halfway through the drama, after Timon has realised his inability to pay his debts, a 'strange event'[55] surfaces. Titus serves a lord who is one of Timon's creditors, and points out that strangeness to Hortensius, who serves another lord, and another of Timon's creditors. The strangeness is that Titus must, for his own lord, collect money owed for jewels that Timon had given to the lord of Hortensius.[56] Dawson and Minton remind us that Titus' master, too, has surely accepted gifts from Timon,[57] resulting in the grim irony that 'the various lords have all received gifts' and 'now demand repayment of the cost of those gifts'.[58] The spirit of measurement and comparison lurches towards parody.

> Timon in this should pay more than he owes
> And e'en as if your lord should wear rich jewels
> And send for money for 'em.[59]

Hortensius confirms, 'I know my lord hath spent of Timon's wealth',[60] and adds the probative conclusion, 'And now ingratitude makes it worse than stealth.'[61] In other words, it is the operation of justice which spawns injustice greater than that of the conventional, positive-law injustice of stealing. 'The law shall bruise 'em.'[62]

The notion of 'new law' pervades Shakespeare. It arises in one form or another in most of the plays, superficially alluding to the mythicised transition from Jewish to Christian law, while in fact denoting the transition from the older, feudal-aristocratic regime towards progressive accommodations of market-driven actors and transactions. That is not a transition from 'no measurement' to 'measurement', since feudal relations entail their own criteria of measurement and comparison, sometimes based on criteria beyond human agency, such as birth, a criterion that Macbeth, Bolingbroke or *King Lear*'s Edmund so dramatically challenge. As John of Gaunt nevertheless reminds us in his 'sceptred isle' speech, a more overtly mythicised unity of the 'old law', the older, feudal regime, stands at least as a notional or symbolic counterweight

---

54 Tim 2.217.
55 Tim 8.19.
56 Tim 8.21–22.
57 ARD3 239.
58 ARD3 239.
59 Tim 8.25–7.
60 Tim 8.29.
61 Tim 8.30.
62 Tim 10.4.

to measurement, whereas modernity will lay bare measurement, and measurement alone, as all that justice can practically be, do or mean. Insofar as the myth of a transition from 'old law' to 'new law' carries longstanding connotations of a Christian 'new' testament supplanting the 'old', the population which so zealously preaches 'new law' values of Christian scripture nevertheless just as avidly practices the 'new law' values of the marketplace.

The cynical Apemantus[63] scorns Timon's guests. 'It grieves me to see so many dip their meat in one man's blood.'[64] The Christological, last-supper reference is clear enough.[65] As Timon rebuffs Apermantus's constant carping, 'let my meat make thee silent',[66] leaving aside any sexual innuendo, it becomes hard to resist an allusion to 'my mete', in the sense of merit as something measured out, recalling Shakespeare's more mercenary sense of the 'new law', and reminiscent, in turn, of the comic irony of Aragon's meritocratic ideal in *The Merchant of Venice* or of the naïveté of Cordelia's in *Lear*.[67] As Rousseau observes, measurement, necessary for justice, breeds comparison. Comparison breeds rivalry, and rivalry triggers endless injustice. Apemantus then retorts doubly in snapping, 'I scorn thy meat.'[68] Timon later, in his mock prayer to the gods aimed at expressing his contempt for his false friends, exclaims, with the same seeming pun, 'Make the meat be beloved more than the man that gives it',[69] precisely as he confronts the 'new law', the marketplace world, where one's being, one's humanity, reduces utterly to that which can be meted out, including one's own marketable skills and talents – merit. That scene ends with Timon's fury against his guests, as he throws stones at them. One guest notes the irony of Timon, suddenly turned from philanthrope to misanthrope, who has not thereby abandoned measurement, which none of us ever does. Rather, Timon has only adopted a new criterion of measurement: 'One day he gives us diamonds, next day stones.'[70]

Heralding his self-banishment, Timon will proclaim an anti-metaphysics, a metaphysics of disorder, precisely counter to Ulysses' myth of unity, order

---

63 See, e.g., Dawson and Minton, 2008, pp. 57–61; Jowett, 2004, pp. 75–78.
64 Tim 2.40–1. Cf. Tim 6.62–63, 74; 8.49; 11.65, 11.74–75; 14.416.
65 See, e.g., Jowett, 2004, pp. 34–36.
66 Tim 2.37.
67 Cordelia, too, emerges as a 'new', marketplace princess, able to conceive of human relations as the market does: precisely measured out to suit its function, 'no more nor less'. Lr 1.83–84, 87–88. She, too, is a seeming 'new law' Christ, reflecting the rigour of the 'new law' of credit and debt precisely meted out. Her two sisters, at the opposite end, in their bogus declarations of an absolute love for the king (Lr 1.49–55, 62–70), parody feudal notions of absolute loyalty, of absolute *unity* with the monarch, defined by an equally bogus, absolute, surprisingly Schmittian enmity towards all else, as, among other things, their separate passions for Edmund will belie.
68 Tim 2.38.
69 Tim 11.74–75.
70 Tim 11.114.

and obedience in *Troilus and Cressida*.[71] Classical Western metaphysics, from Plato and Aristotle through to Aquinas and Dante, always discloses a natural order in which *suum cuique* operates even in nature, measuring out a cosmic justice, as the context and the model for human welfare: 'The heavens themselves, the planets and this centre/Observe degree, priority and place.'[72] In Timon's anti-metaphysics, measurement has not vanished, but instead, like Hobbes's state of nature, accords to all things all that they can either steal or kill. In the place of a human society aspiring to embrace the order of the sun, moon and stars, that cosmos discloses itself as no better than the injustice of humans. All things in nature do nothing more than assail or steal from one another.

> The sun's a thief, and with his great attraction
> Robs the vast sea. The moon's an arrant thief,
> And her pale fire she snatches from the sun.
> The sea's a thief, whose liquid surge resolves
> The moon into salt tears. The earth's a thief,
> That feeds and breeds by a composture stol'n
> From general excrement.[73]

That natural law of injustice as justice, the latter wholly collapsed into the former, reveals all things in the universe following the same *suum cuique*, a cosmic meting-out to each thing whatever it can devour or deceive, as Timon suggests in a compression of Aesopian fables which no longer require a moral tale, as their conclusions are all foregone.

> If thou wert the lion, the fox would beguile thee. If thou wert the lamb, the fox would eat thee. If thou wert the fox, the lion would suspect thee when peradventure thou wert accused by the ass. If thou wert the ass, thy dullness would torment thee, and still thou lived'st but as a breakfast to the wolf.[74]

Human justice mirrors that natural justice such as to render a specific category of 'injustice' superfluous. Justice is and guarantees injustice.

> Each thing's a thief.
> The laws, your curb and whip, in their rough power
> [Have] unchecked theft.[75]

---

71 See this book, Chapter 6, text accompanying n. 3.
72 Tro 1.3.85–6.
73 Tim 14.436–42.
74 Tim 14.328–33.
75 Tim 14.442–44.

Timon's indicative turns imperative. From the ontological 'is' he derives an ethical and legal 'should', which takes the concomitant form of an injunction and a malediction.

> Bankrupts, hold fast!
> Rather than render back, out with your knives,
> And cut your trusters' throats. Bound servants, steal!
> Large-handed robbers your grave masters are,
> And pill [i.e, plunder] by law.[76]

Like Flaminius's Dantesque calibration of punishments, Timon, again far from overcoming obsessive measurement, simply applies it in tragic farce. Instead of money, bankrupts will pay with their creditors' throats. Instead of rendering service, indentured servants will pay their masters by stealing from them, and so on. Later the flattering poet will add hyperbole to the metaphysics, glibly assuring Timon that '[n]ot all the whips of heaven are large enough' to punish Timon's false friends.[77] Measuring out evils tailored to their subjects, or rather meting out moments of justice so that they may be violated, Timon relishes Alcibiades' war against Athens.

> Let not thy sword skip one.
> Pity not honoured age for his white beard;
> He is an usurer. Strike me the counterfeit matron;[78]
> It is her habit only that is honest,
> Herself's a bawd.[79] [. . .]
>
> Spare not the babe
> Whose dimpled smiles from fools exhaust their mercy.
> Think it a bastard.[80]

To the prostitutes who accompany Alcibiades, Timon snaps, '[H]e whose pious breath seeks to convert you,/Be strong in whore,[81] allure him, burn him up.'[82] For legal professionals, Timon reserves a specially measured and tailored wish, exactly targeting those instruments – speech and language – by which

---

76 Tim 12.8–12. Cf. Tim 14.445–49.
77 Tim 14.595.
78 'The married woman whose modesty is a sham.' PEN2 190.
79 'She looks honest only by her outward dress and appearance; inside she is a pander.' ARD3 281.
80 Tim 14.111–21. Cf. 14.703–19.
81 Glossed as 'resolute in whoring' PEN2 192; cf. OXF4 277.
82 Tim 14.141–42.

nominal justice works substantive injustice:[83] 'Crack the lawyer's voice/That he may never more false title plead,/Nor sound his quillets[84] shrilly.'[85] Timon wishes the curse of competition and rivalry even upon unborn twins, with the maternal womb their battlefield.[86]

> Twinned brothers of one womb,
> Whose procreation, residence, and birth
> Scarce is dividant [divided], touch them with several fortunes,
> The greater scorns the lesser. [. . .]
> Raise me this beggar and deject this lord.[87]

A contrary irony emerges from Timon's steward Flavius, charged with the daily calculations of household incomings and expenditures. Flavius had long sought to warn Timon of the mounting debts, but to no avail.[88] Confronted with Timon's ruin, he commiserates with the bleak fates of the other household servants. Not throwing off measurement entirely, which is impossible on any notion of justice, the Steward nevertheless embraces an ideal of equitable shares – the only figure in the play to do so sincerely – and spoken in the language of unity.

> Good fellows all,
> The latest of my wealth I'll share among you.
> Wherever we shall meet . . .
> Let's yet be fellows; [. . .]
> *He gives them money.*
> Let each take some.
> Nay, put out all your hands. Not one word more.[89]

The injustice that follows from just actions echoes through the play as a refrain.

> Strange, unusual blood[90]
> When man's worst sin is he does too much good.
> Who then dares to be half so kind again?
> For bounty, that makes gods, does still mar men.

---

83 Cf. Heinze, 2012b.
84 Glossed as 'verbal niceties, quibbles'. OXF4 279. Cf. 1H6 2.4.17.
85 Tim 14.153–55.
86 On similar, primordially fratricidal imagery in Racine, see Heinze, 2010b.
87 Tim 14.3–9.
88 Tim 2.191–204; 4.119–67.
89 Tim 13.22–28.
90 Glossed as 'temperament, passion', OXF4 264; 'unnatural race of man', ARD3 270. Cf. PEN2 182; ARD2 88.

> My dearest lord, blessed to be most accursed,
> Rich only to be wretched, thy great fortunes
> Are made thy chief afflictions.[91]

Timon curses the earth itself as 'Thou common whore of mankind that puts odds/Among the rout of nations.'[92] According to Dawson and Minton, '[t]he earth is figured as a whore because it is available to all (*common*), and people fight over it as it "puts odds/Among the rout [= mob] of nations".'[93] 'Odds' and 'odd' are common Shakespearen terms of measurement, often ironic, and often appearing in contrast to 'even'.[94] 'Odds' can simultaneously denote 'inequalities' and 'strife'.[95] Timon certainly traces the origin of war to material acquisitiveness, but more primordially, like Rousseau, to measurement, comparison and rivalry as such, with material wealth again as measurement's premier incarnation. 'Religious canons, civil laws', two supposed systems of justice, 'are cruel;/Then what should war be?'[96] In *Much Ado about Nothing*, the 'merry war'[97] between Beatrice and Benedick manifests as measurement and comparison elevated to comically absurd levels.[98]

Justice in this 'new law' world takes the form of 'healths' that constantly 'will make' one's 'state look ill'.[99] The analogy between bodily health and the health of society, justice, is standard in classical thought, already ubiquitous in Plato, and revives in early modernity.[100] Like Plato's *phármakon*, illness's cause and cure, such 'nutriment' readily reveals itself as 'poison',[101] and the physician's 'antidotes are poison'.[102] Still early in the play, detached from Timon's 'last supper' banquet and looking on, Appemantus quips his version of *homo homini lupus*.

> I wonder men dare trust themselves with men.
> Methinks they should invite them without knives:
> Good for their meat, and safer for their lives.
> There's much example for't. The fellow that sits next him, now parts bread with him, pledges the breath of him in a divided draught, is the readiest man to kill him.[103]

---

91 Tim 13.38–44.
92 Tim 14.43.
93 ARD3 275 (editors' emphasis and internal gloss).
94 See, e.g., LLL 3.1.81–94.
95 Crystal and Crystal, 2002, p. 303.
96 Tim 14.60–61.
97 Ado 1.1.59.
98 See, e.g., Gay, 1994, pp. 143–77.
99 Tim 2.56–7.
100 Cf., e.g., Tim 4.191, 5.13–14, 5.52; 7.11–12; 8.70–73; 14.84.
101 Tim 5.57–8.
102 Tim 14.432.
103 Tim 2.43–5.

Apemantus presents, as Dawson and Minton observe, 'the classic outsider/commentator type'.[104] He carps at self-delusion and social hypocrisy, like *King Lear*'s Fool or *Troilus and Cressida*'s Thersites. While Apemantus 'really does aim to do good to Timon',[105] his worldview is less straightforward than he suggests. In Molière's terms, Apemantus, at the outset, spontaneously plays the Alceste, the misanthrope, to Timon's Philinte, or social butterfly. When Timon's fortunes collapse, those roles reverse, as Timon shuns humanity while Apemantus boasts of uses for it. Frequent analogies are drawn between the misanthropic Apemantus and Diogenes, the founder of cynical philosophy, with Apemantus depicted as Timon's opposite extreme, as 'opposite to humanity'.[106] After Timon's fall, however, Apemantus embraces no such extremity, praising instead an Aristotelian golden mean in character and conduct.[107] That synthesis in one person of Diogenes and Aristotle is ironic, as two more incompatible schools are scarcely imaginable. It is unsurprising, then, that Apemantus and Timon, first appearing as opposite equals, become, like Antonio and Shylock, like Socrates and Thrasymachus, different faces of the same principle.

However we may wish to decode Apemantus's person or thoughts, it is clear that he, too, remains an inevitable participant in the injustice he rejects. Much may commend his rejection of wine in favour of '[h]onest water, which ne'er left man i'th'mire'.[108] What nevertheless remains is his framing of the comparison, in terms of measurement, as if his categorical right thereby stands in mutual exclusion to all others' categorical wrong: 'This and my food are equals; there's no odds.'[109] When, after turning towards misanthropy, Timon trades insults with Apemantus, their banter about love and hate collapses into terms of measurement. To Apemantus's praise, 'I love thee better than e'er I did', Timon responds in an equal through opposite measure: 'I hate thee worse.'[110] Apemantus's simultaneously obtuse and platitudinous praise of contented poverty over precarious wealth defeats itself precisely by failing to transcend, by remaining locked within, the logic of measurement and comparison which it purports to question.

> Willing misery
> Outlives uncertain pomp, is crowned before –
> The one is filling still, never complete,
> The other, at high wish. Best state, contentless,

---

104 ARD3 55.
105 ARD3 58.
106 Tim 1.276.
107 Tim 14.302–5.
108 Tim 2.59.
109 Tim 2.60.
110 Tim 14.234–35.

> Hath a distracted and most wretched being,
> Worse than the worst, content.[111]

Timon's retort, one of the play's more striking passages, unmasks Timon less as Apemantus's nemesis, and more as a bird of his feather. Noting Apemantus's humble birth, Timon goes so far as to measure Apemantus against the dissolute person whom Timon speculates that Apemantus *would have* become *if* Apemantus had been better born. As mentioned earlier, far from scorning wealth and privilege, as he purports to do, Timon maintains the aristocrat's disdain for Apemantus's low birth.

> Thou art a slave whom fortune's tender arm
> With favour never clasped, but bred a dog.
> Hadst thou like us from our first swathe proceeded
> The sweet degrees that this brief world affords
> To such as may the passive drudges of it
> Freely command, thou wouldst have plunged thyself
> In general riot, melted down thy youth
> In different beds of lust, and never learned
> The icy precepts of respect, but followed
> The sugared game before thee.[112]

Throughout these volleys, the language of measurement and comparison relentlessly lock Timon's and Apemantus's respective assaults into pat, simplistic, binary formulas of more-*a*-than-*b* and less-*c*-than-*d*. Apemantus chides Timon.

> The middle of humanity thou never knewest, but the extremity at both ends. When thou wast in thy gilt and thy perfume, they mocked thee for too much curiosity;[113] in thy rags thou knowest none, but art despised for the contrary.[114]

The formula straightforwardly reduces the play's eponymous hero to a measurement of one Timon against another Timon. Timon's grasp of injustice descends into a rivalry for misery against Apemantus, a farce of *more miserable than thou*. 'But myself/Who had the world as my confectionary,/[. . .] I to bear this,/That never knew but better, is some burden.'[115] In a quasi-stichomythic follow-up, those more elaborate contests again degenerate to

---

111 Tim 14.243–48.
112 Tim 14.253–60.
113 Glossed as '(a) delicacy, fastidiousness, (b) desire for novelty'. OXF4 289.
114 Tim 14.302–5.
115 Tim 14.260–68.

sheer one-ups. When Timon barks, '[M]end my company: take away thyself',[116] Apemantus's mirror-image retort measures out the same length, 'So I shall mend mine own by th' lack of thine.'[117] Then Timon again: '"Tis not well mended so, it is but botched.'[118] Dawson and Minton gloss that final retort to mean that 'if Apemantus leaves Timon's company and relies merely on his own, this would result in even worse company (for Apemantus would have only himself)'.[119] No rhetorical technique illustrates better than stichomythia Nietzsche's critique of reason as sheer, petty measuring-out, justice collapsed into the unseemly tit-for-tat which is the essence of legalism in what he views as our decline from heroic to mercantile values. Apemantus later mocks, 'When I know not what else to do, I'll see thee again.'[120] Timon first measures back precisely, 'When there is nothing living but thee, thou shalt be welcome.'[121] He then measures out a length further with a new, equally prosaic comparison, another better-*x*-than-*y*: 'I had rather be a beggar's dog than Apemantus.'[122] What follows is full-blown stichomythia, simultaneously a tragedy and a farce of measurement and comparison as sheer one-upping.

> Apemantus
>   Thou art the cap of all the fools alive.
> Timon
>   Would thou wert clean enough to spit upon.
> Apemantus
>   A plague on thee! – Thou art too bad to curse.
> Timon
>   All villains that do stand by thee are pure.
> Apemantus
>   There is no leprosy but what thou speak'st.
> Timon
>   If I name thee.
>   I'll beat thee, but I should infect my hands.
> Apemantus
>   I would my tongue [i.e. words] could rot them off.
> Timon
>   Away thou issue of a mangy dog! [. . .]
> Apemantus
>   Beast!

---

116 Tim 14.286.
117 Tim 14.287.
118 Tim 14.288.
119 ARD3 294.
120 Tim 14.353–54.
121 Tim 14.355–56.
122 Tim 14.356–57.

Timon
  Slave!
Apemantus
  Toad!
Timon
  Rogue, rogue, rogue![123]

Throughout these volleys, the language of measurement and comparison relentlessly lock Timon's and Apemantus's respective assaults into pat, simplistic, binary formulas of more- or less-*x*-than-*y*. Similarly, the divinity of wealth is assessed by a comparative account of the temple in which it is worshipped: 'What a god's gold,/That he is worshipped in a baser temple/Than where swine feed!'[124]

Timon of Athens ends with Timon's death announced, but its means uncertain.[125] Alcibiades returns, triumphant over Athens, whose senators acquiesce in his demand for justice. Superficially, the play seems to end on that note of so-called 'healing', which scholars in our time ever crave to discover in the Bard, indeed re-enforced by the posthumous tribute to Timon.[126] Alcibiades indeed demands strict application of the rule of law.

[N]ot a man
Shall pass his quarter or offend the stream
Of regular justice in your city's bounds
But shall be remedied to your public laws
At heaviest answer.[127]

That decree is curious, since rigorous, rule-bound application of law was what had first spurred Alcibiades to revolt, with the execution of his soldier for committing an honour killing. Admittedly, the imposition of that heavy sentence by Athens's corrupt senate played a decisive role. Yet even the most upright judges would have had to impose the same penalty had they followed Timon's new rule of strict legality. Against which injustice, then, did Timon originally revolt? Against the injustice of the inflexible penalty? Or only against the injustice of its pronouncement by corrupt officials, such that he would have accepted the punishment had it been issued by a more respectable body?

Neither explanation seems wholly supported by the text. On the one hand, Alcibiades stresses too much the senators' corruption to suggest that such a

---

123 Tim 14.358–75.
124 Tim 582–84.
125 See Tim 15.757–58, 17.66–74.
126 Tim 17.75–82.
127 Tim 17.59–63.

charge is irrelevant to the integrity of the soldier's sentence.[128] On the other hand, Alcibiades' strenuous attempts to argue from the standpoint of equity, in order to avoid the harsh result of a strict application of law,[129] are urged in arguments clearly separate from those relating to the senators' corruption. Alcibiades says nothing more about the matter, and indeed seems quick to place Athenian law back in the hands of those who had been governing all along. In the context of the play, and of the treatment of justice throughout Shakespeare, his description of justice as a 'stream' seems nearly an oxymoron, something fleeting and slippery, antithetical to a solid foundation for justice, the lack of which is so persistently lamented throughout the play. The play's superficially satisfying, or 'healing' resolution, in fact leaves Athens with a vague notion of justice, and with dubious stewards for it – the very recipe for restoring justice to its perpetual status as a system of injustice.

7.4 'If things be measured equal to their worth'

Few early modern writers are as singularly concerned with the problem of injustice as Pierre Corneille, who examines it in comic, tragic-comic and tragic genres. While Shakespeare's biographers wonder whether the English playwright's insights into law stem in part from a legal apprenticeship undertaken during his youthful, 'lost' years,[130] Corneille leaves no doubt. Born into a middle-class family,[131] Corneille receives a legal education and enters practice before turning to the stage.[132] As with Shakespeare, and later Molière, Corneillian comedy pokes fun at the ascendant values of the marketplace, and of a bourgeoisie emerging to challenge earlier, feudal and aristocratic power structures. Hence those plays' frequent giggles at injustices, often broken contracts,[133] within private-law contexts. Meanwhile, as with Shakespeare, Corneille's more overtly political dramas turn to constitutional and public-law concerns, raising questions about the foundations of power, law and government.

In *Corneille et la dialectique du héros*, Serge Doubrovsky is right to explain that love in Corneille's tragic compositions will involve what Corneille calls 'a crucial state interest' (*un grand intérêt d'État*).[134] Doubrovsky is wrong, however, to deduce from that observation that sentiment in the early comedies follows solely its own 'internal dialectic', as opposed to a broader, political one.[135] The criticism is worth making, not because an immediate dispute with Doubrovsky's 1963 essay is now required, but because that more general

---

128 Tim 10.96–97.
129 See Tim 10.40–77.
130 See, e.g., Hood-Phillips, 1972, pp. 176–92.
131 Biet, 2005, pp. 11–12.
132 Biet, 2005, p. 20.
133 Cf., e.g., CE 4.1.
134 Doubrovsky, 1963, pp. 88, 120.
135 Doubrovsky, 1963, p. 88.

understanding of Corneille's early comedies as apolitical is not infrequent in the traditional commentaries,[136] if only through their sheer silence on the early work – their tendency to see serious political commentary mostly in Corneille's tragic writing.

Such views display the error of seeing law and justice primarily in conventional and institutional terms, overlooking them as both expressions of, and as factors influencing, the broader matrix of social attitudes and actions. Corneille's theatre stands out for its pervasively 'juridical' character, its dialectical structure, as the title and content of Doubrovsky's analysis reveal. The characters' confrontations of conflicting ideas in a prosecutorial vein, always remains relevant to its broader culture as both source and product of law, even in those plays not placed in any overtly political or judicial context. Those juridical traits, which will recur in Molière and Racine, mark Corneille's earliest play, the comedy *Mélite* (1629), and survive through to his final, bitter tragedy *Suréna* (1674). If Doubrovsky and others are right to see, for example, *Le Cid's* Rodrigue as pre-eminently political, they are wrong to overlook Rodrigue's predecessors in the comedies,[137] when those figures in fact constantly reflect legal modernity emerging in tandem with the marketplace world. Doubrovsky's distinction between 'a simple difference of *goods*' (*une simple différence des* biens) which mark the comedies' protagonists, and 'a difference of *rank*' (*une différence de* rang) which emerge in the tragedies[138] is fair enough, but in no way corresponds to any difference between, on the one hand, 'legal' or 'political', and, on the other hand, 'non-legal' or 'apolitical' worlds. The world of goods is obviously as politically driven, and as legally structured, as is the world of rank.[139]

Insisting that the values at issue in Corneillian theatre are always only aristocratic, Doubrovsky, again reflecting earlier misconceptions, ends up with a false dichotomy between crises of aristocratic values in the tragic writings, and largely apolitical, purely personal crises, in the comedies.[140] The comedies do not, however, display apolitical, but rather bourgeois, 'privatised' crises of law or society, which have perennially lent themselves to comedy. They offer critical social insights, and are, then, not as 'reactionary' as Doubrovsky suggests.[141] Doubrovsky argues that 'the entirety' of Corneillian theatre 'freezes' (*immobilises*) the Hegelian Master-Slave dialectic at 'the moment of the Master's triumph as such' (*le moment de la Maîtrise en tant que tel*).[142] If that

---

136 Others have indeed noted the 'unity of Corneillian theatre' across comic and tragic genres. Prigent, 1986, p. 33 (citing Sweetser and Starobinksi).
137 See, e.g., Doubrovsky, 1963, p. 88.
138 Doubrovsky, 1963, pp. 88–89 (Doubrovsky's italics).
139 Nadal observed long ago the 'radical' shift in early Corneille away from his era's erstwhile theatrical exoticism, towards bourgeois and even 'analytic' realism. See Nadal, 1948, p. 67.
140 Doubrovsky, 1963, p. 87, n. 76.
141 Doubrovsky, 1963, p. 96.
142 Doubrovsky, 1963, pp. 94–95.

observation is exaggerated with respect to the comedies, it is nevertheless fair regarding what Doubrovsky calls 'a complex *internal* dialectic in the ambition of Mastery' (*une complexe dialectique* interne *du projet de Maîtrise*),[143] as applied specifically to the play about which he introduces that point, namely, *Le Cid*, to which I shall return.

Much of Corneille's debut in *Mélite* is deliberately frivolous, even if the talents of the later tragedian are immediately evident.[144] Every Corneillian theme is already germinating in his first, farcical work, completed when the young lawyer is aged 23. The play, whose plot could not be simpler, follows three young men entangled in love intrigues centred on the play's eponymous heroine. The first to fall in love with Mélite is Éraste. In the opening scene, Éraste laments to his friend Tircis that Mélite rebuffs him. They debate the best way to win a woman's love, expressing opposed attitudes, each with a long cultural history. Tircis's initial view is simultaneously misogynist and Machiavellian. He depicts women either as objects for the man to conquer while he avoids the duties of marriage, or as objects of marriage only for acquiring women's wealth.[145]

That latter option plants the action within the ongoing critiques of materialism and mercantilism already evident in Shakespeare, Middleton and other early modern writers. *Mélite* will focus on money as one of a range of instruments of competition, rivalry and measurement. Tircis's attitude anticipates the overtly abusive history of *Médée* (*Medea*) (1635), where Corneille will more chillingly emphasise the self-interested, exploitative dimension of Jason's masculinity. At first, Éraste counters Tircis's philosophy only with standard, blind lover's romanticism, describing Mélite as divine[146] and therefore unattainable. Still introducing the play's themes, the two young men express only flip sides of the same patriarchal notions. Although the play is too light-hearted to deal with injustice in any overt way, it already contains ingredients that will attract weightier consideration in later works.

Rousseau leaves no real comment on *Mélite*, which, by the 18th century, stands in the shadow of Corneille's tragedies. Much of Rousseau's analysis nevertheless pertains, even if Rousseau can scarcely be called a warrior against patriarchy.[147] For Rousseau, injustice first arises among humans not as they are still solely preoccupied with their basic needs, but as they pursue distinctly social enterprises, entering into competition and therefore comparison with

---

143 Doubrovsky, 1963, p. 95 (Doubrovsky's italics).
144 See, e.g., Nadal, 1948, p. 80.
145 Mél 1.1.64–126. George Couton, reading such into such passages an *éducation sentimentale*, PC-OC 11, n. 1 and 17, n. 4, gets more than he bargains for. The young men's sentimental education becomes an initiation into patriarchy.
146 Mél 1.1.70–78, 1.2.167.
147 Perhaps too Aristotelian for his own good, the radical democrat's *La Nouvelle Héloïse*, for example, emphasises his heroine's initiation into personal and social subordination to her husband.

one another. Corneille's first play takes middle-class subjects, not constrained by material necessity, and therefore preoccupied with social matters in that leisurely vein.[148] Tircis advises Éraste in the abstract, creating a competition and therefore an inevitable comparison of views about prevailing over women. More importantly, upon meeting Mélite, and practicing the private Machiavellianism that he preaches, Tircis will become Éraste's rival for Mélite's affections.[149] From the outset, the 'Rousseauvian Fall', the loss of paradise, the moment at which camaraderie turns to rivalry, is triggered, and the comedy, like later Corneillian theatre, will draw largely from the piling of comparison upon comparison, measurement upon measuremnt. In *The Merchant of Venice*, socio-political insiders are defined along religious and ethnic lines as Venetian Christians, forging their inter-group unity, their unified purity, in opposition to ethnic and religious outsiders. As *Mélite* lacks such outsiders, the characters will, in that 'Rousseauvian Fall', move from a primordial, fraternal unity towards the progressive construction of their own disunity, their own alienation of one another, their own self-created injustice. It is remarkable how Racine's first play *La Thébaïde*, in the Theban context, tells that same story of a primordial fratricidal, Cain-and-Abel link, between Antigone's brothers Eteocles and Polyneices,[150] creating the bleakest possible version of a theme of individual and interpersonal alienation which Corneille's first play spins as a sheer frolic (although Corneille's *Horace* will revisit these themes in a more sinister mood). 'Our abiding cruelty is as evident in the horrors of civil war as it is in the pleasures of laughter.'[151]

Reflecting early modern anxieties about the gradual displacement of one questionable regime by another, of status-based aristocracy by marketplace and mercantile values and their 'visible God', themes about benign appearances masking self-serving and even brutal realities pervade early modern literature, as *The Merchant of Venice* or *Timon of Athens* make abundantly clear. Shakespeare typically portrays that tension as hypocrisy. Characters like Antonio, Bassanio, Portia, or Timon's false friends, condemn duplicity in others while practicing it themselves. Corneille's Tircis, by contrast, gleefully announces such deception as his game plan, even if Mélite, who will fall for him anyway, quickly notices it.[152] That overtly acknowledged reality, Tircis's desire for personal advancement, becomes the measure against which his mercenary ends and fraudulent means are to be determined,[153] as his future wife's wealth will decide that criterion's success. Éraste avows having used the same tactics on an earlier woman, before having fallen for Mélite,[154] just as Tircis, after

148 Cf., e.g., Mél 3.7.1143.
149 See, e.g., Mél 1.3.246–50.
150 See Heinze, 2010b, pp. 89–91.
151 Shklar, 1990, p. 36 (discussing Molière).
152 Mél 1.2.198–99, 205–6
153 Mél 1.1.22, 26, 64–67; cf. 1.2.153. Cf. also Mél 1.2.173, and, ironically, 1.2.191, 193.
154 Mél 1.1.69.

meeting her, will avow abandoning them,[155] be it only partially,[156] as if the two young men had tacitly agreed on that patriarchal strategy as the universal male default mode.[157]

Éraste invokes an agelessly comic notion of 'injustice'[158] when he complains of Mélite's refusal to requite his love. That comedy draws precisely from a notion of justice as *suum cuique*: the love shown, or felt, by the lover must be reciprocated to the same extent by the beloved. The lover's feelings being absolute, the beloved must display the same. Molière will explore that comic sense of justice to an extreme, effectively neurotic degree through Alceste in *Le Misanthrope*. Shakespeare's Proteus, spurned by Sylvia, had already exuded it in the final, near-rape scene of *Two Gentlemen of Verona*. Like Proteus and Alceste, Éraste asserts *suum cuique* justice in the patriarchal and proprietary terms of his 'rights' (*mon droit*) to Mélite.[159] Like Proteus in particular,[160] Éraste's duel imagery, referring to Tircis as his 'second',[161] sketches a parallel between the brute force always underlying law, *le droit*, and the implicit violence always inherent in patriarchy, even when it takes ostensibly frivolous forms.[162]

Like Benedick confronting Beatrice in *Much Ado About Nothing*, Éraste will have to hear Mélite rebuff him in quasi-stichomythic retorts precisely measured to his overtures, applying her diametrically opposed criterion of *suum cuique*. Corneille emerges both in form and in content as jurist and dialectician when that comically juridical banter becomes amplified through the equal phonic measurements of Alexandrine couplets. Even that comic pursuit illuminates the pursuer of justice as constantly generative of his own injustice.

> Éraste
> > Votre divin aspect suspendant mes douleurs
> > Mon visage du vôtre emprunte les couleurs.
>
> Mélite
> > Faites mieux, pour finir vos maux et votre flamme
> > Empruntez tout d'un temps les froideurs de mon âme.[163]

155 Mél 1.2.200–1, 1.3.215–19.
156 Mél 1.3.217–19, 228.
157 Cf. Mél 1.4.278.
158 Mél 1.2.69.
159 Mél 1.2.189.
160 TGV 5.4.55–59.
161 Cf. PC-OC 15, n. 2.
162 See, e.g., Shr 4.3.
163 Mél 1.2.167–70.

> Éraste
> > My woes all give way to your divine eyes.
> > From your sweet gaze my face borrows its guise.
>
> Mélite
> > Then give your pains and passion this fine goal:
> > Borrow, for good, the chill within my soul.

Feeling oneself to be under the power of one's beloved is a poetic commonplace, which, in the French Baroque, is frequently expressed as being under the beloved's 'law' (*sous sa loi*). When Éraste employs that self-description,[164] it, too, comically conveys the sense, often reproduced in tragic works, of perceived or actual injustice resulting from some active pursuit of justice.[165] In Cartesian and bourgeois modernity, *suum cuique*, will constantly take the form of that meritocratic ethos – ubiquitous today, while Rousseau had already warned against it – and few words will recur so frequently, or so problematically, throughout the Corneillian corpus as merit, *mérite*, again in both the silliest and the bleakest contexts. When the play's third male lover, Philandre, proclaims his love for the play's other heroine, Tircis's sister Cloris, in the standard hyperbolic terms,[166] that discourse of merit surfaces to produce the paradox that something supposedly limitless, like Philandre's love, can nevertheless be captured in terms of merit, which are terms of limit-setting, indeed of commodification, through measurement, and which can identify boundless virtue only on the supposition that Cloris's virtue might indeed, by that same measurement, be bounded. Cloris coyly recoils, in the same language of measurement,

> Cloris
>   Tu m'en vas tant conter de ma perfection,
>   Qu'à la fin j'en aurai trop de présomption.
> Philandre
>   S'il est permis d'en prendre à l'égal du mérite,
>   Tu n'en saurais avoir qui ne soit trop petite.
> Cloris
>   Mon mérite est si peu.[167]

Philandre insists that Cloris accept the compliment. Her refusal, he contends, would reveal his poor judgment in women. He would then be seen to have squandered his attentions on someone who was not worth them (*qui ne valait pas l'offre de mon service*).[168] Éraste, too, after losing Mélite, ponders the loss in terms of straightforward measurement and comparison.

---

164 Mél 1.3.240.
165 Cf. Mél 2.1.388–92.
166 Mél 1.4.256–82.
167 Mél 1.4.279–83. Cf. Mél 2.2.430, 2.5.529.
> Cloris
>   You have so much to tell of my perfection,
>   That soon I shall be filled up with presumption.
> Philandre
>   If things were measured equal to their worth
>   You'd be filled up within the widest berth.
> Cloris
>   My worth is slight.
168 Mél 1.4.286–89.

> C'est ce que j'ai gagné par deux ans de service?
> C'est ainsi que mon feu s'étant trop abaissé
> D'un outrageux mépris se voit récompensé ?
> Tu me préfères donc un traître qui te flatte ? [. . .]
> . . . tu verras à l'effet
> Par le peu de rapport que nous avons ensemble
> Qu'un honnête homme et lui n'ont rien qui se ressemble.[169]

Like Éraste, Philandre derives that point from a *suum cuique* formula, which measures out his deserts according to his merits. Having faced 'struggle' and 'torment' (*D'avoir tant pris de peine, et souffert de tourment*),[170] his assessment of Cloris's merit merely extrapolates from, being rigorously co-extensive with, his assessment of his own. Cloris replies by, for lack of a better phrase, 'pulling a Cordelia'. She deflates the chivalrous hyperbole of boundless love. She replaces it with the hard-nosed, marketplace reality that, because everything has a price, everything therefore has a limit, and therefore a discrete, appraisable measure. Any suggestion of more is ruse and deception, even from her lover.

> Du moins ne prétends pas qu'à présent je te loue,
> Et qu'un mépris rusé que ton cœur désavoue
> Me mette sur la langue un babil affété
> Pour te rendre à mon tour ce que tu m'as prêté.[171]

Philandre's romantic and hyperbolic measures get their reality check, then, from Cloris's studious measure of virtues against faults,

> Au contraire, je veux que tout le monde sache
> Que je connais en toi des défauts que je cache.[172]

---

169 Mél 2.3.466–74.

> That's my reward for two years of devotion?
> And for my passion, which has stooped so low,
> You've nothing but such raw contempt to show?
> A traitor's lies you'd still choose over me? [. . .]
> . . . the end you'll see:
> From the few fleeting bonds we both can summon,
> An honest man has naught with him in common.

170 Mél 1.4.288. Cf. Mél 1.4.298.
171 Mél 1.4.305–08.

> At least, don't claim I speak praise on your part.
> That sly contempt, disowned within your heart,
> Can put my tongue to chatter fast and free,
> And pay you back for all you've lent to me [i.e. Philandre's exaggerated praise].

172 Mél 1.4.309–10.

> Let everyone instead learn what is true:
> I hush, but know, the faults that lie in you.

As the exchange accelerates, both the substantive content and the literary form of equal measurement, comparison and exchange more overtly take the form of bargaining.

> Philandre
> Quant à toi tu te crois de beaucoup plus aimable?
> Cloris
> Sans doute, et qu'aurais-tu qui me fût comparable?[173]

The volley will reach a point at which Cloris asks whether Philandre's protestations can be taken as 'genuine' or 'hard currency' (*de l'argent comptant*),[174] so that the scene's final kiss,[175] innocent enough, is nevertheless more bartered than bestowed. Cloris's brother Tircis arrives, interrupting the kiss, and Cloris discloses to him her plan to marry Philandre. Tircis replies by announcing his new infatuation with Mélite, in the straightforward language of measuring Cloris as a commodity inferior by comparison.

> Ma foi, si ton Philandre avait vu de mes yeux,
> Tes affaires, ma sœur, n'en iraient guère mieux. [. . .]
> . . . repose-t'en sur moi,
> Que celle que j'ai vue est bien autre que toi.[176]

When Mélite again meets Éraste, she will compare him to Tircis in the same terms.[177] My observations to some degree depart from, although they do not contradict, some classic analyses. According to Doubrovsky, '"love", in Corneille, is something very different from the attraction of mutual "merit". . . . [I]t is, in its essence, *desire*.'[178] Doubrovsky cites a persuasive study by Jean Starobinski, who describes 'the fundamental human relationship in Corneille's theatre', that is, love, as that of *éblouissement*, 'being overwhelmed'.[179] I may

---

173 Mél 1.4.313–14.

> Philandre
> And you? Do you have so much more to love?
> Cloris
> That's without doubt. Who else can stand above?

174 Mél 1.4.323.
175 Mél 1.4.331–2.
176 Mél 1.5.355–60.

> If your Philandre had seen with my eyes,
> Your luck, my sister, might not wholly rise. [. . .]
> . . . to speak true,
> I've seen a lady quite different from you.

177 Mél 2.2.432.
178 Doubrovsky, 1963, p. 101 (original emphasis).
179 Starobinski, 1999, 31–41 (Starobinski's italics). Cf. Doubrovsky, 1963, p. 38.

appear to overlook those insights in casting literary characters as obsessed with measurement, like calculating, profit-maximising rationalists, to the exclusion of any other aspirations or emotions. My aim, however, is no more to deny passion than it is to suggest that measurement explains the totality of these plays' thoughts or actions. Of course, it does not. Bassanio's interest in Portia is mercenary, but need not only be mercenary. Portia's interest in Bassanio may involve social climbing, but need not involve only that. Such characters can fall in love while still reflecting the values of an entire history and culture steeped in the mindset of justice as measurement, just as we do. They can still be in love when, in pursuing justice as measurement, they inflict endless injustice upon each other or upon others.

With the opening of Act II, Éraste suddenly transforms into the first in a line of Corneillian heroes who, having received an offence, now enter to recite a soliloquy to ponder his remedy. Tircis is now his rival. Éraste laments his folly in being the author of that offence. He regrets the breach, the loss of unity, that has now opened between the erstwhile companions. It is in the language of theft, of formal injustice, and indeed of contributory negligence, that Éraste blames himself: 'I myself opened the door to this thief.'[180] With that loss of unity comes, in a second soliloquy, the empire of measurement. Éraste inveighs first against Mélite for failing to repay the measure, two years, of his 'service',[181] and then against his new adversary, his new *affronteur*, of whom Éraste declares he shall, with the Freudian irony scarcely opaque, 'measure' his 'sword' (*mésurer mon épée*).[182] Apparently admitting, for the time being, that Mélite cannot be his, his weapon is now to feign a love letter written to Mélite by Philandre. In one such specimen, Éraste will have Mélite 'beginning to value herself', having learned of Philandre's new love for her.

> Je commence à *m'estimer* quelque chose puisque je vous plais, et mon miroir m'offense tous les jours ne me représentant *pas assez* belle comme je m'imagine qu'il faut être pour *mériter* votre affection. Aussi pauvre Mélite ne le croit posséder que par faveur, ou comme une *récompense* extraordinaire d'un *excès* d'amour, dont elle tâche de suppléer au *défaut* des grâces que le Ciel lui a refusées.[183]

Paying the servant Cliton to deliver the message, Éraste reflects on how that lower caste of humanity see neither 'good' nor 'evil' once they stand to

---

180 Mél 2.1.388.
181 See this chapter, text accompanying nn. 168–169.
182 Mél 2.3.485.
183 Mél 3.2.880 *et seq.* (italics added).

> I now think myself *worth* something, because you're pleased with me. Every day, my mirror offends me, not showing me as beautiful as I surely must be to *deserve* your love. Poor Mélite feels *worthy* only by your favour, or as extraordinary *compensation* for an *excess* of love, which she strives to offer for *lack* of that grace which Heaven has refused her.

gain,[184] displaying his superbly Shakespearean oblivion to the fact that it is he, and his own class, who create that mercenary ethos for which he now reproaches a humble servant. Intervening directly to coax Philandre towards Mélite, Éraste will again resort to the language of straightforward comparison of the two heroines, like goods on a shelf,

> Éraste
> Auprès de sa beauté qu'est-ce que ta Cloris?
> Philandre
> Un peu plus de respect pour ce que je chéris.
> Éraste
> Je veux qu'elle ait en soi quelque chose d'aimable,
> Mais la peux-tu juger à l'autre comparable?[185]

By the next act, Philandre will have fallen into the trap. The hope planted by Mélite's supposed love letters to him 'is worth more' than Cloris's 'embraces' (*Leur attente vaut mieux, Cloris, que tes caresses*).[186] Meanwhile Tircis, pursuing Mélite's — beauty? wealth? — has composed for her a sonnet, reminiscent of lovers' bad verses in Shakespeare. It declares that 'nothing is admirable' *compared* to Mélite,[187] and 'nothing is solid' *compared* to his 'loyalty'.[188] His passion is 'incomparable',[189] and yet his 'love' *compares* precisely to her 'beauty'.[190] As the rivalry for Mélite shifts focus to Philandre and Tircis, Tircis challenges Philandre to a duel.

> Celle qui te chérit *vaut bien* un coup d'épée,
> Fais voir que l'infidèle en se donnant à toi
> A fait choix d'un amant qui *valait mieux* que moi.[191]

---

184 Mél 2.6.622–27.
185 Mél 2.7.661–64.

> Éraste
> Next to her beauty what does Cloris have?
> Philandre
> Please — more respect for someone whom I love.
> Éraste
> Though I suppose she's likeable as such,
> Next to the other does she stack up much?

186 Mél 3.1.780.
187 Mél 2.5.517.
188 Mél 2.5.518.
189 Mél 2.5.518.
190 Mél 2.5.520.
191 Mél 3.3.924–26 (italics added).

> The one you love is surely worth a fight,
> Show that the lying mistress who chose you,
> Took someone who loves better than I do.

Consoling Tircis for his apparent loss, Cloris, too, appropriates the language of measurement and comparison of women. For Cloris, too, Mélite, having so little merit (*si peu de mérite*[192]), can be treated as a mediocre and fungible asset, readily replaced by any number (*tant d'autres*) of other women.

> Apprends aussi de moi que ta raison s'égare,
> Que Mélite n'est pas une pièce si rare
> Qu'elle soit seule ici qui vaille la servir.
> Tant d'autres te sauront en sa place ravir.[193]

Reaching its Baroque heights, the play will include two feigned deaths and an episode of questionable madness before the characters repair back to their middle-class normality. Éraste, thinking he has caused the deaths of Tircis and Mélite, will again damn himself to a vision of Hell, measuring out his own ultimate punishments in an Ovidian masquerade of underworld imagery.[194] It is above all, however, the play's more prosaic moments which, as in Shakespeare, reveal the immersion – not merely of our understandings of justice, but of all reality – so deep in the language of measurement as to render none other imaginable or desirable. The worldly nurse in *Romeo and Juliet*, as always in Shakespeare, proclaims only more bluntly the self-serving values which higher born characters expressly foreswear but inevitably practice. After Romeo's banishment, she advises Juliet to marry the Count Paris, whom she compares to Romeo in no uncertain terms.

> I think it best you married with the County [Paris]
> O, he's a lovely gentleman!
> Romeo's a dish-clout to him. An eagle, madam,
> Hath not so green, so quick, so fair an eye
> As Paris hath. Beshrew my very heart,
> I think you are happy in this second match,
> For it excels your first; or if it did not,
> Your first is dead, or 'twere as good he were,
> As living here and you no use of him.[195]

---

192 Mél 3.5.1076.
193 Mél 3.4.1039–42. Cf. Mél 4.2.1281–82.

> Learn from me, too, that you think like a fool
> And that Mélite is not so rare a jewel,
> That she alone is worthy of high grace.
> So many others can fill up her place.

194 Mél 4.6.1451–92.
195 Rom 3.5.217–25

Even in the brooding *Romeo and Juliet*, that kind of blunt or lower comedy is a convention in early modern drama. It comes as no surprise to hear it in Corneille, who would have had no real knowledge of Shakespeare. Mélite's counterpart, her nurse or *Nourrice*, coaching Mélite in courtship, more candidly advises her pupil to shop around for her men. She advises Mélite that a woman ought to keep all such suitors' hopes up, holding out the appearance of an equal measure to all of them. She should maintain the equilibrium of their rivalry, until such time as she chooses her husband, presumably on financial grounds.

> Qu'ils vivent tous d'espoir jusqu'au choix d'un mari,
> Mais qu'aucun cependant ne soit *le plus* chéri,
> Tiens bon, et cède enfin, puisqu'il faut que tu cèdes,
> À qui *paiera le mieux* le bien que tu possèdes.[196]

The Nourrice's preference for Éraste comes as no surprise, as she reminds Mélite that he possess 'two times' Tircis's wealth, 'and more'.[197] The high-born Mélite objects to her Nourrice's mercenary language. Yet, in replying that not wealth, but merit, ought to guide her choice, she does not, as we do not, overcome measurement, but merely substitutes one criterion, one form of *suum cuique*, for another.

> Mélite
>   Tu te places au rang qui n'est dû qu'au mérite.
> La Nourrice
>   On a trop de mérite étant riche à ce point.[198]

7.5 'My spirit's split in two'

Corneille's most famous drama is *Le Cid* (1637). Written as a tragi-comedy, the weightier material, of the type that will dominate the middle and later Corneille, elicits measurement at work in fiercer, starker, bleaker terms than

---

[196] Mél 4.1.1217–20 (italics added).

> Let them all live in hope 'til you have one,
> Give none of them the best place in the sun,
> Take care – you must give over, but addressed
> To him alone who for your goods pays best.

[197] Mél 4.1.1239.
[198] Mél 4.1.1244–45.

> Mélite
>   Merit alone can mount the heights you seek.
> Nourrice
>   Yet wealth like his is merit high enough.

the early comedies can allow. Drawn from medieval Spanish lore,[199] *Le Cid* opens with a comparison between two rivals for the hand of Chimène, daughter of the Count Don Gomès. In the original, 1637 version, Chimène's confidante, Elvire, directly addresses the Count, singling out Don Rodrigue and Don Sanche as the most eminent among the suitors.

> Entre tous ces amants dont la jeune ferveur
> Adore votre fille, et brigue ma faveur
> Rodrigue et Don Sanche à l'envi font paraître
> Le beau feu qu'en leurs cœurs ses beautés on fait naître.[200]

The 1660 version,[201] opening with that conversation not staged, but instead already completed and reported by Elvire in dialogue with Chimène, diminishes Elvire's suggestion of equipoise, of *indifférence*,[202] between the two suitors. Instead, Chimène now intensifies the terms of measurement and comparison, as she asks whether Elvire has revealed to Don Gomès Chimène's preference for Rodrigue.

> N'as-tu point trop fait voir quelle inégalité
> Entre ces deux amants me penche d'un côté?[203]

Unlike comic subordinates, such as *Mélite's* Nourrice, the confidant role in more serious Corneillian drama sometimes serves to inject principles of prudence and moderation, contrasting with the main protagonists' extremes of ecstasy or despair. Recall the similar role played by Nerissa in *The Merchant of Venice*, as her diplomatic comments on Portia's opening allusions to Aristotle's golden mean underscore not only the indiscretion but the hypocrisy of Portia's criteria of measurement.[204] Elvire contrasts with Chimène's impulsive comparison by refraining from measurement. In the 1637 version,

---

199 Cf. Doubrovsky, 1963, p. 96.
200 Cid 1.1.1–4.

> All for your daughter – these young suitors burn
> With love, which through me they all strive to earn.
> Yet Sancho and Rodrigo shine most bright,
> With passion that her beauty sets alight.

201 PC-OC 1488–89. Aside from the slight discrepancies noted here, the versions differ, for purposes of the present analysis, more in form than in content. They require mention only for the opening of Act I. The remaining action, as printed in the 1637 version, will therefore be cited without recourse to the variants.
202 See this chapter, text accompanying nn. 205–206.
203 Cid-1660 1.1.15–16.

> Did you let on that, for me, they're unequal?
> That I yearn for the hand of just one rival?

204 See this book, Chapter 6, Section 6.6.

and essentially retained in the later one, she assures Don Gomès, about Chimène,

> ... pour tous [all the suitors] dedans l'indifférence
> Elle n'ôte à pas un, ni donne d'espérance,
> Et sans les voir d'un œil trop sévère, ou trop doux.[205]

Yet even that non-judging, non-measuring *indifférence* betrays a mind, or at least a father, that measures. As to Chimène's father, Elvire confides, 'He values Rodrigue *as much* as you love him.'[206] If Mélite and her Nourrice, like Portia and Nerissa, each represent a high-born woman and her confidante in a new, proto-capitalist world, their feudal forerunners have not disappeared in early modernity. Like Shakespeare, Corneille constantly evokes the challenge of the emerging, non-aristocratic classes to the ancient aristocratic privileges, embodied in *Le Cid* by Rodrigue. Those old and new orders are sometimes presented as mutually exclusive criteria of measurement, and then other times presented as similar, as merely two different variations of the same theme of measurement.

Accordingly, once Chimène's love for Rodrigue, in comparison to Don Sanche, has been announced, the play's second, secret rivalry, appears. The King's daughter, the Infanta, also in love with Rodrigue, despairs that she can hold out no hope for him. His rank, of 'a simple gentleman' remains inferior.[207]

> ... j'épandrai mon sang
> Plutôt que de rien faire indigne de mon rang.[208]

Closer to Corneille's 17th century than to her medieval model, the Infanta is aware of the competing, meritocratic criterion, modernity's new measuring scheme. Again, as in *Mélite*, and as if preparing Rousseau's critique, the Corneillian corpus makes constant, obsessive reference to *mérite*. At first, that criterion is of no avail to the Infanta. In measuring Rodrigue's birth against her lineage, she measures the meritocratic criterion against the feudal, but as

---

205 Cid 1.1.7–9; cf. Cid-1660 1.1.17–19. Cf. Doubrovsky, 1963, p. 88.

> ... shows indifference for all,
> True hope she gives to none, but lets none fall,
> She looks on each with neither smile nor frown. ...

206 Cid 1.2.38. (Il estime Rodrigue *autant* que vous l'aimez.) (emphasis added). Cf. Cid-1660 1.1.4.
207 That is, 'un simple Chevalier', Cid 1.3.81; 'un simple cavalier', Cid-1660 1.3.76^b.
208 Cid 1.3.85–86.

> ... my blood I'd spend,
> But nothing 'gainst my rank would I intend.

a matter of duty both to the law and the ethos of monarchy, as a 'crucial interest of state',[209] must choose feudal tradition.

> Le seul mérite a droit de produire des flammes [. . .]
> Mais je n'en veux point suivre où ma gloire s'engage [. . .]
> Un noble orgueil m'apprend qu'étant fille de Roi[210]
> Tout autre qu'un Monarque est indigne de moi.[211]

The Infanta will later take more seriously the meritocratic criterion insofar as it can blend with the feudal, as she predicts that Rodrigue's military prowess could result in his ennoblement.[212] Her criteria for measurement will indeed precisely reverse once Rodrigue becomes a *de facto* prince, after conquering two Moorish kings, and being hailed by them as the 'Cid'.[213] That substitute of a feudal for a meritocratic criterion never overcomes, but only varies, and so perpetuates the assumption of justice as measurement. Such competing criteria of measurement travel to the heart of Corneillian tragedy. Chimène can reconcile them as a matter of duty, but in inevitable existential revulsion against – self-alienation and therefore internal division, and internal contradiction, generated by – the feudal criterion of measurement to which she binds herself, committing herself to the injustice of the justice upon which her status depends,

> Je sens en deux parties mon esprit divisé,
> Si mon courage est haut, mon cœur est embrasé :
> Cet hymen m'est fatal, je le crains, et souhaite [. . .]
> . . . je meurs s'il s'achève, et ne s'achève pas.[214]

What immediately follows is the drama's third rivalry, which will unleash the tragic plot. To supervise the education of his son,[215] the King, contrary to the

---

209 See this chapter, text accompanying n. 135.
210 The later variant reads, 'Et je me dis toujours qu'étant fille de Roi . . .'. Cid-1660 1.3.93^d ('Reminding myself always, a King's daughter . . .').
211 Cid 1.3.88–94.

> Desert alone can rightly spark a passion [. . .]
> Yet I shall not endanger rank and station [. . .]
> The daughter of a king learns noble pride,
> Only a monarch may stand by my side.

212 Cid 2.6.534–47.
213 Cid 4.3.1231–35.
214 Cid 1.3.111–18. Cf. Doubrovsky, 1963, p. 89.

> My spirit's split in two, I feel each part:
> My will is strong, yet fire's in my heart.
> This fatal marriage, I both crave and shun [. . .]
> I die for it yet die if it's not done.

215 See PC-OC 710, n. 1.

Count's expectation,[216] appoints not the Count, but rather Rodrigue's father, Don Diègue. While the Count is an aristocrat of the old order, the lower-born Diègue represents, as will his son, the emerging meritocracy. The ambiguity between, on the one hand, the rapprochement between different social orders in the Count's original favouring of Rodrigue for Chimène, and, on the other hand, this affront to the aristocracy represented by that lower social rank, echoes that clash of feudal and proto-capitalist criteria of justice, one being as generative of injustice as the other. The insulted Count confronts Diègue, in one of Western literature's eeriest, most unseemly, contests of grinding, tit-for-tat measurement. The Count certainly cannot accuse the monarch of a breach of law, the appointment being discretionary. The Count nevertheless complains of injustice on meritocratic grounds. He rebukes an injustice generated by the very system of which he and his ancestors are the architects, recalling the language measuring 'low' and 'high' in *The Merchant of Venice* or *Richard II*.[217]

> Enfin vous l'emportez, et la faveur du Roi
> Vous élève en un rang qui n'était dû qu'à moi.[218]

Like the Infanta, the Count cherishes his aristocratic rank, but grasps the meritocratic criterion, often reasoning ambiguously, even embarrassingly, between those two poles, as he must deflate precisely the system of feudal rank upon which he depends, by measuring the King as equal to his subjects. In the new, meritocratic world, a bad appointment can result only from human error, which sits uneasily in the figure of the monarch.

> Pour grands que soient les Rois, ils sont ce que nous sommes,
> Ils peuvent se tromper comme les autres hommes.[219]

Diègue's lower rank endows him with greater freedom from such ambiguity or embarrassment. Lacking higher lineage, he can loudly trumpet the King's measurement of his worth in the contractual, market-driven terms of compensation due for services rendered.

---

216 Cid 1.1.28–32; Cid-1660 1.1.43–48.
217 See this book, Chapter 6, text accompanying n. 38
218 Cid 1.4.145–46.

> You win. The King is pleased for you to be
> Raised to a rank that ought to go to me.

219 Cid 1.3.151–52.

> Kings may be great, yet they're like me or you,
> They make mistakes as other men may do.

Reading the play in part as portraying a 'regime in crisis', see Prigent, 1986, p. 116. Cf. generally Elias, 1983.

> Cette marque d'honneur qu'il met dans ma famille
> Montre à tous qu'il est *juste*, et fait connaître assez
> Qu'il sait *récompenser* les services passés.[220]

The Count retorts in kind:

> Et ce choix sert de preuve à tous les Courtisans
> Qu'ils savent mal *payer* les services présents.[221]

His accomplishments become the measure of Diègue's:

> Et qu'a fait après tout ce grand nombre d'années
> Que ne puissent *égaler* une de mes journées?[222]

His present measures Diègue's past:

> Si vous fûtes vaillant, je le suis aujourd'hui
> Et ce bras du Royaume est le plus ferme appui.[223]

The absurdity, the transparent reflexivity, of the contest, whereby justice and injustice become interchangeable, manifests as Diègue mechanically inverts that last criterion:

> Vous êtes aujourd'hui ce qu'autrefois je fus.[224]

---

220 Cid 1.3.148–50 (my emphasis). Cf. this chapter, text accompanying n. 168. See also Doubrovsky, 1963, p. 90.

> He tenders to my family this honour,
> He does what's *just*. To all he makes it known:
> He *pays what's due* for past services shown.

221 Cid 1.3.153–54 (my emphasis).

> For everyone at court this choice has proven
> How poor's their *pay* for services still given.

222 Cid 1.3.187–88 (my emphasis). The Count refers at line 187 to Diègue's years of military service. See also PC-OC 715, n. 1.

> In all your years what have you really done
> That, of my days, can *equal* even one?

223 Cid 1.3.189–90.

> If you had valour, I have it today
> This arm makes sure our Kingdom's here to stay.

224 Cid 1.3.206.

> You are today the man I used to be.

He then reverts to the monarch as the arbiter of measure:

> Vous voyez toutefois qu'en cette concurrence
> Un Monarque *entre nous met de la différence*.[225]

Like Timon and Apemantus, the Count and Diègue degenerate into a simultaneously farcical and tragic stichomythia, as competition of form mirrors that of content. The Count begins by reducing the measurement as concisely as possible to straightforward measurement of merit:

> Ce que je *méritais* vous l'avez emporté.[226]

Diègue replies with the same criterion:

> Qui l'a gagné sur vous l'avez mieux *mérité*.[227]

The Count narrows the measurement further, indeed in a distinctly modern vein, singling out the 'exercise' of the function, as opposed, for example, to meritorious character or reputation:

> Qui peut mieux l'exercer en est bien *le plus* digne.[228]

Diègue again responds with the same criterion:

> En être refusé n'en est pas un bon signe.[229]

Having acknowledged merit in himself, the Count accuses Diègue of winning on non-meritorious grounds. He accuses Diègue of pulling strings at Court.[230]

---

225 Cid 1.3.207–8 (my emphasis).

> Yet still you see that in our competition
> The King *between us draws a clear distinction*.

226 Cid 1.3.209 (my emphasis).

> What I *deserve* you've stolen from my store.

227 Cid 1.3.210 (my emphasis).

> The one who seized it from you *merits* more.

228 Cid 1.3.211 (my emphasis).

> The *worthiest's* the one who'd do it best.

229 Cid 1.3.212.

> To be refused can scarcely pass that test.

230 Again emphasising the displacement of unwieldy, old aristocrats, or *noblesse d'épée* by a loyal, ascendant, but non-aristocratic class.

The phrase used, *par brigue*, sometimes translated as 'by intrigue', relates to the verb *briguer*, used benignly in 1637 to describe the attempts of Chimène's rivalrous suitors to curry individual favour with Elvire, and sharpened, again as a noun, in the 1660 text (*la secrète brigue*):[231]

> Vous l'avez eu par brigue étant vieux Courtisan.[232]

Diègue denies it:

> L'éclat de mes hauts faits fut mon seul partisan.[233]

The Count then attributes Diègue's success to his seniority:

> Parlons-en mieux, le Roi fait honneur à votre âge.[234]

Diègue returns to the meritocratic measure:

> Le Roi, quand il en fait, le mesure au courage.[235]

As does the Count:

> Et par là cet honneur n'était dû qu'à mon bras.[236]

Diègue concludes:

> Qui n'a pu l'obtenir ne le méritait pas.[237]

---

231 Cid 1.1.2; Cid-1660 1.1.15–16. The otherwise provocative phrase is neutralised in that context, then, solely by the amorous subject matter.
232 Cid 1.3.213.
    You're old at court, you won by pulling strings.
233 Cid 1.3.214.
    For me, my worth itself's a voice that sings.
234 Cid 1.3.215.
    Be frank. The king does honour to your age.
235 Cid 1.3.216.
    The king accords it only to true courage.
236 Cid 1.3.217.
    And that is why my honour should have won it.
237 Cid 1.3.218.
    Whoever missed that honour lacked such merit.

190 The Concept of Injustice

That supreme injustice moves the Count to slap Diègue,[238] and, reverting to the feudal ethos, the competition of words then turns to arms.[239] Aggrieved in turn by that open disgrace,[240] Diègue revives the feudal measurement (at least as interpreted retrospectively in early modernity[241]) for the redress of an injustice done to personal and familial honour:[242] 'Only in blood can such outrage be cleansed.'[243] He commands his son: 'Die or kill!' (*Meurs, ou tue*),[244] requiring that Rodrigue slay Diègue, and attaching the corresponding measure of justice in categorical, either-or terms: 'One who will bear shame deserves no life.'[245] In his famous soliloquy, Rodrigue draws from that view the arch-Corneillian paradox that redressing his father's injustice – in, of course, the only way that his society would recognise – requires committing an injustice against the innocent Chimène. Yet failing to kill Diègue entails the injustice of leaving his father's injustice un-redressed, indeed making him, doubly paradoxically on that society's standards, an unworthy husband for Chimène.[246]

Rodrigue's soliloquy reveals differences between Shakespearean and Corneillian reflections of injustice. The powerful insiders of Christian Venice, that is, Antonio, Portia and their friends, like protagonists elsewhere in Shakespeare, may well recognise that *we in general* are often the architects of our own misfortunes,[247] but they often reveal little insight into the ways in which *they in particular* engineer justice so as to create the injustices they inflict upon others and upon themselves. Corneille's characters, by contrast, frequently recite those socio-political paradoxes and hypocrises at length,[248] even if they are no abler than are Shakespeare's to overcome them.

When Rodrigue does slay the Count, the King will approve and indeed ratify it.

> Ce que le Comte a fait semble avoir mérité
> Ce juste châtiment de sa témérité.[249]

238 Cid 1.3.220 (stage direction).
239 Cf. Doubrovsky, 1963, p. 98. Cf. Heinze, 2009c, pp. 143–49 (examining recourse to force as the underpinning of verbal disputes about justice).
240 Cid 1.4.236, 1.6.269–71. Cf. Doubrovsky, 1963, p. 95.
241 Cf. Doubrovsky, 1963, p. 89.
242 Cf. Doubrovsky, 1963, pp. 91–92, 96, 98.
243 Cid 1.6.276. Ce n'est que dans le sang qu'on lave un tel outrage.
244 Cid 1.6.277. Cf. Doubrovsky, 1963, p. 95; Prigent, 1986, p. 36.
245 Cid 1.6.286. [Q]ui peut vivre infâme est indigne du jour. Cf. Doubrovsky, 1963, pp. 96–97, 112.
246 Cid 1.7.325–26. Cf. Cid 3.4.897–8. Cf. also Doubrovsky, 1963, pp. 99–102.
247 See, e.g. MV 3.2.73–104.
248 See, e.g., Doubrovsky, 1963, p. 100. See also Doubrovsky, 1963, p. 102 (discussing Rodrigue's *prise de conscience*).
249 Cid 2.6.645–46.

> The Count's audacity has well deserved
> That just chastisement with which he's been served.

Chimène, now impelled by her society's criteria of Justice as measurement to implore the King for her lover's death, insists on revenge in the same language of measurement. She offers a glimpse into a point of overlap between feudal notions of vengeance and modern notions of exact compensation – sometimes opposites, but now welded by the early modern poet into an identical result.

> Enfin mon père est mort, j'en demande vengeance, [. . .]
> Vous perdez en la mort d'un homme de son rang,
> Vengez-la par une autre, et le sang pour le sang, [. . .]
> Le soleil qui voit tout ne voit rien sous les Cieux
> Qui vous puisse payer un sang si précieux.[250]

Rodrigue speaks in kind, equally marrying the feudal-chivalrous measurement of vengeance to that of *suum cuique* precisely apportioned on merit.

> Je cherche le trépas après l'avoir donné,
> Mon Juge est mon amour, mon Juge est ma Chimène,
> Je mérite la mort de mériter sa haine.[251]

The other rival for Chimène's hand, Don Sanche, had already jumped at the chance to take Chimène's revenge and eliminate his competitor. When Chimène acknowledges that she must first await the King's remedy, Sanche urges her to accept his pursuit of Rodrigue as justice above law, to avoid what Hamlet had called 'law's delay',[252] which denies justice in protracting its delivery.[253] Chimène's arch-typically Corneillian vacillation between two equally necessary yet mutually exclusive resolutions witnesses her compulsively weighing one against another, each formulation proving as aporetic as the last.

> Par où sera jamais mon âme satisfaite
> Si je pleure ma perte, et la main qui l'a faite?

---

250 Cid 2.7.699–706.

>   My father's dead, and I demand revenge, [. . .]
>   You lose much with this high ranked man's last breath,
>   Revenge him with another – death for death, [. . .]
>   The sun sees all, but shan't on earth behold
>   Repayment for this blood worth more than gold.

251 Cid 3.1.762–764.

>   I've given death, so death is what I seek,
>   My judge, my love, Ximena, she must speak:
>   I've merited her hate and merit death.

252 Ham 3.1.71. Cf. Heinze, 2012b.
253 Cid 3.2.792–97. Cf. Cid 3.4.947–48.

> Et que puis-je espérer qu'un tourment éternel
> Si je poursuis un crime aimant le criminel? [. . .]
> Ma passion s'oppose à mon ressentiment. [. . .]
> Je cours sans balancer où mon honneur m'oblige ;
> Rodrigue m'est bien cher, son intérêt m'afflige,
> Mon cœur prend son parti, mais contre leur effort
> Je sais que je suis fille, et que mon père est mort.[254]

Both Chimène and Rodrigue here limit themselves to the classical binarism of justice measured out to correct injustice. Rodrigue continues shortly afterward, as if taking inventory in accountant's terms.

> Je t'ai fait une offense, et j'ai dû m'y porter,
> Pour effacer ma honte et pour te mériter.
> Mais quitte envers l'honneur, et quitte envers mon père,
> C'est maintenant à toi que je viens satisfaire,
> C'est pour t'offrir mon sang qu'en ce lieu tu me vois,
> J'ai fait ce que j'ai dû, je fais ce que je dois.[255]

Chimène almost parodies justice as measurement, not merely crying for vengeance, but insisting that her call for it responds precisely to that pursued by Rodrigue upon her father.

> Tu n'as fait le devoir que d'un homme de bien;
> Mais aussi, le faisant, tu m'as appris le mien.
> Ta funeste valeur m'instruit par ta victoire;
> Elle a vengé ton père et soutenu ta gloire,

---

254 Cid 3.3.815–34.

> How can my soul ever accept this dictum:
> To cry for both the slayer and the victim?
> What hope have I but torment ever after
> If I revenge the death yet love the killer? [. . .]
> My passion stands opposed to my resentment. [. . .]
> My duty calls. It will brook no delay.
> I love Rodrigo; for his good I pray.
> My heart's on his side. But, despite my dread,
> I am a daughter and my father's dead.

255 Cid 3.4.905–10.

> I have offended you; I had to fight,
> To ward off shame, be worthy of your sight.
> But with my and father's name restored,
> Your turn is next, I'm ready to be gored.
> I'm here for you to spill my blood on dust.
> I acted, and will still act as I must.

Même soin me regarde, et j'ai, pour m'affliger,
Ma gloire à soutenir, et mon père à venger. [. . .]
Ma générosité doit répondre à la tienne :
Tu t'es, en m'offensant, montré digne de moi,
Je me dois par ta mort montrer digne de toi.[256]

Once again, Rodrigue replies with a mirror-image measurement, this dialogue of justice acting as surrogate for a dialogue of love.

Ta générosité doit répondre à la mienne. [. . .]
Ma main seule du mien a su venger l'offense,
Ta main seule du tien doit prendre la vengeance.[257]

Rodrigue then rejoins his other loving relationship, with his father Diègue, who at first deems the son to have fulfilled the call of justice, as measured by his ancestors.

. . . ton illustre audace
Fait bien revivre en toi les Héros de ma race ; [. . .]
Ton premier coup d'épée égale tous les miens.
Et d'une belle ardeur ta jeunesse animée
Par cette grande épreuve atteint ma renommée.[258]

Rodrigue prefers a different measure. He agrees to view the revenge as performed out of sheer filial duty, but not as heroic. It was, after all, Chimène's

---

256 Cid 3.4.921–44.

> You did your duty like a decent man;
> I must do mine, for you taught me that plan.
> Your fateful valour shows me, in your victory,
> How you avenged your father and your glory.
> My business is the same, that's what I rue:
> To save my honour, pay father his due. [. . .]
> My courage must be measured against yours:
> You wronged me, proving yourself worthy of me
> To you my death must prove me just as worthy.

257 Cid 3.4.956–60.

> Your courage must be measured against mine. [. . .]
> My hand alone took vengeance for our wrong,
> Take your revenge, let your hand be as strong.

258 Cid 3.6.1039–42.

> . . . your bravery's fine,
> And revives the heroes of our line; [. . .]
> Your first blow equals all that I have struck.
> Through passion, through your youthful animation,
> You've proved yourself, extolled my reputation.

father who was killed. He and we are surprised when Diègue rejects that compromise, insisting upon the feudal view that personal 'glory' and 'honour' must determine justice and injustice. He, too, displays that feudal ideal as a mercenary one, in the unvarnished terms of measuring out the *quid pro quo*.

> Je t'ai donné la vie, et *tu me rends* ma gloire,
> Et *d'autant* que l'honneur m'est *plus cher* que le jour,
> D'*autant plus* maintenant je te *dois* de retour.[259]

Rodrigue is all the more horrified to hear Chimène reduced, on that criterion, to a fungible commodity: 'Honour's but one, yet mistresses are many.'[260] Diègue avoids Rodrigue's objection by introducing the next of the play's central themes, the King's need for Rodrigue to join forces against a Moorish invasion,[261] which, emblematic of the forging of the early modern nation state, will also have consequences for Castillian rivalries with Grenada and Toledo.[262] After Rodrigue returns from the war a hero, with two kings as his capture, Chimène's criteria of measurement must shift. She can no longer weigh Rodrigue her father's slayer against Rodrigue her lover, but must instead weigh him against the state's new and greatest hero: 'Two kings he did defeat, but killed my father.'[263] For Ronald Dworkin that case must be easy. Chimène's rights asserted to redress Rodrigue's murder of Diègue must trump even the greatest utility that Rodrigue may offer the state.

The King, however, is no Dworkinian. He places collective interest, the safety of the state and Rodrigue's immediate ability to prevent present and future Castillian deaths, above individual interests resting on either side of the squabble between Diègue and the Count. He congratulates Rodrigue, '[T]he salvaged state pleads in your defence.'[264] He reminds Chimène, 'To render justice all points must be weighed,'[265] that is, without claims of individual right necessarily trumping state interest, *raison d'état*, indeed as a matter of 'equity' (*équité*)[266] in an Aristotelian sense.[267] Rodrigue's injustice must be

---

259 Cid 3.6.1064–66 (my emphasis).

> I gave you life, *you pay me* with my honour,
> Because my life is *worth less* than my glory,
> I *owe* you *so much more* for your victory.

260 Cid 3.6.1068. Nous n'avons qu'un honneur, il est tant de maîtresses.
261 Cid 3.6.1085–100. The parallel between Venetian unity forged against the Jew and the Moor in *The Merchant of Venice*, and Spanish unity formed in *Le Cid* remains a standard early modern theme. See, e.g., Said 2003; Longino 2002.
262 Cid 4.3.1236.
263 Cid 4.1.1140. S'il a vaincu deux Rois, il a tué mon père.
264 Cid 4.3.1264. [L]'État défendu me parle en ta défense.
265 Cid 4.5.1396. Quand on rend justice on met tout en balance.
266 Cid 4.5.1398.
267 See this book, Chapter 2, text accompanying n. 81

balanced against the justice he does in securing Castillian survival. The King's daughter the Infanta expressly reverses the Dworkinian calculus, explaining to Chimène that 'yesterday' her duty was admirable, but criteria of measurement must change to accord with state interest.

> Hier ce devoir te mit en un haute estime. [. . .]
> Ce qui fut bon alors ne l'est pas aujourd'hui,
> Rodrigue maintenant est notre unique appui [. . .]
> Le soutien de Castille et la terreur du More, [. . .]
> Tu poursuis en sa mort la ruine publique,
> Quoi? Pour venger un père est-il jamais permis
> De livrer sa patrie aux mains des ennemis?[268]

Like Diègue, the King measures Rodrigue with reference to his illustrious ancestors, but also in mercenary terms.

> Généreux héritier d'une illustre famille
> Qui fut toujours la gloire de la Castille,
> Race de tant d'aïeux en valeur signalés
> Que l'essai de la tienne a si tôt *égalés*,
> Pour te *récompenser* ma force est trop petite,
> Et j'ai *moins* de pouvoir que tu n'as de *mérite*.[269]

When Chimène reminds the King of Sanche's offer to take revenge,[270] the King adds the further argument, reflecting emerging policy in early modernity,[271] that duelling, which can unjustly favour the culpable while

---

268 Cid 4.2.1179–94.

> Your duty yesterday won high esteem. [. . .]
> What was good then is not so good today,
> To save us now Rodrigo's our sole way [. . .]
> Castille's hope is terror for the Moors. [. . .]
> Demanding his death risks death to us all,
> A father's vengeance? Must it even land
> Our very nation in our enemy's hand?

269 Cid 4.3.1219–24 (my emphasis). Cf. Prigent, 1986, p. 123.

> Brave offspring from a family that glows,
> Whose glory in Castille always grows,
> Distinguished by the valour of its men,
> Now your own courage *equals* what was then.
> *To pay you back*, I've too small a reserve,
> My means all come to *less* than you *deserve*.

270 Cid 4.5.1407–10.
271 See, e.g., PC-OC 762, n. 3.

killing the innocent party, must no longer remain lawful in the kingdom.[272] Only on Chimène's insistence does he nevertheless authorise the combat.[273] Yet neither resolution, neither for nor against Chimène, can do justice without injustice. Were Chimène's right to prevail, then many might later die in a defensive or defeated Castille lacking so able a soldier. The King instead prevails. But his solution to redress Chimène's wrongs by giving her in marriage to the victor, universally presumed to be Rodrigue,[274] has long stood as one of literature's more embarrassing resolutions.[275] Chimène at first protests.[276] Later feigning[277] an acquiescence that will become genuine[278] – and conspicuously indifferent to the death of Sanche, which, she rightly assumes, will result[279] – she recognises herself as the 'prize' or 'price' (*le prix*[280]) of the combat, just as Portia becomes the prize, or price, of her father's lottery. Chimène pleads with Rodrigue.

> Sort vainqueur d'un combat dont Chimène est le prix.
> Adieu, ce mot lâché me fait rougir de honte.[281]

The absurdity of justice as measurement chimes both farce and tragedy as Chimène's confidante Elvire supposes she can comfort her mistress, seeing only a just outcome regardless of who wins the duel.

> D'un et d'autre côté je vous vois soulagée,
> Ou vous avez Rodrigue, ou vous êtes vengée.[282]

Chimène is scarcely comforted. From precisely that justice, Chimène can deduce only injustice.

---

272 Cid 4.5.1416–20.
273 Cid 4.5.1435.
274 Cid 4.5.1466–74.
275 At the time, it spawned a lively controversy about plausibility, taste and appropriateness (*la vraisemblance, la bienséance, les bonnes mœurs*) in drama. See, e.g., Scudéry, in PC-OC 785–88.
276 Cid 4.5.1470.
277 See Cid 5.4.1687–94, 5.5.1733–36.
278 See Cid 5.7.1830, 1847, 1859–66.
279 Cid 5.1.1483–89.
280 See this book, Chapter 6, Section 6.10.
281 Cid 5.1.1566–67.

> Go, win the fight. Ximena is the prize.
> Farewell. These words have made me blush with shame.

282 Cid 5.4.1663–64.

> And yet you have good reason to take heart,
> When vengeance – or Rodrigo – takes your part.

> Quoi? L'objet de ma haine, ou bien de ma colère!
> L'assassin de Rodrigue, ou celui de mon père![283]

When Chimène presumably accepts a deferred marriage to Rodrigue,[284] the King's 'time heals all wounds' maxim seems calculated more to dissimulate than to disprove the injustice that flows from justice.

> Le temps assez souvent a rendu légitime
> Ce qui semblait d'abord ne se pouvoir sans crime.[285]

The problem of injustice within legal modernity was never one of finding this or that correct measure, which would prove itself the pristine opposite of injustice as mismeasurement. The problem was of justice as measurement *per se*, insofar as justice is, in modernity, inconceivable as anything else, yet is always – on any criterion of measurement, simply because it *is* measurement – productive of injustice. The failure to perceive justice not as injustice's infirmary, but as its cauldron, intractably entails our incessant, compulsive hunt for the criterion, the better criterion, the best criterion, the sole and final criterion of measurement, while injustice – measurement – bites at our heals, not as the beast hunted, but as the beast ancillary to the chase itself, as Chimène chases Rodrigo, Timon chases Appemantus, Shylock chases Antonio, Socrates chases Thrasymachus.

---

283 Cid 5.4.1667–68.

> The object of my hate or of my spite!
> Rodrigo's killer or my father's blight!

284 See this chapter, text accompanying n. 278.
285 Cid 5.7.1839–40.

> Things often end up justified by time,
> Which seemed impossible without some crime.

Bibliography

Alighieri, D. (1949) *On World-Government (De Monarchia)* (H. Schneider, trans.), Indianapolis, IN: Bobbs-Merrill.
Alighieri, D. (1954) *The Inferno* (J. Ciardi, trans.), New York, NY: Mentor.
Alighieri, D. (1957) *The Purgatorio* (J. Ciardi, trans.), New York, NY: Mentor.
Alighieri, D. (1970) *The Paradiso* (J. Ciardi, trans.), New York, NY: Mentor.
Alighieri, D. (2007) *La Divina Commedia* (A. M. Chiavacci-Leonardi, ed.), Milan: Mondadori.
Annas, J. (1981) *An Introduction to Plato's Republic*, Oxford: Oxford University Press.
Aquinas, T. (2000) *Summa Theologica*, New York, NY: Random House.
Arendt, H. (2006) *Eichmann in Jerusalem*, London: Penguin Classics.
Aristotle (1894) *Ethica Nicomachea*. (J. Bywater, ed.), Oxford: Clarendon Press.
Aristotle (1984) *The Complete Works of Aristotle: The Revised Oxford Translations* (Vols 1 and 2) (J. Barnes, ed.), Princeton, NJ: Princeton University Press.
Aristotle (1992) *The Politics* (rev'd edn) (T. J. Saunders, ed.; T. Sinclair, trans.), London: Penguin.
Aristotle (1993) *Posterior Analytics* (2nd edn) (J. Barnes, trans.), Oxford: Oxford University Press.
Aristotle (1995) *Aristotle: Selections* (T. Irwin and G. Fine, trans.), Indianapolis, IN: Hackett.
Aristotle (1998) *Politics* (C. Reeve, trans.), Indianapolis, IN: Hackett.
Aristotle (1999) *Nicomachean Ethics* (2nd edn) (T. H. Irwin, trans.), Indianapolis, IN: Hackett.
Augustine (1984) *City of God* (H. Bettenson, trans.), Oxford: Oxford University Press.
Austin, J. (1998) *The Province of Jurisprudence Determined* (H. L. A. Hart, ed.), Indianapolis, IN: Hackett.
Bach, J. S. (2000a) Tritt auf die Glaubensbahn, Cantata BWV 152 (text attributed to Solomo Frank) *Bach Sacred Cantatas, 4*, 148–50 (B. Wohlert, ed.), Hamburg: Teldec.
Bach, J. S. (2000b) Nur Jedem das Seine, Cantata BWV 163 (text attributed to Salomo Franck) *Bach Sacred Cantatas, 4*, 174–76 (B. Wohlert, ed.), Hamburg: Teldec.
Barthes, R. (1977) Introduction à l'analyse structurale des récits. In R. Barthes, W. Kayser, W. C. Booth and P. Hamon, *Poétique du récit*, Paris: Éditions du Seuil, pp. 7–57.

Benjamin, W. (1965) Zur Kritik der Gewalt. In *Zur Kritik der Gewalt und andere Aufsätze*, Frankfurt a.M.: Suhrkamp, pp. 29–65.
Bentham, J. (1843) *A Critical Examination of the Declaration of Rights* (Vol. 2), Edinburgh: William Tait.
Biet, C. (1994) *Oedipe en monarchie: Tragédie et théorie juridique à l'Âge classique*, Paris: Klincksieck.
Biet, C. (2005) *Moi, Pierre Corneille*, Paris: Gallimard.
Black's Law Dictionary (8th edn) (2004) St Paul, MN West.
Boose, L. (1988) The Comic Contract and Portia's Golden Ring, *Shakespeare Studies*, 20: 241–54.
Bostock, D. (2000) *Aristotle's Ethics*, Oxford: Oxford University Press.
Brockbank, P., *et al.* gen. eds (1984–) *New Cambridge Shakespeare*, Cambridge: Cambridge University Press. [individual vols.].
Brown, J. R. (2001) *Shakespeare: The Tragedies*, Basingstoke: Palgrave.
Brunssen, F. (2010) 'Jedem das Seine': Zum Umgang mit nationalsozialistisch belasteten Wörtern und Wendungen in Deutschland seit 1945, *Oxford German Studies*, 39: 290–311.
Bruster, D. (1992) *Drama and the Market in the Age of Shakespeare*, Cambridge: Cambridge University Press.
Cahn, S. M. (ed.) (2002) *Classics of Political and Moral Philosophy*, Oxford: Oxford University Press.
Cairns, H. (1942) Plato's Theory of Law, *Harvard Law Review*, 56: 359.
Camus, A. (1951) *L'Homme révolté*, Paris: Gallimard.
Candido, J. (1997) Dining Out in Ephesus: Food in The Comedy of Errors. In R. S. Miola (ed.), *The Comedy of Errors: Critical Essays*, New York, NY: Garland, pp. 199–225.
Cerasano, S. (2003a) Contextual Overview. In S. Cerasano (ed.), *William Shakespeare's The Merchant of Venice*, London: Routledge, pp. 7–21.
Cerasano, S. (ed.) (2003b) *William Shakespeare's The Merchant of Venice: A Sourcebook*, London: Routledge.
Chevallier, J. (2004) *L'État post-moderne* (2nd edn), Paris: LGDJ.
Cohen, W. (1982) The Merchant of Venice and the Possibilities of Historical Criticism, *English Literary History*, 49: 765–89.
Copenhaver, B. P. and Schmitt, C. B. (1992) *Renaissance Philosophy*, Oxford: Oxford University Press.
Corneille, P. (1975) *The Cid, Cinna, The Theatrical Illusion* (J. Cairncross, trans.), London: Penguin.
Corneille, P. (1980a) Mélite. In *Oeuvres complètes* (Vol. 1), Paris: Gallimard (Pléiade), pp. 1–89.
Corneille, P. (1980b) Médée. In *Oeuvres complètes* (Vol. 1), Paris: Gallimard (Pléiade), pp. 533–609.
Corneille, P. (1980c) Le Cid. In *Oeuvres complètes* (Vol. 1), Paris: Gallimard (Pléiade), pp. 689–777.
Corneille, P. (1987) Oedipe. In *Oeuvres Complètes* (Vol. 3), Paris: Gallimard (Pléiade), pp. 13–93.
Cotterrell, R. (2003) *The Politics of Jurisprudence* (2nd edn), London: Butterworths Lexis Nexis.
Crystal, D. and Crystal, B. (2002) *Shakespeare's Words*, London: Penguin.

Dawson, A. B. and Minton, G. E. (2008) Introduction. In W. Shakespeare, *Timon of Athens*, London: Arden (Third Series), pp. 1–145.
Delgado, R. (1989) Storytelling for Oppositionists and Others: A Plea for Narrative, *Michigan Law Review*, 87: 2411.
Derrida, J. (1967a) *De la grammatologie*, Paris: Éditions de Minuit.
Derrida, J. (1967b) *L'Écriture et la différence*, Paris: Éditions du Seuil.
Derrida, J. (1972) La pharmacie de Platon. In *La dissémination*, Paris: Éditions du Seuil, pp. 77–213.
Derrida, J. (1992) Force of Law: The 'Mystical Foundation of Authority'. In D. Cornell, M. Rosenfeld and D. G. Carlson (eds), *Deconstruction and the Possibility of Justice*, London: Routledge, pp. 3–67.
Dollimore, J. (1994) Transgression and Surveillance in *Measure for Measure*. In J. Dollimore and A. Sinfield (eds), *Political Shakespeare: Essays on Cultural Materialism* (2nd edn), Manchester: Manchester University Press, pp. 72–87.
Dollimore, J. (2004) *Radical Tragedy* (3rd edn), Basingstoke: Palgrave.
Dollimore, J. and Sinfield, A. (eds) (1994) *Political Shakespeare: Essays on Cultural Materialism* (2nd edn), Manchester: Manchester University Press.
Dollimore, J. and Sinfield, A. (2002) The Instance of Henry V. In J. Drakakis (ed.), *Alternative Shakespeares* (2nd edn), London: Routledge, pp. 210–31.
Doubrovsky, S. (1963) *Corneille et la dialectique du héros*, Paris: Gallimard.
Drakakis, J. (1996) Historical Difference and Venetian Patriarchy. In N. Wood (ed.), *The Merchant of Venice*, Buckingham: Open University Press, pp. 23–53.
Drakakis, J. (ed.) (2002) *Alternative Shakespeares* (2nd edn), London: Routledge.
Drakakis, J. (2010) Introduction. In W. Shakespeare, *The Merchant of Venice*, London: Arden Shakespreare (Third Series), pp. 1–159.
Dubus III, A. (2001) *House of Sand and Fog*, New York, NY: Vintage.
Duden Deutsches Universal Wörterbuch (2nd edn) (1989) Mannheim: Dudenverlag.
Dworkin, R. (1977) *Taking Rights Seriously*, Cambridge, MA: Harvard University Press.
Dworkin, R. (1986) *Law's Empire*, Cambridge, MA: Harvard University Press.
Eagleton, T. (1986) *William Shakespeare*, Oxford: Basil Blackwell.
Elias, N. (1983) *Die höfische Gesellschaft* (12th edn), Frankfurt: Suhrkamp.
Ellis-Fermor *et al.*, gen. eds (1951–82) *The Arden Shakespeare*, Second Series, London: Methuen [individual vols.].
Erasmus, D. (1997) *The Education of a Christian Prince* (L. Jardine, ed.; N. M. Cheshire and M. J. Heath, trans.), Cambridge: Cambridge University Press.
Forker, C. (2002) Introduction. In W. Shakespeare, *Richard II*, London: Arden Third Series, pp. 1–169.
Fortin, E. L. (1987) St Augustine. In L. Strauss and J. Cropsey, *History of Political Philosophy* (3rd edn), Chicago, IL: University of Chicago Press, pp. 176–205.
Foucault, M. (1972) *Histoire de la folie à l'âge classique*, Paris: Gallimard.
Foucault, M. (1975) *Surveiller et punir: Naissance de la prison*, Paris: Gallimard.
Foucault, M. (1976) *Histoire de la sexualité I: La volonté de savoir*, Paris: Gallimard.
Freud, S. (1999a) Massenpsychologie und Ich-Analyse. In *Sigmund Freud: Gesammelte Werke* (Vol. 13), Frankfurt a.M.: Fischer, pp. 71–161.
Freud, S. (1999b) Das Unbehagen in der Kultur. In *Sigmund: Freud Gesammelte Werke* (Vol. 14), Frankfurt a.M.: Fischer, pp. 419–506.
Fuller, L. (1969) *The Morality of Law* (rev'd edn), New Haven, CT: Yale University Press.

Gay, P. (1994) *Shakespeare's Unruly Women*, London: Routledge.
Girard, R. (2004) To Entrap the Wisest. In R. McDonald (ed.), *Shakespeare: An Anthology of Criticism and Theory 1945–2000*, Malden, MA: Blackwell, pp. 353–64.
Goyard-Fabre, S. (1992) *Les Fondements de l'ordre juridique*, Paris: Presses Universitaires de France.
Goyard-Fabre, S. (1998) *Qu'est-ce que la démocratie?*, Paris: Armand Colin.
Greenblatt, S. (1988) *Shakespearean Negotiations*, Oxford: Oxford University Press.
Greenblatt, S. (1994) Invisible Bullets: Renaissance Authority and Its Subversion, Henry IV and Henry V. In J. Dollimore and A. Sinfield (eds), *Political Shakespeare: Essays on Cultural Materialism* (2nd edn), Manchester: Manchester University Press, pp. 18–48.
Greenblatt, S. *et al.*, eds (2008) *The Norton Shakespeare*, 2nd edn, New York, NY: Norton & Co.
Grosz, G. (1917) *Metropolis*, Madrid: Museo Thyssen-Bornemisza.
Grosz, G. (1920a) *Republican Automatons*, New York, NY: Museum of Modern Art.
Grosz, G. (1920b) *Ohne Titel*, Düsseldorf: Kunstsammlung Nordrhein-Westfalen.
Halio, J. (1993) Introduction. In W. Shakespeare, *The Merchant of Venice*, Oxford: Oxford University Press, pp. 1–83.
Hall, K. (1992) Guess Who's Coming to Dinner? Colonisation and Miscegenation in *The Merchant of Venice*, *Renaissance Drama*, 23: 87–111.
Hart, H. L. A. (1994) *The Concept of Law* (2nd edn) (P. A. Bulloch and J. Raz, eds), Oxford: Oxford University Press.
Hegel, G. W. (1970a) *Phänomenologie des Geistes*. In *Georg Wilhelm Friedrich Hegel: Werke* (Vol. 3), Frankfurt: Suhrkamp.
Hegel, G. W. (1970b) *Grundlinien der Philosophie des Rechts*. In *G.W.F. Hegel: Werke* (Vol. 7), Frankfurt: Suhrkamp.
Hegel, G. W. (1970c) *Vorlesungen über die Ästhetik I*. In *Georg Wilhelm Friedrich Hegel: Werke* (Vol. 13), Frankfurt: Suhrkamp.
Heidegger, M. (1979) *Sein und Zeit*, Tübingen: Max Niemeyer.
Heidegger, M. (1995) *Logik: Die Frage nach der Wahrheit* (2nd edn) Frankfurt a.M.: Klostermann.
Heinze, E. (1999) The Construction and Contingency of the Minority Concept. In B. Bowring and D. Fottrell (eds), *Minority and Group Rights Toward the New Millennium*, Dordrecht: Kluwer, pp. 25–74.
Heinze, E. (2003a) *The Logic of Liberal Rights*, London: Routlege.
Heinze, E. (2003b) *The Logic of Equality*, Aldershot: Ashgage.
Heinze, E. (2005) *The Logic of Constitutional Rights*, Aldershot: Ashgate.
Heinze, E. (2007a) Epinomia: Plato and the First Theory of Law, *Ratio Juris*, 20: 97–135.
Heinze, E. (2007b) The Status of Classical Natural Law: Plato and the Parochialism of Modern Theory, *Canadian Journal of Law and Jurisprudence*, 20: 323–50.
Heinze, E. (2009a) Heir, Celebrity, Martyr, Monster: Legal and Political Legitimacy in Shakespeare and Beyond, *Law & Critique*, 20(1): 79–103.
Heinze, E. (2009b) Imperialism and Nationalism in Early Modernity: The 'Cosmopolitan' and the 'Provincial' in Shakespeare's *Cymbeline*, *Journal of Social & Legal Studies*, 18(3): 139–68.
Heinze, E. (2009c) Power Politics and the Rule of Law: Shakespeare's First Historical Tetralogy and Law's 'Foundations', *Oxford Journal of Legal Studies*, 29: 230–63.

Heinze, E. (2009d) The Metaethics of Law: Book One of Aristotle's *Nicomachean Ethics*, *International Journal of Law in Context*, 6(1): 23–44.
Heinze, E. (2009e) 'Were It Not Against Our Laws': Oppression and Resistance in Shakespeare's *Comedy of Errors*, *Legal Studies*, 29: 230–63.
Heinze, E. (2010a) 'He'd Turn the World Itself into a Prison': Empire and Enlightenment in Jean Racine's *Alexander the Great*, *Law & Humanities*, 4(1): 63–89.
Heinze, E. (2010b) 'This Power isn't Power if it's Shared': Law and Violence in Jean Racine's *La Thébaïde*, *Law & Literature*, 22(1): 76–109.
Heinze, E. (2012a) Victimless Crimes. In R. Chadwick (ed.), *Encyclopedia of Applied Ethics* (2nd edn) (Vol. 4), London: Elsevier/Academic Press, pp. 471–82.
Heinze, E. (2012b) 'Where be his Quiddities Now?': Law and Language in *Hamlet*. In M. Freeman and F. Smith (eds), *Law and Language: Current Legal Issues* (Vol. 15), Oxford: Oxford University Press.
Heinze, E. (2012c) 'The Reality and Hyperreality of Human Rights: Public Consciousness and the Mass Media'. In R. Dickenson *et al.* (eds), *Examining Critical Perspectives on Human Rights: The End of an Era?*, Cambridge: Cambridge University Press (2012), pp. 193–216.
Héritier, F. (2012) M. Guéant est relativiste, *Le Monde*, 68 (20859), 12–13 February, p.15.
Herodotus (2008) *The Histories* (C. Dewald, ed.; R. Waterfield, trans.), Oxford: Oxford University Press.
Hobbes, T. (1998) *Leviathan* (J. C. Gaskin, ed.), Oxford: Oxford University Press.
Holderness, G. (2000) *Shakespeare: The Histories*, New York, NY: St Martins Press.
Holland, P. (2005) Introduction. In W. Shakespeare, *The Merchant of Venice*, London: Penguin, pp. xxi–lxiii.
Homiak, M. (1993) Feminism and Aristotle's Rational Ideal. In G. Lloyd (ed.), *Feminism and History of Philosophy*, Oxford: Oxford University Press, pp. 80–102.
Hood-Phillips, O. (1972) *Shakespeare and the Lawyers*, London: Methuen.
Hsi, C. and Tsu-Ch'ien, L. (1967) *Chin-ssu lu (Reflections on Things at Hand)* (W.-t. Chan, trans.), New York, NY: Columbia University Press.
IBS-UK (ed.) (2009) *The Holy Bible*, London: Hodder & Stoughton.
Jowett, J. (2004) Introduction. In W. Shakespeare, *Timon of Athens*, Oxford: Oxford University Press, pp. 1–153.
Kant, I. (1968a) *Kritik der praktischen Vernunft*. In *Werkausgabe* (Vol. 7), Frankfurt: Suhrkamp, pp. 102–305.
Kant, I. (1968b) *Grundlegung zur Metaphysik der Sitten*. In *Werkausgabe* (Vol. 7), Frankfurt: Suhrkamp, pp. 5–104.
Kant, I. (1968c) *Die Metaphysik der Sitten*. In *Werkausgabe* (Vol. 8), Frankfurt: Suhrkamp, pp. 303–634.
Kant, I. (1968d) *Zum ewigen Frieden*. In W. Weischedel (ed.), *Werkausgabe* (Vol. 11), Frankfurt, a.M.: Suhrkamp, pp. 191–251.
Karst, K. (1996) Integration Success Story (book review), *Southern California Law Review*, 69: 1781.
Kelly, P. (2003) J.S. Mill on Liberty. In D. Boucher and P. Kelly (eds), *Political Thinkers: From Socrates to the Present*, Oxford: Oxford University Press, pp. 324–42.
Kelsen, H. (1960) Das Problem der Gerechtigkeit. In *Reine Rechtslehre* (2nd edn), Vienna: Franz Deuticke, pp. 355–444.

King, M. L. (2002) The March on Washington Address. In S. M. Cahn (ed.), *Classics of Moral and Political Philosophy*, Oxford: Oxford University Press, pp. 1209–11.
Klosko, G. (2006) *The Development of Plato's Political Theory* (2nd edn), Oxford: Oxford University Press.
Knox, B. (1984) *Antigone*: Introduction. In Sophocles, *The Three Theban Plays* (R. Fagles, trans.), London: Penguin, pp. 35–53.
Kojève, A. (1947) *Hegel: Introduction à la lecture de Hegel* (R. Queneau, ed.), Paris: Gallimard.
Kojève, A. (1975) *Kommentar zur Phänomenologie des Geistes* (I. Fetscher, ed.; I. Fetscher and G. Lehmbruch, trans.), Frankfurt a.M.: Suhrkamp.
Kraut, R. (2002) *Aristotle: Political Philosophy*, Oxford: Oxford University Press.
Kraut, R. (ed.) (2006) *The Blackwell Guide to Aristotle's* Nicomachean Ethics, Oxford: Blackwell.
Kristeva, J. (2011) Public Lecture: 'Is There a Feminine Genius? Hannah Arendt, Melanie Klein, Colette', 7 December, London: Queen Mary University of London.
Leggatt, A. (1988) *Shakespeare's Political Drama*, London: Routledge.
Le Petit Robert – Dictionnaire de la langue française (1977) Paris: Le Robert.
Lévinas, E. (1990a) *Totalité et infini: Essai sur l'extériorité*, Paris: Livre de poche.
Lévinas, E. (1990b) *Autrement qu'être ou au-delà de l'essence*, Paris: Livre de poche.
Lévi-Strauss, C. (1987) *Race et histoire*, Paris: Gallimard.
Locke, J. (1988) *Second Treatise of Civil Government*. In *Two Treatises of Government*, Cambridge: Cambridge University Press.
Longino, M. (2002) *Orientalism in French Classical Drama*, Cambridge, UK: Cambridge University Press.
Löw, K. (2001) *Marx und Marxismus: Eine deutsche Schizophrenie*, Munich: Ölzog.
Macchiavelli, N. (1995) *Il Principe* (G. Inglese, ed.), Turin: Einaudi.
MacIntyre, A. (2007) *After Virtue* (3rd edn), Notre Dame, IN: University of Notre Dame Press.
Mahood, M. (2003) Introduction. In W. Shakespeare, *The Merchant of Venice*, Cambridge: Cambridge University Press, pp. 1–65.
Malinowski, G. (2001) Many-Valued Logics. In L. Goble (ed.), *The Blackwell Guide to Philosophical Logic*, Oxford: Blackwell, pp. 309–35.
Marcuse, H. (1965) Nachwort. In W. Benjamin, *Zur Kritik der Gewalt und andere Aufsätze*, Frankfurt a.M.: Suhrkamp, pp. 97–107.
Martin, R. (2001) Introduction. In W. Shakespeare, *Henry VI, Part 3*, Oxford: Oxford University Press, pp. 1–132.
Martin, T. R. (1996) *Ancient Greece: From Pre-Historic to Hellenic Times*, New Haven, CT: Yale University Press.
Marx, K. (1956a) Zur Kritik der Hegelschen Rechtsphilosophie. In Institut für Marxismus-Leninismus beim Zentralkomitee der Sozialistische Einheitspartei Deutschlands (ed.), *Karl Marx – Friedrich Engels: Werke* (6th edn) (Vol. 1), Berlin: Dietz, pp. 201–333.
Marx, K. (1956b) Zur Judenfrage. In Institut für Marxismus-Leninismus beim Zentralkomitee der Sozialistische Einheitspartei Deutschlands (ed.), *Karl Marx – Friedrich Engels: Werke* (6th edn) (Vol. 1), Berlin: Dietz, pp. 347–77.

Marx, K. and Engels, F. (1956c) Manifest der kommunistischen Partei. In Institut für Marxismus-Leninismus beim Zentralkomitee der Sozialistische Einheitspartei Deutschlands (ed.), *Karl Marx – Friedrich Engels: Werke* (6th edn) (Vol. 4), Berlin: Dietz, pp. 461–93.

Marx, K. (1956d) *Das Kaptial*. In Institut für Marxismus-Leninismus beim Zentralkomitee der Sozialistische Einheitspartei Deutschlands (ed.), *Karl Marx – Friedrich Engels: Werke* (6th edn) (Vol. 16), Berlin: Dietz.

Marx, K. (1956e) Kritik des Gothaer Programms. In Institut für Marxismus-Leninismus beim Zentralkomitee der Sozialistische Einheitspartei Deutschlands (ed.), *Karl Marx – Friedrich Engels: Werke* (6th edn) (Vol. 19), Berlin: Dietz, pp. 11–34.

Maus, K. E. (2008) Commentary on *Richard II*. In S. Greenblatt, W. Cohen, J. E. Howard and K. E. Maus (eds), *The Norton Shakespeare* (2nd edn), New York, NY: Norton & Co, pp. 943–50.

Merleau-Ponty, M. (1945) *La phénoménologie de la perception*, Paris: Gallimard.

Mill, J. S. (1957) *Utilitarianism* (O. Piest, ed.), Indianapolis, IN: Hackett.

Mill, J. S. (1982) *On Liberty* (G. Himmelfarb, ed.), London: Penguin.

Milton, J. (1991) *Paradise Lost* (S. Orgel and J. Goldberg, eds), Oxford: Oxford University Press.

Mitchell, B. and Lucas, J. R. (2003) *An Engagement with Plato's Republic*, Aldershot: Ashgate.

Modern Language Association (MLA) (2003) *Shakespeare Variorum Handbook*, R. Knowles (ed.) (2nd edn), Web publication.

Molière (2010) *Le Misanthrope*. In G. Forestier and C. Bourqui (eds), *Oeuvres complètes* (Vol. 1), Paris: Gallimard (Pléiade), pp. 633–726.

Morrison, W. (1997) *Jurisprudence: From the Greeks to Post-Modernism*, London: Cavendish.

Nadal, O. (1948) *Le sentiment de l'amour dans l'oeuvre de Pierre Corneille*, Paris: Gallimard.

Nietzsche, F. (1999) *Also sprach Zarathustra*. In *Kritische Studienausgabe* (Vol. 4), Berlin: De Gruyter.

Oxford English Dictionary (2nd edn) (1989) Oxford: Oxford University Press.

Pappas, N. (2003) *Plato and the Republic* (2nd edn), London: Routledge.

Perelman, C. (1990) La justice. In *Éthique et droit*, Brussels: Éditions de l'Université de Bruxelles, pp. 13–305.

Pitcher, J. (2005) Commentary. In W. Shakespeare, *Cymbeline*, London: Penguin, pp. 161–310.

Plato (1903) *Platonis Opera* (J. Burnet, ed.), Oxford: Oxford University Press.

Plato (1961) *The Collected Dialogues* (E. Hamilton and H. Cairns, eds), Princeton, NJ: Princeton University Press.

Plato (1968) *The Republic* (A. Bloom, trans.), New York, NY: Basic Books.

Plato (1997) *Plato: Complete Works* (J. M. Cooper, ed.), Indianapolis, IN: Hackett.

Popper, K. (2002a) *The Open Society and Its Enemies* (Vols 1 and 2), London: Routledge.

Popper, K. (2002b) *The Poverty of Historicism*, London: Routledge.

Pradeau, J.-F. (2000) Introduction. In Platon, *Alcibiade*, Paris: Flammarion, pp. 9–81.

Préposiet, J. (2002) *Histoire de l'Anarchisme* (rev'd edn), Paris: Tallandier.

Prigent, M. (1986) *Le héros et l'État dans la tragédie de Pierre Corneille* (3rd edn), Paris: Presses Universitaires de France.
Proudfoot, R. *et al.*, gen. eds (1995–) *The Arden Shakespeare*, Third Series, London: Thompson [individual vols.].
Pugliatti, P. (1996) *Shakespeare The Historian*, Basingstoke: Palgrave Macmillan.
Quotations from the Langdell Reading Room (n.d.) Harvard Law School Library, www.law.harvard.edu/library/about/history/reading-room-quotations.html (accessed 5 May 2012).
Racine, J. (1999) *Andromaque*. In *Oeuvres complètes* (Vol. 1), Paris: Gallimard (Pléiade), pp. 193–256.
Rackin, P. (1990) *Stages of History: Shakespeare's English Chronicles*, Ithaca, NY: Cornell University Press.
Radio-Sweden (2012) *Banks' Funds Invest in Controversial Oil Company*, 20 January, http://sverigesradio.se/sida/artikel.aspx?programid=2054&artikel=4920674 (accessed 1 March 2012).
Raffield, P. (2010) *Shakespeare's Imaginary Constitution*, Oxford: Hart.
Rawls, J. (1999) *A Theory of Justice* (2nd edn), Oxford: Oxford University Press.
Rice, D. (1998) *A Guide to Plato's Republic*, Oxford: Oxford University Press.
Rousseau, J.-J. (1980a) Discours sur les arts et les sciences. In B. Gagnebin (ed.), *Oeuvres Complètes* (Vol. 3), Paris: Gallimard (Pléiade).
Rousseau, J.-J. (1980b) Discours sur l'origine et les fondements de l'inégalité parmi les homes. In B. Gagnebin (ed.), *Oeuvres Complètes*, Paris: Gallimard (Pléiade).
Rousseau, J.-J. (1980c) *Du Contrat social*. In B. Gagnebin (ed.), *Oeuvres Complètes* (Vol. 3), Paris: Gallimard (Pléiade).
Rousseau, J.-J. (1980d) Discours sur l'Économie Politique. In B. Gagnebin (ed.), *Oeuvres Complètes* (Vol. 3), Paris: Gallimard (Pléiade), pp. 241–78.
Rousseau, J.-J. (1997) *The Discourses and Other Early Political Writings*. (V. Gourevitch, trans.), Cambridge: Cambridge University Press.
Russell, B. (2000) *History of Western Philosophy* (2nd edn), London: Routledge.
Said, E. (2003) *Orientalism*, London, UK: Penguin.
Schiller, F. (2003) *Wilhelm Tell*, Stuttgart: Ernst Klett.
Schleiermacher, F. (1996) *Über die Philosophie Platons* (P. M. Steiner, ed.), Hamburg: Meiner.
Schmitt, C. (1982) *Der Leviathan in der Staatslehre des Thomas Hobbes*, Stuttgart: Klett-Cotta.
Schmitt, C. (1996) *Der Begriff des Politischen* (6th edn), Berlin: Duncker & Humblot.
Shapiro, J. (1996) *Shakespeare and the Jews*, New York, NY: Columbia University Press.
Shklar, J. N. (1990) *The Faces of Injustice*, New Haven, CT: Yale University Press.
Sinfeld, A. (1994) Heritage and the Market, Regulation, and Desublimation. In J. Dollimore and A. Sinfeld (eds), *Political Shakespeare: Essays on Cultural Materialism* (2nd edn), Manchester: Manchester University Press, pp. 255–79.
Sinfeld, A. (1996) How to Read *The Merchant of Venice* without being Heterosexist. In *Alternative Shakespeares* (Vol. 2), London: Routledge, pp. 122–39.
Sokol, B. J. and Sokol, M. (2003) *Shakespeare, Law, and Marriage*, Cambridge: Cambridge University Press.
Sophocles (1891) *The Antigone of Sophocles* (R. Jebb, ed.), Cambridge: Cambridge University Press.

Sophocles (1984) *Antigone.* In *The Three Theban Plays* (B. Knox, ed.; R. Fagles, trans.), London: Penguin, pp. 55–128.
Spencer, T., gen. ed. (1967–) *The New Penguin Shakespeare*, London: Penguin [individual vols.].
Starobinski, J. (1999) Sur Corneille. In *L'oeil vivant* (rev'd edn), Paris: Gallimard, pp. 29–70.
Taylor, C. (1992) Atomism. In S. Avineri and A. de-Shalit (eds), *Communitarianism and Individualism*, Oxford: Oxford University Press, pp. 29–50.
Tennenhouse, L. (1986) *Power on Display: The Politics of Shakespeare's Genres*, New York, NY: Methuen.
Tennenhouse, L. (1991) The Counterfeit Order of *The Merchant of Venice*. In T. Wheeler (ed.), *The Merchant of Venice: Critical Essays*, New York, NY: Garland, pp. 195–215.
The New Oxford Dictionary of English (1989) Oxford: Oxford University Press.
The Oxford Dictionary of Law (7th edn) (2009) Oxford: Oxford University Press.
Tolstoy, L. (1993) Second Epilogue. In *War and Peace* (L. Maude and A. Maude, trans.), Ware: Wordsworth, pp. 929–64.
Voltaire (1958) *Le Siècle de Louis XIV*. In R. Pomeau (ed.), *Voltaire: Oeuvres historiques*, Paris: Gallimard (Pléiade), pp. 603–1274.
Voltaire (1964) *Dictionnaire philosophique* (R. Pomeau, ed.), Paris: GF-Flammarion.
Ward, I. (1999) *Shakespeare and the Legal Imagination*, London: Butterworths.
Watt, G. (2008) The Law of Dramatic Properties in *The Merchant of Venice*. In P. Raffield and G. Watt (eds), *Shakespeare and the Law*, Oxford: Hart, pp. 237–51.
Weber, M. (1972) *Wirtschaft und Gesellschaft* (5th edn) (J. Winckelmann, ed.), Tübingen: J.C.B Mohr.
Webster's New Universal Dictionary of the English Language (1976) New York, NY: Webster's International Press.
Webster's Third New International Dictionary, VI (1976) Springfield, MA: G. & C. Merriam Co.
Wells, S. gen. ed. (1982–) *The Oxford Shakespeare*, Oxford: Oxford University Press [individual vols.].
White, R. (1996) *Natural Law in English Renaissance Literature*, Cambridge: Cambridge University Press.
Wilcox, M. (1976) *A Companion to the Iliad*, Chicago, IL: University of Chicago Press.
Wilson, R. (1993) *Will Power: Essays on Shakespearean Authority*, Detroit, MI: Wayne State University Press.
Wittgenstein, L. (1984) *Philosophische Untersuchungen*. In *Werkausgabe*, Frankfurt a.M.: Suhrkamp, pp. 225–580.
Wolters' Woordenboek Nederlands (1992) Groningen: Wolters-Noordhoff.
Zehnpfennig, B. (2001) *Platon zur Einführung* (2nd edn), Hamburg: Junius.

Index

Adeimantus 3, 57–58
afterlife, *see* Christianity, Plato (myths)
Alcibiades
   Plato's, *see* Plato (*Alcibiades*)
   Shakespeare's, *see* Shakespeare (*Timon of Athens*)
Alexander the Great 106
Alexandrine couplets 175
Alighieri, D 11, 50, 65–67, 75, 163, *see also* Christianity
   Divina Commedia, 50, 65–66
   Inferno 66, 158, 164
   De Monarchia 66–67
   Paradiso 50, 65
   Purgatorio 66
anarchism 56, 67–68
Antigone, *see* Sophocles
anti-rationalism, *see* rationalism
anti-Semitism, *see* Judaism, Nazism (Holocaust), Shakespeare (*The Merchant of Venice*)
apartheid 81, *see also* discrimination, racism
Aquinas, T 4, 5, 8, 45, 64, 75, 163, *see also* Christianity
   lex aeterna 64
   lex humana 64
Arendt, H 5, 41–42
aristocracy, 27, 100–13, 168, 172, 182–97, *see also* constitutions, feudalism, monarchy, oligarchy
Aristotle 4, 5, 5 n29, 8, 11, 19, 21, 24–26, 27, 37, 38–39, 40–41, 42, 44, 55, 60–63, 64, 68, 70, 72, 73, 74, 76, 79, 87–95, 103, 122 n56, 133 n135, 134, 138, 141, 142, 154, 163, 173 n145, 194, *see also* equity
   conventional v. natural justice 61
   distributive justice 87–89, *see also suum cuique*

   general justice 87
   'golden mean' 24
   ideal polity 88
   Nicomachean Ethics 122
   phronesis 88, 93
   Plato, critique of 60–63
   Politics 24, 101
   rectificatory justice 87–88, 89, *see also suum cuique*
   reciprocity 90–93
   special justice 87
Athens 3, 43, 61, 64, 71, 73, 80, 84, 86, 87, 103, 104, *see also* Hegel, Rousseau, Shakespeare (*Timon of Athens*)
Augustine (of Hippo) 4, 8, 63, 64, 76, 106, *see also* Christianity
   civitas dei 63
   civitas terrena 63
Auschwitz, *see* Nazism
Austin J 87, 117
autarchy 145, 147, *see also* anarchy, Rousseau
autres pays, autres moeurs 76

Bach, JS 79, 108
Baroque 31, 68, 176
Beauvoir, S de 103 n17
Being, *see* Alighieri, Christianity, cosmos, Hegel, Heidegger, phenomenology, soul
Benjamin, W 5, 104, 106
Bentham, J 17, 75, 76, 153
Bible 68, 69, 81, 122, *see also* Alighieri, Aquinas, Augustine, Christianity, cosmos, God(s), Hell, Milton, Satan
   Cain and Abel 174
   Romans 81
Blanc, L 90, *see also* Marx
body 138–40, *see also* health, medicine, racism

Bolingbroke, H (Henry IV), 110 *see also* Shakespeare (*Richard II; Henry IV, Part One*)
Buchenwald 81
Buddhism 10
bureaucracy 115

Caesar Augustus, 79 n 1, *see also* Corneille (Cinna)
Callicles, 53
Camus, A 103 n 17.
capitalism 44, 107, 114–82, 151–52, *see also* feudalism, Marx, Rousseau, Shakespeare (*The Merchant of Venice, Timon of Athens*)
capital punishment, *see* death penalty
Cephalus 79–80, 91, 141, *see also* Plato (*Republic*), Polemarchus, *suum cuique*
Cerasano, S 136 n150
Christianity 4, 9, 10, 49, 51, 63–67, 73, 76, 105, 126, 127, 128, 129, 131, 132, 133, 134, 135, 137–38, 139, 141, 142 n201, 153, 161, 162, *see also* Alighieri, Aquinas, Augustine, cosmos, God(s), Hell, Milton, Satan, Shakespeare (*The Merchant of Venice*)
citizenship 43, 61, 64, 74, 88, *see also* Aristotle, democracy, Rousseau
civil disobedience 100–02
'civilisation' 30–31, 71, 72, 145, 147, 148, *see also* Rousseau
civitas dei, see Augustine
civitas terrena, see Augustine
colonialism, *see* imperialism, Euro-centrism
commerce, *see* Aristotle (reciprocity), capitalism, communism, free markets, property, Marx, money
commodification, *see* capitalism, communism, Corneille (*Mélite*), free markets, injustice (and measurement), Marx, property, Shakespeare (*The Merchant of Venice; Timon of Athens*)
common law 115 n5
communism, 74–75, 78, *see* Engels, Marx
communitarianism 60
compassion, *see* rationalism
competition, *see* capitalism, free markets, meritocracy
Confucianism 10
congeries 139
conscientious objectors, *see* civil disobedience
constitutions 5, 60, 62
consumerism, *see* capitalism, communism, free markets, property, Marx, money

Corneille, P 11, 12, 27, 95, 107, 171
Cinna 68–69
Horace 174
Le Cid 11, 114, 172, 173, 182–97
Médée 120, 173
Mélite 11, 172–82
Rodogune 69
Suréna 69, 172
cosmos 50–52, 64
Couton, G 173 n145
Critical Race Theory 29
currency, *see* money

Dante, *see* Alighieri
Dawson and Minton 158, 160, 161, 166, 167, 169
death penalty 18, 30 n63, 159
Delgado, R 29–30
democracy 59–60, 61, 64, 74, 84, 86, 92, 110, 116 n9, *see also* Athens, Plato (*Republic*)
Derrida, J 32–33, 57, 78, 85, 104, 106, *see also phármakon*
De la Grammatologie 78
'La Pharmacie de Platon' 78
Descartes, R 94, 176
despotism 67, 86, *see also* dictatorship, fascism, totalitarianism, tyranny
dialectics 36–44, 88, 107, 109 *see also* injustice, Aristotle, Hegel, Marx, Plato (*Meno*)
dictatorship 55–56, *see also* despotism, monarchy, totalitarianism, tyranny
discrimination 81, *see also* Judaism, racism, women
divine retribution, *see* Plato (myths)
Doubrovsky, S 171–73, 178–79
Drakakis, J 120, 121
Dworkin, R 4, 17, 79, 89, 117, 117 n13, 194–95

Eagleton, T 132
economics, *see* capitalism, communism, free markets, Marx, money, Shakespeare (*The Merchant of Venice; Timon of Athens*)
equity 35, 194
emotion, *see* rationalism
Edward III, *see* Shakespeare (*Richard II*)
Engels, F 74, 153
Erasmus, D 11, 67
The Education of a Christian Prince 67
ethical relativism 53

ethnicity *see* racism
eudaimonía 76
Euro-centrism 70, 147
Europe 72–73, 76, 77, 95, 101, 109, 147,
 see also Euro-centrism, imperialism,
 Renaissance
existentialism, *see* Camus, phenomenology

factions (political), 53, 61–62, 64, 66, 71,
 72, 84–85, 159, *see also* injustice (and
 unity)
fascism 55–56
federalism (global) 73
feelings, *see* rationalism
feminism *see* women
feudalism 44, 109, 113, 114, 115, 162,
 182–97, *see also* capitalism, meritocracy,
 monarchy, Shakespeare
Fletcher, J 110
Florence 70
freedom (individual) 59, 117, 148, *see also*
 anarchy, autarchy, liberalism,
 libertarianism, Rousseau
free markets 76, 86, 91, 91, 103, 114–82,
 see also capitalism, liberalism
Foucault, M 32, 69
Fortune, *see* Lady Fortune
Freud, S 30 n65, 179

Geist, *see* Hegel
genocide 41
golden fleece, 120–21, 126, *see also* Jason
 and the Argonauts
Gerechtigkeitsnorm 20, 81, *see also* Kelsen
Girard, R 135
Glaucon 2, 3, 57, 59
God(s) 3–4, 9, 31, 64, 65, 66, 68, 73, 82,
 107–09, 127, 154, *see also* Alighieri,
 Augustine, Aquinas, Christianity, Milton,
 Satan
 Higgs boson ('God') particle 95
Gorgias, 53, *see also* Plato
Gourevitch, V 145
Greenblatt, S 106
Grosz, G 94

harmony, *see* cosmos, injustice (and unity),
 music, soul
Hart HLA 87, 116–17
Harvard Law School 81
health, 93,166, *see also* medicine
hēdonē 76

Hegel GWF 4, 5, 8, 27, 33, 42, 43–44, 46,
 47, 54 64, 69, 70, 71, 73, 74, 77, 89,
 109, 110, 153
 Athens 43, 64
 Being, 43
 citizenship 43
 Geist (mind, spirit) 43
 Grundlinien der Philosophie des Rechts
  (Elements of the Philosophy of Right)
  43–44, 74, 110
 master-slave dialectic 172–73
 Rome 43, 64, 77
 world history 43
Heidegger, M 29, 94
Hell 66, 181, *see also* Alighieri (Inferno),
 Christianity, Milton, Satan
Héritier, F 102–03
historicism 43
Hobbes, T 30–31, 61, 68, 69, 70, 71, 74,
 75, 95, 115, 147, 163
 Leviathan 61, 68, 94
Holocaust, *see* Nazism
Homer, 52 n13
homo homini lupus 166
hubris 49, 51
humanism 67, *see also* liberalism,
 Renaissance
human rights 77
Hydra 86

imperialism 70, 75, 77, *see* Euro-centrism
incest 101
individualism, *see* capitalism, democracy,
 freedom, liberalism
injustice, *see also* Aristotle, *Gerechtigkeitsnorm*,
 litigiousness, natural justice, rule of law
 commensurability with justice 45–49
 dialectics of 36–44
 etymology (bi-polar) of, 10, 15, 16–17,
  19, 28–29, 33, 42, 45–49
 incommensurability with justice
  45–49
 isolated contexts of 22–28
 logical analysis of, 45–49
 and measurement, 7, 10–11, 33, 50, 54,
  55, 78, 79–95, 99, 114–97, *see also*
  suum cuique
 systemic contexts of 33–36
 and unity 7, 10–11, 33, 50–78, 85,
  99–113, 123, *see also* faction
international law, *see* human rights
Islam 9, 10, 76

Jason and the Argonauts 120–21, 173, *see also* golden fleece
John of Gaunt, *see* Shakespeare (*Richard II*)
Jowett, J 156, 158
Judaism 9, 10, 123 n67, 124–25, 126, 128, 130–38, 139, 159, 161, *see also* Shakespeare (*The Merchant of Venice*)
justice, *see* injustice
  programmatic theories of 5, 6, 8, 9, 10, 11, 18, 19, 26, 33, 35, 41, 42, 47, 48, 50, 56, 59, 62, 66, 77, 78, 79, 89, 92, 93, 99, 108, 113, 129, 149, 153

Kafka, F 114
Kant, I 4, 8, 19, 20, 21, 25, 26, 27, 33, 37, 41, 43, 44, 46–47, 54, 73, 74, 79, 89
  categorical imperative 26, 46–47, 73
  Zum ewigen Frieden (Perpetual Peace) 73
Kasuistik 26
Kelsen, H 19, 20, 54–55, 56, 81, 83

Lady Fortune 156
laissez-faire 142, *see also* capitalism, free markets, liberalism
law and literature 29, 99
lawsuits, *see* litigation, litigiousness
legal profession, *see* litigiousness
Levi, P 42
Lévinas, E 32, 41–42, 77–78
lex aeterna, *see* Aquinas
lex humana, *see* Aquinas
liberalism 56, 70–71, 72, 76, 79, 86, 89, 114–52, *see also* Dworkin, Locke, Kant, Mill, Rawls
libertarianism 56, 67–68
lineal descent, *see* monarchy
litigation 15, 19, 36, 85, 86, 89, 90, 99, *see also* litigiousness
litigiousness 85, 86, 90, 110, *see also* litigation
Locke, J 4, 5, 8, 11, 35, 47, 69, 70–71, 72, 73, 74, 79, 95, 147
  'Letter on Toleration' 70
Louis XIV 70

Machiavellianism 104 n22, 120, 156, 173, 174, *see also* 'might makes right', Thrasymachus
mafia 4
Medea, *see* Corneille (*Médée*)
Mahood, M 120, 121
majoritarianism 72, *see also* democracy
Manicheanism 49

melancholy 119, 122
Martin, R 112
Marx, K 4, 5, 7, 8, 11, 17, 19, 20, 21, 25, 33, 42, 43, 44, 46, 54, 56, 69, 71, 73, 74–75, 78, 89–90, 92, 93, 107, 117–18, 129, 130, 142 n201, 143, 147, 150, 151–52, 153–54, 155
  Das Kapital 74–74
McCleskey v Kemp 30
medicine 51, 83, 85, 166, *see also* health, *phármakon*
Meno, *see* Plato (*Meno*)
'Meno's paradox', *see* Plato (*Meno*)
mercantilism 114–82, *see also* capitalism
meritocracy 110, 113, 140–52, 172–97, Corneille (*Mélite*), free markets, injustice (and measurement), liberalism, Rousseau, Shakespeare (*The Merchant of Venice; Timon of Athens*)
Merleau-Ponty M 29
metaphysics, *see* Aristotle, Christianity, cosmos, Hegel, Heidegger, Plato, soul
Middle Ages, *see* feudalism
Middleton, T 11, 107, 154, 173, *see also* Shakespeare (*Timon of Athens*)
'might makes right' 68, *see also* Machiavellianism, Thrasymachus
militarism 75
Mill, JS 4, 5, 8, 21, 26, 27, 47, 76, 79
  harm principle 26, 47
  On Liberty 26
Milton, J 95, 107–09, *see also* Christianity
  Paradise Lost 107–09
misanthropy, 167, *see also* Molière, Shakespeare (*Timon of Athens*)
miscegenation 127 n81, *see also* racism
modernity 67–78, 95, 101, 103–97, 114–97
  concept of 153
Molière 167, 171, 172
  Le Misanthrope 175
monarchy 62, 86–87, 101, 109–10, 113, 185 *see also* aristocracy, Alighieri (*De Monarchia*), feudalism, meritocracy
money 90–93, 94, 95, 114–97, *see also* Aristotle (reciprocity), capitalism, communism, free markets, property, Marx, Shakespeare (*The Merchant of Venice; Timon of Athens*)
Montaigne, M de 5
Moors, 142, 185, 194–95, *see also* Islam, racism, Corneille (*Le Cid*), Shakespeare (*The Merchant of Venice; Othello*)
music, 50, 51, 55, *see also* harmony

Nadal, O 172 n139
national interest, *see* raison d'état
national security, *see* raison d'état
natural justice, *see* Aristotle, Aquinas, Augustine, Christianity, gods, Hegel, Judaism, Islam, Kant, Plato
Nazism 30, 56
  Holocaust 48, 135, 136, 136 n150, *see also* anti-Semitism, Buchenwald, Third Reich
Nero, *see* Racine *(Britannicus)*
Nietzsche, F 1, 8, 34, 169
nihilism 6, 34, 113
noblesse d'épée 110
noblesse de robe 110

Oedipus, *see* Sophocles
oligarchy 62, *see also* aristocracy, constitutions, feudalism, monarchy
ontology, *see* Aristotle, Hegel, Heidegger, phenomenology, Plato
Ovid 181

paragone 156 n24
paterfamilias 140
patriarchy, *see* women
Paul (of Tarsus), *see* Bible *(Romans)*
Perelman, C 20, 21, 54–55, 56
phármakon 85, 106, 109, 129, 147, 158, 166, *see also* Derrida, medicine
phenomenology 32, 42, *see also* Heidegger, Lévinas, Merleau-Ponty, rationalism
philosopher rulers 88, *see also* Plato *(Republic)*
phronesis, see Aristotle
plague 101 n12
Plato 1, 2, 3, 5, 6, 7, 8, 11, 21, 22, 23, 24, 25, 48, 50–60, 62–63, 64, 68, 72, 73, 75, 76, 77, 78, 86, 87, 88, 92, 93, 103, 118, 122 n56, 144, 145, 147, 150, 163, 166, *see also* Adeimantus, Glaucon, injustice (and unity), medicine, music, Polus, Socrates, Thrasymachus
  Alcibiades 39–40
  Apology 19
  Gorgias 19, 106, *see also* Callicles, Polus
  Laws 19, 24, 25, 52, 59, 62, 82, 101
  Meno 23–25, 37–40, 61
    'Meno's paradox' 38
  myths (of afterlife), 3, 51
  Parmenides 52
  Phaedo 24 n34
  Phaedrus, see Derrida, *phármakon*

Protagoras 19
Republic 1, 2, 3, 5, 5 n31, 6, 11, 17, 19, 24, 24 n34, 38, 40, 51, 52, 53, 54, 55, 57–58, 60–62, 61 n58, 70, 79–80, 81–86, 90, 91, 101, 106
Statesman 52, 58
pleonexia 49
poetics, *see* Alexandrine couplets, congeries, *paragone*, poetry, stichomythia
poetry 82, *see also* poetics
Polemarchus 80, 83, 84, 88, 91, 141, *see also* Cephalus, Plato *(Republic)*, Simonides, *suum cuique*
Polus 3 n21
Pope, A 120
pragmatism 25
Prigent, M 186 n219
property 57, 59, 75, 84, 147, *see also* capitalism, communism, Marxism, Plato *(Republic)*
Priam, *see* Racine *(Andromaque)*
pro bono publico 128
public order, *see* raison d'état
Purgatory, *see* Alighieri *(Purgatorio)*
Pythogoreanism 50, *see also* harmony, Plato

Racine, J, 95, 107, 172, 174
  Andromaque 31
  Britannicus 69
  La Thébaïde 69, 174
racism 29–30, 127, 128, 129, 138–39, 141–42, *see also* apartheid, body, Critical Race Theory, discrimination, Shakespeare *(The Merchant of Venice)*
raison d'état 68–69, 70–71, 73–74, 106, 194, *see also* Corneille, Hobbes, Racine, Shakespeare *(Macbeth)*
rationalism 28–33, 47–48, *see also* modernity
Rawls, J 4, 5, 6, 19, 21, 79, 89, 153
religion, *see* Alighieri, Augustine, Aquinas, Christianity, God(s), Hell, Judaism, Islam, Milton, Paul, Satan
Renaissance 67–68, 70, 104, 122 n56, *see also* Erasmus, Shakespeare
republicanism, *see* Aristotle (ideal polis), citizenship, Rousseau
rex non potest peccare 116, *see also* monarchy
rhetoric *see* poetics
Rome 61, 71, 104, 118 *see also* Hegel,
Rousseau, J-J 4, 5, 8, 11, 19, 21, 30–32, 33, 35, 37, 54, 56, 69, 71–74, 75, 77, 78, 89, 92, 110, 118, 144–52, 154, 155, 160,

162, 166, 173–74, *see also* meritocracy, rationalism
Contrat social (Social Contract) 56, 72, 144, 149
Discours sur les sciences et les arts (Discourse on the Sciences and Arts) 71, 144, 150
Discours sur l'origine et les fondements de l'inégalité (Discourse on the origin of Inequality) 71, 144, 150
La Nouvelle Héloïse 173 n147
volonté générale (general will) 72
volonté de tous (will of all) 72
rule of law 88, 116

Satan 66, 68, 107–09, *see also* Alighieri (*Inferno*), Christianity, God(s), Hell, Milton
Schiller, F
Wilhelm Tell 31
Schleiermacher, F 39 n 98
Schmitt, C 30, 78, 104, 162
Scotus, D 94
Second World War 77
secularism, *see* liberalism, humanism, modernity
Seneca 69 n101
sexism, *see* women
Shakespeare, W 11, 95, 107, 122 n56, 150, 173, 180, 181, 182, 184
All's Well That Ends Well 157
As You Like It 116
The Comedy of Errors 116, 117, 123–24, 133, 157
Coriolanus 116, 117 n13
Cymbeline 157
Hamlet 23, 105, 132, 157, 191
Henry IV, Part One 104, 111–13, 139 n180
Henry IV, Part Two 117, 139 n180
Henry V 22, 27, 112, 115, 117, 117 n13, 122
Henry VI, Part One 27–28, 122
Henry VI, Part Two 105 n32
Henry VI, Part Three 105 n32
Henry VIII 110
Julius Caesar 116, 117 n13
King John 104
King Lear 104, 140–41, 161, 162, 167, 177
Love's Labours Lost 157
Macbeth 103–09, 110–11, 112, 113, 114, 122, 123, 129, 161

Measure for Measure 116, 117
The Merchant of Venice 11, 114–44, 150, 153, 154, 155, 158–59, 162, 174, 179, 183, 186, 197
The Merry Wives of Windsor 117, 139 n180, 153
A Midsummer Night's Dream 116, 126
Much Ado about Nothing 117, 157, 166, 175
Othello 116, 117, 126, 128, 159
Richard II 104, 112, 117 n13, 122, 136, 161, 186
Richard III 105, 105 n32
Romeo and Juliet 116, 117, 181–82
The Taming of the Shrew 157
The Tempest 115
Timon of Athens 11, 153–71, 174, 188, 197, *see also* Middleton
Titus Andronicus 117 n13, 128
Troilus and Cressida 99, 115, 162–63, 167
Twelfth Night 138
Two Gentlemen of Verona 115, 157, 174
A Winter's Tale 117, 157
Shintoism 10
Shklar, J 174
Simonides 80, 82
slavery 41, 88, 90
sociology 107
Socrates 1, 2, 3, 4, 5, 6, 7, 22, 23, 24, 37–38–40, 42, 53, 57–58, 80, 82, 83, 84, 101, 197, *see also* Plato *(Republic)*
trial and death of 84
sophists 80, 101, *see also* Gorgias, Polus, Thrasymachus
Sophocles
Antigone vi, 11, 100–03, 105, 106, 108, 109, 113, 114
soul 37, 50–52
Spain, *see* Corneille (*Le Cid*), Shakespeare (*The Merchant of Venice*)
speculum principum 136
Starobinski, J 178
stichomythia 168–70
stoicism 76
storytelling, *see* law and literature
suum cuique 58, 79–90, 147, 159, 163, 175, 176, 182, *see also* Aristotle, Cephalus, Polemarchus, Simonides
surveillance state 69, *see also* Foucault

Talbot, J, *see* Shakespeare (*Henry VI, Part One*)
Taoism 10
taxation 89

Third Reich 4, *See also* Nazism
Thrasymachus 1, 2, 4, 5, 6, 7, 8, 22, 34, 37–38, 53, 197
'to each his own', *see suum cuique*
totalitarianism 55–56
trade, *see* Aristotle (reciprocity), capitalism, communism, free markets, property, Marx, money
tyranny 62, 67, 84, *see also* dictatorship, fascism, totalitarianism

unconscionability 49
United States of America
 Supreme Court 30
Universal Declaration of Human Rights 77
usury 133

utilitarianism 75–76, *see also* Bentham, Mill

Venice, *see* Shakespeare (*The Merchant of Venice*)
Voltaire 5, 47, 70

Weimar Republic 4
Wiesel, E 42
Wittgenstein, L 29
women 88, 102, 107, 123–26, 155, 173–97, *see also* Beauvoir, Corneille (*Médée*), Shakespeare (*The Merchant of Venice*) Sophocles (*Antigone*)
Woolsey, T 100
World War II, *see* Second World War